ERIK H. ERIKSON

Identity

Youth and Crisis

faber and faber

LONDON · BOSTON

First published in England in 1968
by Faber and Faber Limited
3 Queen Square London WC1
First published in paper covers in 1971
Reprinted 1974
This reissue published in 1983
Printed in Great Britain by
Whitstable Litho Ltd, Whitstable, Kent
All rights reserved

© 1968 by *W. W. Norton & Co. Inc.*

British Library Cataloguing in Publication Data

Erikson, Erik H.
Identity: youth and crisis
1. Adolescent psychology
I. Title
155.5   BF721
ISBN 0-571-09715-4

Contents

Contents

Preface

ONE OF MY TEACHERS in the Vienna Psychoanalytic Institute in the late twenties was Dr. Paul Federn, a fascinating man equally inventive in new concepts and in slips of the tongue. At the time, his concept of "ego boundaries" was much discussed as important but opaque. We students, in some desperation, asked him to give us as many seminars in succession as he deemed necessary to explain it to us. For three long evenings he held forth; and on concluding the last one he folded up his papers with the air of one who has finally made himself understood, and asked: "*Nun—hab ich mich verstanden?*" ("*Now*—have I understood myself?").

I have asked myself this question more than once in rereading what I have written on identity, and I hasten to declare that I will not offer a definitive explanation of it in this book. The more one writes about this subject, the more the word becomes a term for something as unfathomable as it is all-pervasive. One can only explore it by establishing its indispensability in various contexts.

Each chapter of this book, then, is a revision of a major essay of the last two decades, supplemented by excerpts from papers written at about the same time. Some of these essays have appeared in a psychological monograph series, with an introduction by David Rapaport which staunchly assigns me my place in

9

psychoanalytic theory as he saw it a decade ago. I have never learned to feel comfortable in the role of a writer on human development who must publish clinical observations as part-evidence. But this matter has been taken, almost torn, out of our hands by students and readers. For writings originally meant for professional circles have found their way into class-rooms and bookstores, and therefore may appropriately be included in a revised review of the kind offered in this book. Nor is such curiosity mainly morbid: in his search for a more inclusive self-definition the student of today is determined to be informed about human deviation as well as human variation, and this in sufficient detail to permit identification, empathy, and distance.

Today, also, there are new reasons, beyond the usual hoarding instinct, for a worker in my field to collect and to reprint the stray work not previously contained in a book. For one thing, single essays and papers are always ahead of themselves in suggestiveness and behind in firmness of established ground. Not until one tries to make a book of them can one really know what each meant to deal with, and what they gradually have come to mean together. On revising them years later, it is disquieting to hear oneself talk in different tongues to different audiences, especially if one has forgotten to whom in a given audience—and against whom—one was talking at the time. Yet I have left to each "period piece" its emphasis of tone and to the whole the character of a record. The record reveals that I am the kind of clinical worker in whose mind a few observations linger for a long time. Such observations, when first made, are always marked by a combination of surprise at the unexpected and yet also of a confirmation of the long awaited. For this reason, I am apt to present the same observation to different audiences in various contexts, hoping each time that understanding may be deepened.

And finally, to write or to have written about identity presents a special object lesson to the writer on human development: he cannot escape the necessity of re-evaluating his own thinking in the light of acute historical change. In fact, in a retrospective prologue, I will try to throw some light on the singular and often erratic appeal of the terms "identity" and "identity crisis" during the two decades when the material on which this book is based was written. The reader, in turn, will have to mobilize his historical awareness in order to judge what long-range trend in this body of writing may seem to be confirmed by contemporary developments, and what observations appear to have been convincing only in their transient setting. To help the reader in this, the original publications and their dates are listed on page 321. The last entry, it will be noted, antedates the recent publicity given to some new forms of display and some new inner adventures (some chemically induced) on the part of the most flamboyant and un-violent section of to-day's youth. This is just as well. For only a long look, through and past fads and antics, can help us to read what age-old message they are trying to bring to our attention. Nor had the problem of street violence reached its explosive momentum when this was written. But here, too, the role of the young and of the young adult leader calls for concerted attention.

IF THIS UNDERTAKING proves to be at all readable, it is due to the preparatory work of Joan Erikson and Pamela Daniels.

Pamela Daniels, chief assistant in my course on the Life Cycle at Harvard, has gone over the original papers, ably cutting down repetitiousness to a necessary minimum and gently clarifying what she knew puzzled our students.

Joan Erikson always edits what I write. Nobody knows better what I want to say, and nobody could be more careful to let me say it in my own way and, if need be, in overlong sentences. But this book also is witness to the years of our joint work in the Austen Riggs Center where she established a novel "Activities Program" for the patients. This program has become an indispensable counterpart to psychotherapy, and has proven fertile in testing and promoting the inner resources of young people in acute crisis.

In each chapter some acknowledgments are made, but a man's indebtedness over two decades of practicing and teaching, consulting and traveling cannot be compressed into references. I am dedicating this book to two friends who have died, and I do so not only because they are sorely missed, but because they live in what is alive in this book, as they do in the work of others. Robert P. Knight was the medical director and David Rapaport the research director of the Austen Riggs Center in the Berkshires. An astonishing pair, marked by extreme differences in background and appearance, temperament and mental style, they yet established together, in addition to their eminent work as individuals, a rare therapeutic and theoretical center which no doubt some day will find its historian. There, also, I experienced the longest stretch of intimate work association in the two decades recorded here.

It was to the Austen Riggs Center that the Field Foundation gave the initial grant for the study of the problem of Identity; and I am writing this preface while working on another errand, a book on Gandhi's middle years, as the first Field Foundation Fellow. Later the Ford Foundation, in a general grant to Riggs, provided further opportunities for travel and study. In smaller explorations, the Shelter Rock Foundation has remained a steady support. The Foundations' Fund for Research in Psychiatry, finally, sponsored my work on *Young Man Luther*, a companion book to this volume, for it applies to one life history what this book roamingly explores in many lives and times.

By title, however, this book is a successor to *Childhood and Society*. Being close relatives, all three books bear similarities and even repetitions which, I hope, will be as forgivable as family likenesses are—among friends.

Many eyes and hands have typed the manuscripts collected here, but none more ably and more cheerfully than Ann Burt of Santuit.

E.H.E.

Cotuit, Massachusetts, 1967.

Identity
Youth and Crisis

C H A P T E R

I

Prologue

1.

To REVIEW THE CONCEPT OF IDENTITY means to sketch its history. In the twenty years since the term was first employed in the particular sense to be discussed in this book, its popular usage has become so varied and its conceptual context so expanded that the time may seem to have come for a better and final delimitation of what identity is and what it is not. And yet, by its very nature, what bears such a definitive name remains subject to changing historical connotations.

"Identity" and "identity crisis" have in popular and scientific usage become terms which alternately circumscribe something so large and so seemingly self-evident that to demand a definition would almost seem petty, while at other times they designate something made so narrow for purposes of measurement that the over-all meaning is lost, and it could just as well be called something else. If, to give examples of the wider use of the term, the papers run a headline "The Identity Crisis of Africa" or refer to the "identity crisis" of the Pittsburgh glass industry; if the outgoing president of the American Psychoanalytic Association titles his farewell address "The Identity Crisis of Psychoanalysis"; or if, finally, the Catholic students at Harvard announce that they will hold an "Identity Crisis" on Thursday night at eight o'clock sharp, then the dignity of the term seems to vary greatly. The quotation marks are as important as the term they bracket: everybody has heard of "identity crisis" and it arouses a mixture of curiosity, mirth, and discomfort which yet promises, by the very play on the word "crisis," not to turn out to be something quite as fatal as it sounds. In other words, a suggestive term has begun to lend itself to ritualized usage.

Social scientists, on the other hand, sometimes attempt to achieve greater specificity by making such terms as "identity crisis," "self-identity," or "sexual identity" fit whatever more measurable item they are investigating at a given time. For the sake of logical or experimental maneuverability (and in order to keep in good academic company) they try to treat these terms as matters of social roles, personal traits, or conscious self-images, shunning the less manageable and more sinister—which often also means the more vital—implications of the concept. Such usages have, in fact, become so indiscriminate that the other day a German reviewer of the book in which I first used the term in the context of psychoanalytic ego theory called it the pet subject of the *amerikanische Populaerpsychologie*.

But one may note with satisfaction that the conceptualization of identity has led to a series of valid investigations which, if they do not make clearer what identity is, nevertheless have proved useful in social psychology. And it may be a good thing that the word "crisis" no longer connotes impending catastrophe, which at one time seemed to be an obstacle to the understanding of the term. It is now being accepted as designating a necessary turning point, a crucial moment, when development must move one way or another, marshaling resources of growth, recovery, and further differentiation. This proves applicable to many situations: a crisis in individual development or in the emergence of a new elite, in the therapy of an individual or in the tensions of rapid historical change.

The term "identity crisis" was first used, if I remember correctly, for a specific clinical purpose in the Mt. Zion Veterans'

Rehabilitation Clinic during the Second World War, a national emergency which permitted psychiatric workers of different persuasions and denominations, among them Emanuel Windholz and Joseph Wheelwright, to work together harmoniously. Most of our patients, so we concluded at that time, had neither been "shellshocked" nor become malingerers, but had through the exigencies of war lost a sense of personal sameness and historical continuity. They were impaired in that central control over themselves for which, in the psychoanalytic scheme, only the "inner agency" of the ego could be held responsible. Therefore, I spoke of a loss of "ego identity." [1] Since then, we have recognized the same central disturbance in severely conflicted young people whose sense of confusion is due, rather, to a war within themselves, and in confused rebels and destructive delinquents who war on their society. In all these cases, then, the term "identity confusion" has a certain diagnostic significance which should influence the evaluation and treatment of such disturbances. Young patients can be violent or depressed, delinquent or withdrawn, but theirs is an acute and possibly passing crisis rather than a breakdown of the kind which tends to commit a patient to all the malignant implications of a fatalistic diagnosis. And as has always been the case in the history of psychoanalytic psychiatry, what was first recognized as the common dynamic pattern of a group of severe disturbances (such as the hysterias of the turn of the century) revealed itself later to be a pathological aggravation, an undue prolongation of, or a regression to, a normative crisis "belonging" to a particular stage of individual development. Thus, we have learned to ascribe a normative "identity crisis" to the age of adolescence and young adulthood.

Referring to the first use of the term "identity crisis," I said "if I remember correctly." Perhaps one should be able to remember such things. But the fact is that a term which later becomes so distinctive is often first used as something one takes, and thinks others take, for granted. This brings to mind one of the innumerable stories with which Norman Reider could be counted on to lighten those often weary war days. An old man, he recounted, used to vomit every morning, but he showed no inclination to consult a doctor about it. His family finally prevailed on him to go to Mt. Zion for a general checkup. When Dr. Reider approached him cautiously, "How are you?" he was told promptly, "I'm fine. Couldn't be better." And, indeed, on further examination the constituent parts of the old man seemed to be in as good shape as could be expected. Finally, Dr. Reider became a bit impatient. "But I hear you vomit every morning?" The old man looked mildly surprised and said, "Sure. Doesn't everybody?"

In telling this story, I am not implying that "identity crisis" is a symptom of mine that I simply assumed everybody else had also—although there is, of course, something to that too. But I did assume that I had given the most obvious name to something that everybody had had at one time and would, therefore, recognize in those who were having it acutely.

Judged by the clinical origin of these terms, then, it would seem reasonable enough to link the *pathological* and the *developmental aspects* of the matter and to see what might differentiate the identity crisis typical for a case history from that of a life history. This emphasis on individual lives, however, would make the other and wider uses of the terms "identity" and "identity crisis" appear all the more suspect as mere analogies not admissable in any court of definition. That Catholic students would try to pool their individual crises, enjoy them together, and get them over with in one evening makes at least humorous sense. But what possible connection could adolescence as such have with the state of an African nation or of a scientific body? *Is* this a mere analogistic usage such as is employed, with a mixture of boastfulness and apology, when a nation is said to be in its historical and economic "adolescence," or to have developed a "paranoid political style"? And if a nation cannot be said to be "adolescent," can a type of individual identity crisis be shared by a significant section of the young population? And further, to return to the faddish use of the term "identity confusion," would some of our youth act so openly confused and confusing if they did not *know* they were *supposed* to have an identity crisis?

The history of the last twenty years seems to indicate that there are clinical terms which are taken over not only by diagnosticians, but also by those who have been overdiagnosed, and, in this case, by a section of a whole age group who echo our very terms and flamboyantly display a conflict which we once regarded as silent, inner, and unconscious.

2.

Before we try to understand the meaning of the present-day echo of our terms, let me take a long look back to our professional and conceptual ancestors. Today when the term identity refers, more often than not, to something noisily demonstrative, to a more or less desperate "quest," or to an almost deliberately confused "search" let me present two formulations which assert strongly what identity feels like when you become aware of the fact that you do undoubtedly *have* one.

My two witnesses are bearded and patriarchal founding fathers of the psychologies on which our thinking on identity is based. As a *subjective sense* of an *invigorating sameness* and *continuity*, what I would call a sense of identity seems to me best described by William James in a letter to his wife:[2]

A man's character is discernible in the mental or moral attitude in which, when it came upon him, he felt himself most deeply and intensely active and alive. At such moments there is a voice inside which speaks and says: "*This* is the real me!"

Such experience always includes

. . . an element of active tension, of holding my own, as it were, and trusting outward things to perform their part so as to make it a full harmony, but without any *guaranty* that they will. Make it a guaranty . . . and the attitude immediately becomes to my consciousness stagnant and stingless. Take away the guaranty, and I feel (provided I am *ueberhaupt* in vigorous condition) a sort of deep enthusiastic bliss, of bitter willingness to do and suffer anything . . . and which, although it is a mere mood or emotion to which I can give no form in words, authenticates itself to me as the deepest principle of all active and theoretic determination which I possess . . .

James uses the word "character," but I am taking the liberty of claiming that he describes a sense of identity, and that he does so in a way which can in principle be experienced by any man. To him it is both mental and moral in the sense of those "moral philosophy" days, and he experiences it as something that "comes upon you" as a recognition, almost as a surprise rather than as something strenuously "quested" after. It is an active tension (rather than a paralyzing question)—a tension which, furthermore, must create a challenge "without guaranty" rather than one dissipated in a clamor for certainty. But let us remember in passing that James was in his thirties when he wrote this, that in his youth he had faced and articulated an "identity crisis" of honest and desperate depth, and that he became *the* Psychologist-Philosopher of American Pragmatism only after having experimented with a variety of cultural, philosophic, and national identity elements: the use in the middle of his declaration of the untranslatable German word "*ueberhaupt*" is probably an echo of his conflictful student days in Europe.

One can study in James's life history a protracted identity crisis as well as the emergence of a "self-made" identity in the new and expansive American civilization. We will repeatedly come back to James, but for the sake of further definition, let us now turn to a statement which asserts a unity of *personal and cultural* identity rooted in an ancient people's fate. In an address to the Society of B'nai B'rith in Vienna in 1926,[3] Sigmund Freud said:

What bound me to Jewry was (I am ashamed to admit) neither faith nor national pride, for I have always been an unbeliever and was brought up without any religion though not without a respect for what are called the "ethical" standards of human civilization. Whenever I felt an inclination to national enthusiasm I strove to suppress it as being harmful and wrong, alarmed by the warning examples of the peoples among whom we Jews live. But plenty of other things remained over to make the attraction of Jewry and Jews irresistible—many obscure emotional forces, which were the more powerful the less they could be expressed in words, as well as a clear consciousness of inner identity, the safe privacy of a common mental construction. And beyond this there was a perception that it was to my Jewish nature alone that I owed two characteristics that had become indispensable to me in the difficult course of my life. Because I was a Jew I found myself free from many prejudices which restricted others in the use of their intellect; and as a Jew I was prepared to join the Opposition, and to do without agreement with the "compact majority."

No translation ever does justice to the distinctive choice of words in Freud's German original. "Obscure emotional forces" are *"dunkle Gefuehlsmaechte"*; the "safe privacy of a common mental construction" is *"die Heimlichkeit der inneren Konstruktion"*—not just "mental," then, and certainly not "private," but a deep communality known only to those who shared in it, and only expressible in words more mythical than conceptual.

These fundamental statements were taken not from theoretical works, but from special communications: a letter to his wife from a man who married late, an address to his "brothers" by an original observer long isolated in his profession. But in all their poetic spontaneity they are the products of trained minds and therefore exemplify the main dimensions of a positive sense of identity almost systematically. Trained minds of genius, of course, have a special identity and special identity problems often leading to a protracted crisis at the onset of their careers. Yet we must rely on them for formulating initially what we can then proceed to observe as universally human.

This is the only time Freud used the term identity in a more than casual way and, in fact, in a most central ethnic sense. And as we would expect of him, he inescapably points to some of those aspects of the matter which I called sinister and yet vital —the more vital, in fact, "the less they could be expressed in words." For Freud's "consciousness of inner identity" includes a sense of bitter pride preserved by his dispersed and often despised people throughout a long history of persecution. It is anchored in a particular (here intellectual) gift which had victoriously emerged from the hostile limitation of opportunities. At the same time, Freud contrasts the *positive identity* of a fearless freedom of thinking with a *negative* trait in "the peoples among whom we Jews live," namely, "prejudices which restrict others in the use of their intellect." It dawns on us, then, that one person's or group's identity may be relative to another's, and that the pride of gaining a strong identity may signify an inner emancipation from a more dominant group identity, such as that of the "compact majority." An exquisite triumph is suggested in the claim that the same historical development which restricted the prejudiced majority in the free use of their intellect made the isolated minority sturdier in intellectual matters. To all this, we must come back when discussing race relations.[4]

And Freud goes farther. He admits in passing that he had to suppress in himself an inclination toward "national enthusiasm" such as was common for "the peoples among whom we Jews live." Again, as in James's case, only a study of Freud's youthful enthusiasms could show how he came to leave behind other aspirations in favor of the ideology of applying the methods of natural science to the study of psychological "forces of dignity." It is in Freud's dreams, incidentally, that we have a superb record of his suppressed (or what James called "abandoned," or even "murdered") selves—for our "negative identity" haunts us at night.[5]

3.

The two statements and the lives behind them serve to establish a few dimensions of identity and, at the same time, help to explain why the problem is so all-pervasive and yet so hard to grasp: for we deal with a process "located" *in the core of the individual* and yet also *in the core of his communal culture*, a process which establishes, in fact, the identity of those two identities. If we should now pause and state a few minimum requirements for fathoming the complexity of identity we should have to begin by saying something like this (and let us take our time in saying it): in psychological terms, identity formation employs a process of simultaneous reflection and observation, a process taking place on all levels of mental functioning, by which the individual judges himself in the light of what he perceives to be the way in which others judge him in comparison to themselves and to a typology significant to them; while he judges their way of judging him in the light of how he perceives himself in comparison to them and to types that have become relevant to him. This process is, luckily, and necessarily, for the most part unconscious except where inner conditions and outer circumstances combine to aggravate a painful, or elated, "identity-consciousness."

Furthermore, the process described is always changing and developing: at its best it is a process of increasing differentiation, and it becomes ever more inclusive as the individual grows aware of a widening circle of others significant to him, from the maternal person to "mankind." The process "begins" somewhere in the first true "meeting" of mother and baby as two persons who can touch and recognize each other,[6] and it does not "end" until a man's power of mutual affirmation wanes. As pointed out, however, the process has its normative crisis in adolescence, and is in many ways determined by what went before and determines much that follows. And finally, in discussing identity, as we now see, we cannot separate personal growth and communal change, nor can we separate (as I tried to demonstrate in *Young Man Luther*) the identity crisis in individual life and contemporary crises in historical development because the two help to define each other and are truly relative to each other. In fact, the whole interplay between the psychological and the social, the developmental and the historical, for which identity formation is of prototypal significance, could be conceptualized only as a kind of *psychosocial relativity*. A weighty matter then: certainly mere "roles" played interchangeably, mere self-conscious "appearances," or mere strenuous "postures" cannot possibly be the real thing, although they may be dominant aspects of what today is called the "search for identity."

In view of all this, it would be obviously wrong to let some terms of personology and of social psychology often identified with identity or identity confusion—terms such as self-conception, self-imagery, or self-esteem, on the one hand, and role ambiguity, role conflict, or role loss, on the other—take over the area to be studied, although teamwork methods are, at the moment, the best approach in this general area. What these approaches as yet lack, however, is a theory of human development which attempts to come closer to something by finding out wherefrom and whereto it develops. For identity is never "established" as an "achievement" in the form of a personality armor, or of anything static and unchangeable.

The traditional psychoanalytic method, on the other hand, cannot quite grasp identity because it has not developed terms to conceptualize the environment. Certain habits of psychoanalytic theorizing, habits of designating the environment as "outer world" or "object world," cannot take account of the environment as a pervasive actuality. The German ethologists introduced the word "*Umwelt*" to denote not merely an environment which surrounds you, but which is also in you. And indeed, from the point of view of development, "former" environments are forever in us; and since we live in a continuous process of making the present "former" we never—not even as a newborn—meet any environment as a person who never had an environment. One methodological precondition, then, for grasping identity would be a psychoanalysis sophisticated enough to include the environment; the other would be a social psychology which is psychoanalytically sophisticated; together they would obviously institute a new field which would have to create its own historical sophistication. In the meantime, we can only try to see where a historical instance or a bit of normative development, a fragment of case history, or an event in a biography becomes clearer when something like identity development is assumed to exist. And, of course, it helps to note down in detail what and why and how an item seems to become clearer.

But once we accept a historical perspective, we face the probability that the quotations which I have offered as a massive motto are really tied to a kind of identity formation highly dependent on cultural conditions of a sedentary middle class. True, both James and Freud belonged to the middle class of the early industrial era which migrated from country to city or from city to city, and James, of course, was the grandson of an immigrant. Nevertheless, their homes and their studies, their academic and their clinical associations were, even when revolutionary in scientific matters, highly stable in their morals and ideals. It may well be that what "you can take for granted" (a phrase which Freud used in order to characterize his attitude toward morality) also determines what chances you can fruitfully take with it. And chances they took, the revolutionary minds of the middle class of the nineteenth century: Darwin, by making man's very humanity relative to his animal ancestry; Marx, by exposing the middle-class mind itself as classbound; and Freud, by making our ideals and our very consciousness relative to an unconscious mental life.

Since then there have been national wars, political revolutions, and moral rebellions which have shaken the traditional foundations of all human identity. If we wish to find witnesses to a radically different awareness of the relation of positive and negative identity, we only have to change our historical perspective and look to the Negro writers in this country today. For what if there is nothing in the hopes of generations past nor in the accessible resources of the contemporary community which would help to overcome the negative image held up to a minority by the "compact majority"? Then, so it seems, the creative individual must accept the negative identity as the very base line of recovery. And so we have in our American Negro writers the almost ritualized affirmation of "inaudibility," "invisibility," "namelessness," "facelessness"—a "void of faceless faces, of soundless voices lying outside history," as Ralph Ellison puts it. But the responsible Negro writers continue to write and write strongly, for fiction even in acknowledging the depth of nothingness can contribute to something akin to a collective recovery.[7] This, as we shall see, is a universal trend among the exploited. It is no coincidence that one of the most telling autobiographic documents of India's liberation as a nation also bears the "negative" title *Autobiography of an Unknown Indian*. No wonder that in young people not inclined toward literary reflection, such deepseated negative identities can be reabsorbed only by a turn to militancy, if not transient violence.

4.

Now let us take a look ahead from the vantage point of twenty years ago and, forgetting concepts and clinics, *see* the youth of today. Youth, in any period, means first of all the noisier and more obvious part of that subrace, plus the quiet sufferers who come to the attention of psychiatrists or are brought to life by the novelists. In the most picturesque segment of the younger generation we are witnessing an exacerbated "identity-consciousness" which seems to play havoc not only with our formulations of the positive and negative identity, but also with our assumptions concerning manifest and latent behavior and conscious and unconscious processes. What appears to us to be profoundly relative is displayed by them as a relativistic "stance."

The youth of today is not the youth of twenty years ago. This much any elderly person would say, at any point in history, and think it was both new and true. But here we mean something very specifically related to our theories. For whereas twenty years ago we gingerly suggested that some young people might be suffering from a more or less unconscious identity conflict, a certain type today tells us in no uncertain terms, and with the dramatic outer display of what we once considered to be inner secrets, that yes, indeed, they have an identity conflict—and they wear it on their sleeves, Edwardian or leather. Sexual identity confusion? Yes, indeed; sometimes when we see them walking down the street it is impossible for us to tell, without indelicate scrutiny, who is a boy and who is a girl. Negative identity? Oh yes, they seem to want to be everything which "society" tells them not to be: in this, at least, they "conform." And as for such fancy terms as psychosocial moratorium, they will certainly take their time, and take it with a vengeance, until they are sure whether or not they want any of the identity offered in a conformist world.

But is what they lay claim to exactly what we meant? And have we and what we meant not also changed with the same events which changed the status of the identity conflict? This very question opens a psychohistorical perspective which we can only begin to discuss here. But begin we must, for the acceleration of change in future generations and in current world conditions is here to stay, or (to hastily adjust our figures of speech) to move along with us—and ahead of us.

In a way, it makes supreme sense that the age group which can never sacrifice the actuality of growing and participating to what the older generation tiredly calls "reality" should also be the one which transposes theory into conduct and demonstrates to us that teaching, too, is acting. It is in adolescence, we said, that the ideological structure of the environment becomes essential for the ego, because without an ideological simplification of the universe the adolescent ego cannot organize experience according to its specific capacities and its expanding involvement. Adolescence, then, is a stage in which the individual is much closer to the historical day than he is at earlier stages of childhood development. While the infantile antecedents of identity are more unconscious and change very slowly, if at all, the identity problem itself changes with the historical period: this, in fact, is its job. To discuss the identity problem, then, and to describe its dimensions at the very time when we clinicians are listened to, means to play into cultural history, or, perhaps, to become its tool.

Thus we see much of what at first we interpreted as latent now expressed in slogans, demonstrated on the streets, and spread out in the illustrated magazines. But if bisexual confusion has now become in some young people a posture and a blatant challenge, does that mean that they—as a generation— are less clear about essential sex differences, or are paralyzed, or, indeed, are without fidelities in their sexual lives? I would not think so. The traditional sex-typing which they object to was by no means uniformly beneficial to sexual life. Or are they truly dominated by their negative identities as their display of irreverence seems to indicate? I would not think so at all. True, it gratifies them that parents are dismayed by their appearances, for the display is really a declaration insisting on some positive identity not primarily based on the parental type of conformism or pretension. That such nonconformism, in turn, is a plea for fraternal confirmation and thus acquires a new ritualized character that is part of the paradox of all rebellious identity formation. There is, of course, a more dangerous display of truly negative and ugly possibilities such as those flaunted by some motorcycle youths with the motto, "When you enter a town, look as repulsive as you can." This would be closer to the potentially criminal identity which feeds on rejection by others who are only too eager to confirm it.

Some young people actually seem to read what we write and use our terms almost colloquially. Sometimes they merely acknowledge that we seem to know what they are talking about, and I am not always above accepting this as a compliment. But I would also recognize it as an aspect of the old game of what Freud called "turning passive into active" and thus a new form of youthful experimentation. Often the demonstration seems to declare: "Who says we *suffer* from an identity 'crisis'? We are choosing it, having it actively, we are playing at *making it happen*." The same applies to the acceptance of other previously latent themes and, above all, to the inbuilt ambivalence of the generations. While at one time we cautiously tried to prove to sensitive young people that they also hated the parents they depended on, they now come to us with an overtly ugly or indifferent rejection of all parents and we have difficulty proving to them that they also really like them—in a way. And as we say this, many know it already. Maybe this is a new and more open form of an adaptation to psychiatric enlightenment which in the past has employed seemingly less dangerous because mostly verbal forms: for from Freud's early days onward, enlightened people have adapted to his insights by mouthing the names of their neuroses—and keeping the neuroses, too.

This game may, in fact, have been more dangerous in the past. If we should write a history of hysteria, we would certainly find that sexual wishes, repressed while hysteria dominated the psychopathological market, became strenuously overt as a consequence of psychiatric enlightenment: hysterical symptoms decreased, and character problems replaced them. What in Freud's day, then, was a neurotic epidemiology with social implications has, in our time, become a series of social movements with neurotic implications. This at least opens up many hidden problems to the joint scrutiny and, maybe, the mastery of a young generation which is intent on developing its own ethics and its own kind of vitality in view of the moral abrogation of its parents.

At the same time, we clinicians must remain alert to the possibility that in all the flamboyant identity confusion there is also much of what in those Mt. Zion days we used to refer to as the Pinsk-Minsk mechanism, one of the more timeless contributions of Jewish wit to the understanding of the tricks of the unconscious. In a railroad station in Poland a man runs into a business competitor and asks him where he is going. "To Minsk," the other says, trying to run off. "To Minsk!" the first cries after him, "you say 'to Minsk' so that I should think you are going to Pinsk! You liar—you *are* going to Minsk!"

In other words, some youths who seem to have a somewhat more malignant identity confusion, do. It helps to know, however, that this at least is the crisis appropriate to their age, and also that some are now having it more openly because they know that they are supposed to have it. But our clinical vigilance must not rest, whether the crisis becomes manifest in faddish manners or in psychoticlike conditions, in delinquentlike behavior or in fanatic movements, in creative spurts or even in all too erratic social commitment. When consulted, we can only try to estimate the ego strength of the individual by attempting to diagnose the extent to which conflicting infantile stereotypes still dictate his behavior, and what his chances are of finding himself by losing himself in some absorbing social issue.

5.

In looking at the youth of today, one is apt to forget that identity formation, while being "critical" in youth, is really a *generational issue*. So we must not overlook what appears to be a certain abrogation of responsibility on the part of the older generation in providing those forceful ideals which must antecede identity formation in the next generation—if only so that youth can rebel against a well-defined set of older values.

A recent television documentary dealt with young people in Lexington, Massachusetts. This town was selected, I assume, because it was the cradle of American liberty. The documentary showed with remarkable frankness what has happened to "free" young Americans, or at any rate how they behave publicly. But the parents were hardly there. True, there was one mother who seems to have opened her home to adolescents, and twelve to fifteen teen-agers would gather to study and play the afternoon away in her house and in her garden. But there was hardly a word about the other homes. Parents were seen only at a meeting called to discuss teen-agers, as if they were an invasion from another planet. And that is, indeed, the way youth is now reflected in the "media." And these media, we must note, are no longer content to mediate communication; brashly and efficiently, they make themselves the mediators between the generations. This sometimes forces youth into being caricatures of the reflections of the images they had more or less experimentally "projected," and drives the parents farther away from the eerie happenings. But parental sanction, too, diminishes with parental indignation, and one often senses that youth would rather get rid (as it were) of strong-minded parents than not have any worth mentioning. For if I am not mistaken, parents often impress the young as having remained overgrown boys and girls themselves, taken up with a world of gadgetry and buying power, which permits them to circumvent the whole formidable issue of the new meaning of the generations in a technological universe including the Bomb and the Pill.

Where, then, *are* some of the principal contemporary sources of identity strength? By contemporary I mean a present with an *anticipated future*, for we must do our best to overcome clinical habits which make us assume that we have done our part if we have clarified the past. I will, therefore, not dwell now on the problem of what the traditional remnants of identity strength are—economic, religious, or political; regional or national—all of which are in the process of allying themselves with ideological perspectives in which the vision of an anticipated, and in fact of a planned, future of technological progress will take over much of the power of tradition. And if I call such sources "ideological," I am using the word to denote a universal psychological need for a system of ideas that provides a convincing world image.

It must be confessed that at least those of us who are occupied with making sense of case histories or of biographies (which so often superficially resemble case histories) and who are teaching either young psychiatrists or the humanistically privileged college youth, are often out of touch with the resources of identity available to that majority of youths whose ideology is a product of the machine age. That youth, on the whole, does not need us, and those who do assume the "patient role" created by us. Nor do we seem to think that our theories need to include them. And yet we must assume that masses of young people both here and abroad are close enough both by giftedness and by opportunity to the technological trends and the scientific methods of our time to feel at home in it as much as anybody ever felt at home in human life. I, for one, have never been able to accept the claim that in mercantile culture or in agricultural culture, or, indeed, in book culture, man was in principle less "alienated" than he is in technology. It is, I believe, our own retrospective romanticism which makes us think that peasants or merchants or hunters were less determined by their techniques. To put it in terms of what must be studied concertedly: in every technology and in every historical period there are types of individuals who ("properly" brought up) can combine the dominant techniques with their identity development, and *become* what they *do*. Independently of minor superiorities or inferiorities, they can settle on that *cultural consolidation* which secures them what joint verification and what transitory salvation lies in doing things together and in doing them right—a rightness proven by the bountiful response of "nature," whether in the form of the prey bagged, the food harvested, the goods produced, the money made, or the technological problems solved. In such consolidation and accommodation a million daily tasks and transactions fall into practical patterns and spontaneous ritualizations which can be shared by leaders and led, men and women, adults and children, the privileged and the underprivileged, the specially gifted and those willing to do the chores. The point is that only such consolidation offers the coordinates for the range of a period's identity formations and their necessary relation to a sense of inspired activity, although for many or most it does so only by also creating compartments of pronounced narrowness, of enforced service, and of limited status. Each such consolidation, by dint of its very practicality (the fact that "it works" and maintains itself by mere usage and habituation), also works for entrenched privileges, enforced sacrifices, institutionalized inequalities, and built-in contradictions, which become obvious to the critics of any society. But how such consolidation leads to a sense of embeddedness and natural flux among the very artifacts of organization; how it helps to bring to ascendance some style of perfection and of self-glorification; and how it permits man at the same time to limit his horizon so as *not* to see what might destroy the newly won familiarity of the world and expose him to all manner of strangeness and, above all, to the fear of death or of killing—all of this we have hardly approached from the point of view of depth psychology. Here the discussion of the "ego" should take on new dimensions.

The history of cultures, civilizations, and technologies is the history of such consolidations, while it is only in periods of marked transition that the innovators appear: those too privileged in outlook to remain bound to the prevailing system; too honest or too conflicted not to see the simple truths of existence hidden behind the complexity of daily "necessities"; and too full of pity to overlook "the poor" who have been left out. As therapists and ideologists, we understand the uppermost and the lowest fringe better, because of our own therapeutic ideology. Thus we often take for granted the vast middle which, for reasons of its own, maintains us. Yet insofar as we aspire to contribute to "normal psychology" we must learn to understand cultural and technological consolidation, for it, ever again, inherits the earth.

And always with it comes a new definition of adulthood, without which any question of identity is self-indulgent luxury. The problem of adulthood is how to *take care* of those to whom one finds oneself committed as one emerges from the identity period, and to whom one now owes *their* identity.

Another question is what the "typical" adult of any era's consolidation is able and willing to renounce for himself and demand of others, for the sake of a style of cultural balance and, perhaps, perfection. Judging from the way Socrates, the philosopher, in his Apologia, exposed the fabric of Athenian consolidation, it was probably not only for himself that, at the very end, he pronounced death to be the only cure for the condition of living. Freud, the doctor, revealed for the mercantile and early industrial period what havoc the hypocritical morality was wreaking, not only in his era, but in all of human history. In doing so, he founded what Philipp Rieff has described as the *therapeutic orientation*, which goes far beyond the clinical cure of isolated symptoms. But we cannot know what technological conformity does *to* man unless we know what it does *for* him. The ubiquitous increase in mere number, of course, at first transforms many erstwhile problems of quality into matters of mere quantitative management.

If the majority of young people, therefore, can go along with their parents in a kind of fraternal identification, it is because they jointly leave it to technology and science to carry the burden of providing a self-perpetuating and self-accelerating way of life. This would make it plausible that the young are even expected to develop new values-as-you-go. But the fact is that the values associated with indefinite progress, just because it strains orientation as well as imagination, are often tied to unbelievably old-fashioned ideas. Thus technological expansion can be seen as the due reward of generations of hard-working Americans. No need is felt to limit expansionist ideals, as long as —together with technical discipline—old-fashioned decencies and existing political machineries survive, with all their home-town oratory. There is always hope (a hope which has become an important part of an implicit American ideology) that in re-gard to any possible built-in evil in the very nature of super-machines, appropriate brakes and corrections will be invented in the nick of time, without any undue investment of strenuously new principles. And while they "work," the supermachineries, organizations, and associations provide a sufficiently "great," or at any rate adjustable, identity for all those who feel actively en-gaged in and by them.

Thus, also, that major part of youth which sees no reason to oppose the war in Vietnam is animated by a combination of a world-war patriotism, anticommunism, obedience to the draft and to military discipline, and finally by that unshakable solidar-ity, the highest feeling among men, which comes from having renounced the same pleasures, facing the same dangers, and hav-ing to obey the same obnoxious orders. But there is a new ele-ment in all this which comes from the technological ideology and makes a soldier an expert whose armament is mechanized and whose fidelity is an almost impersonal technical compliance with a policy or strategy which puts a certain *target* into the range of one of the admirable weapons at hand. No doubt cer-tain "character structures" fit such a world view better than others, and yet, on the whole, each generation is prepared to participate in a number of consolidated attitudes in one lifetime.

But until a new ethics catches up with progress, one senses the danger that the limits of technological expansion and national as-sertion may not be determined by known facts and ethical con-siderations or, in short, by a certainty of identity, but by a will-ful and playful testing of the range and the limit of the super-machinery which thus takes over much of man's conscience. This could become affluent slavery for all involved, and this seems to be what the new "humanist" youth is trying to stop by putting its own existence "on the line" and insisting on a modicum of a self-sustaining quality of living.

6.

Now let us turn to that other, and to many of us more familiar, ideological source of identity, namely, the neohumanism which in fact makes youth so acutely aware of identity problems. Those who, in the contemptuous view of youth consolidated in technological expansion, are the "peaceniks," are the humanists whose style of consolidation also includes quite old-fashioned sentiments and ideals (in appearance, they often seem to be emerging from an underground medieval town) while it is hospitable to ideals of civil disobediance and nonviolence which in their modern form originated (but by no means ended) with Mahatma Gandhi.[8] Here opposition to thoughtless mechanization goes together with a dislike of regimentation and of the military kind of enthusiasm, and with a sensitive awareness of the existential individuality of anyone in the range of a gun sight. This and the technocratic view must obviously oppose and repel each other, for the acceptance of even a part of one view causes a slide leading to a reconversion of the whole configuration of images. Often, therefore, these two views face one another as if the other were *the* enemy, although he may be brother, friend—or oneself at a different stage of one's own life.

Twenty years ago we related identity problems with much hesitation (for the term was then highly suspect) to the *ideological needs* of youth, ascribing, in fact, much acute confusion to a kind of ideological undernourishment on the part of those youths who had come too late to share either the military fervor of the world wars "over there" or the radicalism of the first postwar years over here. American youth, we said, was anti-ideological, glorifying instead a "way of life"—and a comfortable one. We were afraid, of course, that the "materialist" trend so vastly reinforced by technology would find little balance in a youth to whom all ideology had become political and foreign,

the more so since McCarthyism had succeeded in creating in almost all Americans a fear of radical thinking amounting to a
traumatic transformation of a previously cherished identity into
a negative one.

Since then some American youths have proven themselves in
the civil rights movement as well as in the Peace Corps, showing
that they can accept unaccustomed hardship and discipline when
moved by a convincing ideological trend applied to real and universal needs. In fact, in such universal matters as the opposition
to unrestricted armament or to a thoughtless consent to the acceleration of the war in Vietnam, youth has proven more fore-
sighted than many, many adults. To the horror of a parent generation brainwashed by McCarthyism they have reinstated some
of their own parents' abandoned ideals.

But only after having discussed, as far as my conceptual means
permit, that majority of youth which derives a certain strength
of identity from the whole ideological package of technological
expansion can I discuss our new-humanist youth from a more
balanced viewpoint. For does not an interplay between a new
dominant class of *specialists*—those who "know what they are
doing"—and an intense new group of universalists—those who
"mean what they are saying"—always determine the identity
possibilities of an age? And those who mean it often care deeply
for and become the champions of a third group—those who
have been left behind by all concerned. In our time these are the
technologically or educationally underprivileged who are cut off
from all ideologies because of lack of capacity or opportunity or
(of course) both. In revolutionary times, then, the overprivileged
and the underprivileged often reach out to each other, both being marginal to the vast consolidation of the "compact majority."

The more mature among our new young humanists are seeking a common denominator in human life—some kind of worldwide identity bridging affluence and underdevelopment. For
some individuals who might otherwise have rebelled unfruitfully
or withdrawn completely, the capacity to employ their conflict
in a socially relevant and activist movement undoubtedly has po-

tential therapeutic value. At the same time it seems clear that the "therapeutic" as well as the political value of all these groups depends on the vitality of their communal potential—and on the discipline and inventiveness of their leaders.

The protests of humanist youth range from romantic Edwardianism and jazzy *Wandervogeltum* to the deeply committed "New Left," and to an identification with naked heroism anywhere in the world where "machines" threaten to crush man's will. They range, in other words, from a reactionary resistance to all machine conformity to a reformulation of human rights and dignities in an irreversibly technological future. If they seem perplexed and sometimes bizarre in the light of these demands, we should remind ourselves that it was the tradition of enlightenment which, taking a stable middle class or a liberal world for granted, opened all values to ruthless inquiry. Now the young must experiment with what is left of this "enlightened" and "analyzed" world. The psychoanalytic enlightenment, for example, assumed that infantile sexuality and perversions could be brought to public attention with an advocacy of enlightened judgment as a replacement for age-old repression. Now perversions, as, indeed, all kinds of perversity, must find their own limits of attractiveness in print and deed. Therefore, only a relative freedom of experimentation can find its own correction where the parental combination of radical enlightenment and old-fashioned morality has failed. Yet the search of youth, I believe, is not for all-permissibility, but rather for new ways of directly facing up to what truly counts.

We will undoubtedly see a tragic re-evaluation of the first attempts of youth to ritualize life for themselves and by themselves and against us, and of the way in which, in the face of provocation and challenge, the elder generation abdicates too willingly and too quickly their vital role as sanctioners and critics. For without some leadership—and, if need be, leadership that can be lustily resisted—the young humanists are in danger of becoming irrelevant and ending up, each individual and each clique, stewing in strictly episodical "consciousness expansion."

And now from speculation to utopia. The possibility of a true polarization of the new specialized-technological identity and the universalist-humanist one must be allowed for the simple reason that such a polarization is the mark of the over-all identity of any period. A new generation growing up with and in technological and scientific progress as a matter of course will be prepared by the daily confrontation with radically new practical possibilities to entertain radically new modes of thought. This may form a link between a new culture and new forms of society, allowing for ways of balancing specialization with new inner freedom. And neohumanist youth will find some accommodation with the machine age in which they already fully participate in their daily habits. Thus each group may reach in the other that sensitivity or sturdiness which may be ready for activation. Polarization, however, is continued tension and dynamic interplay. I do not mean, then, to predict or even to wish that the clarity of opposition of the technological and the neohumanist identity be blurred, for dynamic interply needs clear poles. What I mean to suggest is that youth, in all its diversities, will share a common fate, namely, a change in the generational process itself. In saying this, I am not abandoning my conception of the human life cycle or of the place of identity in it. Rather I will submit that subdivisions in the stages of greatest importance for identity will distribute generational functions somewhat differently. Already today the mere division into an older, i.e., parent, generation and a younger, i.e., pre-parent, generation is, as you may have noted in what I have said, becoming rather superannuated. Rapid technological change makes it impossible for any traditional way of being older to become so institutionalized that the younger generation can step right into it or, indeed, resist it in revolutionary fashion. Aging, for example, will be (or already is) a quite different experience for those who find themselves occupationally outdated than for those who have something somewhat more lasting to offer. By the same token, young adulthood will be divided into older and younger young adults, the not too young and not too old specialists probably moving

into the position of principal arbiters—each for the limited period of the ascendance of a particular stage of his speciality. His
power, in many ways, will replace tradition as the sanction of
parenthood. But this also means that the "younger generation"
will be (or already is, as I would testify from my observations as
college teacher) divided more clearly into the older and the
younger young generation, where the former will have to take
(and is eager to take) much of the direction of the conduct of
the latter. Thus the relative waning of the parents and the emergence of the young adult specialist as the permanent and perma-
nently changing authority is bringing about a shift by which
older youth guided by such young authority will have to take
increasing responsibility for the conduct of younger youth—
and we for the orientation of the specialists and of older youth.
This, however, we can only do by recognizing and cultivating
an age-specific *ethical* capacity in older youth—which is the true
criterion of identity. That we consistently neglect this potential
and even deny it in good paternalistic fashion is probably re-
sented much more by youth than our dutiful and feeble attempts
to keep order by prohibition. At any rate, the ethics of the future will be less concerned with the relationship of generations
to each other than with the interplay of individuals in a scheme
in which the whole life-span is extended; in which new roles for
both sexes will emerge in all life stages; and in which a certain
measure of choice and identity must be the common value, to be
guaranteed in principle to every child planned to be born—
anywhere.

As this can never again become a matter of fixed tradition, it
probably cannot be the concern of old-fashioned "movements."
New social inventions will replace both, but they can emerge
only from a new and young sense of ethics which values the vital
moment in relentless change.

7.

Having gone so far in utopian directions, I will, in conclusion,
revert to man's past, and this time to a very long time span in his
development, namely, sociogenetic evolution—with a brief

glance back to the Garden of Eden.

How did man's need for individual identity evolve? Before Darwin, the answer was clear: because God created Adam in His own image, as a counterplayer of His Identity, and thus bequeathed to all man the glory and the despair of individuation and faith. I admit to not having come up with any better explanation. The Garden of Eden, of course, has had many utopian transformations since that expulsion from the unity of creation —an expulsion which tied man's identity forever to the manner of his toil and of his co-operation with others, and with technical and communal pride.

A certain New Englander was once working in his garden when a parson walked by and congratulated him on what God and he had wrought together as evidenced in such a commendable yield. "Yep," the man said, "and you should have seen it when God had it all to himself." In such a story, God is not dead, just put in his place. Each cultural consolidation around a state of technology has its way of creating familiarity with the Unfamiliar. Technological and enlightened man, however, seems to flatter himself more than any man before him that he has the universe to himself and that an experimentally inclined God, very much made in man's image, is glad to step aside for him. At any rate, I have heard very clever men (but never a woman) claim that in principle there is nothing in nature that man cannot now learn to understand. "Death, too?" I heard a woman ask one of these metaphysical technocrats, and he nodded with an enigmatic smile. And man, he continued, therefore can, in principle, change anything in nature or in his own nature to fit any blueprint. "Whose blueprint?" the woman asked. Another smile. Thus, it is part of today's consolidation that man re-internalizes the eternal Identity whom he had projected on the (now, in principle, conquerable) heavens, and tries to remake himself in the blueprint of a manufactured identity In conjunction with the fact that man also can now totally *un*make himself, however, an all-human identity becomes an inescapable goal.

In this, however, revived forms of humanisms and libertarian-isms will not do. Their original proponents, we must remember, did not know of the two objects already mentioned, the gigantic bomb and the tiny pill, which, if they do not give man power over life and death, certainly give him the decision as to whose life and death it shall be—decisions which will call for new "political" forms.

This brings me to a final perspective which will, at any rate, help to throw light on the over-all significance of the problem of identity and provide the best argument yet for our *not* settling on any methodology or any definition too early. For man's need for a psychosocial identity is anchored in nothing less than his sociogenetic evolution. It has been said (by Waddington) that authority-accepting is what characterizes man's sociogenetic evolution. I would submit that identity formation is inseparable from this, for only within a defined group identity can true authority exist.

Man as a species has survived by being divided into what I have called *pseudospecies*. First each horde or tribe, class and nation, but then also every religious association has become *the* human species, considering all the others a freakish and gratuitous invention of some irrelevant deity. To reinforce the illusion of being chosen, every tribe recognizes a creation of its own, a mythology and later a history: thus was loyalty to a particular ecology and morality secured. One never quite knew how all the other tribes came to be, but since they did exist, they were at least useful as a screen of projection for the negative identities which were the necessary, if most uncomfortable, counterpart of the positive ones. This projection, in conjunction with their territoriality, gave men a reason to slaughter one another *in majorem gloriam*. If, then, identity can be said to be a "good thing" in human evolution—because good things are those which seem to have been necessary for what, indeed, has survived—we should not overlook the fact that this system of mortal divisions has been vastly overburdened with the function of reaffirming for each pseudospecies its superiority over all others. Maybe we and our youth are turning to thoughts of identity precisely because the world wars have shown that a glorification of the pseudospecies can now spell the end of the species, wherefore an all-inclusive human identity must be part of the anticipation of a universal technology. It is this anticipation, also, which will unite some of the majority and of the minority among our youths in one universe. But this places all older identities in deadly danger. "Prejudiced" people, wherever they are, may therefore fight a murderous rear-guard battle; and ascending nations and even ancient ones endangered in their "young" national identities may well delay and endanger a worldwide identity.

The pseudospecies, then, is one of the more sinister aspects of all group identity. But there are also "pseudo" aspects in all identity which endanger the individual. For man's development does not begin or end with identity; and identity, too, must become relative for the mature person. Psychosocial identity is necessary as the anchoring of man's transient existence in the here and the now. That it is transient does not make it expendable. If, to those who seek an identity, Norman Brown advocates "Get lost" and Timothy Leary "Drop out," I would suggest that to get lost one must have found oneself, and to drop out one must have been in. The danger of all existentialism which chooses to remain juvenile is that it shirks the responsibility for the generational process, and thus advocates an abortive human identity. We have learned from the study of lives that beyond childhood, which provides the moral basis of our identity, and beyond the ideology of youth, only an adult ethics can guarantee to the next generation an equal chance to experience the full cycle of humanness. And this alone permits the individual to transcend his identity—to become as truly individual as he will ever be, and as truly beyond all individuality.

We realize, then, the widening context of the problem of identity. Beginning with veterans of war and severely disturbed young people, we have come to formulate a normative crisis in individual development. From that of delinquent and violent upheavals we have come to suspect a significance of identity in the whole scheme of sociogenetic evolution. And from the social boundness of identity we have come to envisage its own transcendance. In what follows we will review these steps in all the fragmentary details of our original observations, so that we may at least know where we came from when we started to use the term and, maybe, see where it may yet lead us.

When it comes to central aspects of man's existence, we can only conceptualize at a given time what is relevant to us for personal, for conceptual, and for historical reasons. And even as we do so, the data and the conclusions change before our eyes. Especially at a time when our conceptualizations and interpretations become part of a historically self-conscious scene, and when insight and conduct influence each other with an immediacy that hardly leaves a pause for any new "tradition" to form —in such a time all thinking about man becomes an experiment in living. The newness of man's self-awareness and of his attention to his awareness has, at first, led to a scientific mythology of the mind or to a mythological use of scientific terms and methods, as if social science could and would repeat in a short time, and in view of immediate practical goals, the whole long progress of natural science from nature philosophy to pure and applied science. But man, the subject of psychosocial science, will not hold still enough to be divided into categories both measurable and relevant. In reviewing and discussing two decades of work, we cannot present it as a system expected to survive discarded systems, but as a bit of conceptual living both limited and enhanced by what historical relevance and consequence it may possess for a time.

Foundations in Observation

1. A CLINICIAN'S NOTEBOOK

THE STUDY OF THE EGO in psychoanalysis has hardly begun to account for the relationship of this "inner agency" to social life. Men who share the concerns of an *ethnic group*, who are contemporaries in a *historical era*, or who compete and co-operate in *economic pursuits* are also guided by common images of good and evil. Infinitely varied, these images reflect the elusive nature of cultural differences and of historical change; in the form of contemporary social models they assume decisive concreteness in every individual's struggle for ego synthesis—and in every patient's failure. In the traditional case history, however, the patient's residence, ethnic background, and occupation are the first items to be radically altered when it is necessary to disguise his personal identity. The essence of the inner dynamics of a case, it is judged, is thereby left intact. The exact nature, then, of the values common to the patient's background are considered to be so close to the "surface" that they are not necessarily of "psychoanalytic" interest. I will not now discuss the rationale for such neglect [1] but merely offer observations from my notebook which seem to indicate that contemporary social models are both clinically and theoretically relevant and cannot be shunted off by brief and patronizing tributes to the role "also" played by "social factors." [2]

The general neglect of these factors in psychoanalysis naturally has not furthered a rapprochement with the social sciences. Students of society and history, on the other hand, blithely continue to ignore the simple fact that all individuals are born by mothers; that everybody was once a child; that people and peoples begin in their nurseries; and that society consists of generations in the process of developing from children into parents, destined to absorb the historical changes of their lifetimes and to continue to make history for their descendants.

Only psychoanalysis and social science together can eventually chart the course of individual life in the setting of a changing community. Ambitious steps in this direction have been made by eminent psychoanalysts, generally called neo-Freudians, who bypass the efforts of "ego psychology." Instead of adopting some of their terminology, which, to my mind, over-adjusts some basic Freudian notions to a new climate of discourse, I will restrict myself here to offering a collection of observations which may help to prepare the way for a new formulation of the ego's relation to the social order.

I. GROUP IDENTITY AND EGO IDENTITY

a

Freud's original formulations concerning the ego and its relation to society necessarily depended on the general state of psychoanalytic theory at the time and on the sociological formulations of his era. The focus of theorizing was the "id," the instinctual force driving man from within; while in his first group-psychological discussions, Freud referred to observations on mass behavior made by the postrevolutionary French sociologist Le Bon. This has left its mark on consequent psychoanalytic discussions of "multitudes" of men, for Le Bon's "masses" were society on the rebound, shiftless mobs enjoying the anarchy between two consolidated stages of society and, at their best and worst, leader-led mobs. Such mobs exist; their definition stands. However, there is a wide gap between this sociological model and the psychological one governing the psychoanalytic method —namely the reconstruction of the individual's history from the evidence of transferences and countertransferences, in a therapeutic situation strictly *à deux*. The resulting methodological divergence has perpetuated in psychoanalytic thought an artificial overdifferentiation between the isolated individual forever projecting his infantile family constellation on the "outer world," and the "individual-in-the-mass," submerged in what Freud calls an "indistinct aggregate" of men. Yet that a man could ever be psychologically alone; that a man, "alone," is essentially different from the same man in a group; that a man in a temporary solitary condition or when closeted with his analyst has ceased to be a "political" animal and has disengaged himself from social action (or inaction) on whatever class level—these and similar stereotypes demand careful revision.

The concept of the ego, then, was first delineated by the definitions of these counterplayers, the biological id and the sociological "masses." The ego, the individual center of organized experience and reasonable planning, stood endangered by both the anarchy of the primeval instincts and the lawlessness of the group spirit. If Kant gave as the co-ordinates of the moral burgher "the stars above him" and "the moral law within him," the early Freud placed his fearful ego between the id within him and the mob around him.

To safeguard the encircled individual's precarious morality, Freud instituted within the ego the superego. Here, too, the emphasis was at first on the foreign burden which was thus imposed upon the ego. The superego, as Freud pointed out, is the internalization of all the restrictions to which the ego must bow. It is forced upon the child (*"von aussen aufgenoetigt"*) by the critical influence of the parents and, later, of professional educators and the "vague multitude of fellow men" (*"die unbestimmte Menge der Genossen"*) who make up the "milieu" and "public opinion."[3]

Surrounded by such mighty disapproval, the child's original state of naive self-love is said to be compromised. He looks for models by which to measure himself, and seeks happiness in trying to resemble them. Where he succeeds he achieves self-esteem, a not too satisfactory facsimile of his original narcissism and sense of omnipotence.

These early conceptual models have continued to determine the trend of discussions and the aims of practice in clinical psychoanalysis, although the focus of our research has shifted to a variety of genetic problems, including observations which attest to the constructive necessity of social organization in the individual's development. From the study of the ego's dissipation in an amorphous multitude of others, we must turn to the problem of the infantile ego's very origin in social life. Instead of emphasizing what the pressures of social organization are apt to deny the child, we wish to clarify what the social order may first grant to the infant as it keeps him alive and as, in administering to his needs in specific ways, it introduces him to a particular cultural style. Instead of accepting such instinctual "givens" as the Oedipus trinity as an irreducible schema for man's irrational conduct, we are exploring the way in which social forms co-determine the structure of the family; for, as Freud said toward the end of his life, ". . . what is operating in the superego is not only the personal qualities of these parents but also everything that produced a determining effect upon them themselves, the tastes and standards of the social class in which they live and the characteristics and traditions of the race from which they spring." [4]

b

Freud has shown that sexuality begins with birth, and he has also given us tools for demonstrating the fact that social life begins with each individual's beginnings.

These tools can be applied to the study of so-called primitive societies where child training seems to be integrated with a well-defined economic system and a small, static inventory of social prototypes. Child training in such groups is the method by which a group's basic ways of organizing experience, or what

we may call group identity, is transmitted to the infant's early
bodily experiences and, through them, to the beginnings of his
ego.

Let me first illustrate the concept of group identity by a brief
reference to anthropological observations made by H. S. Mekeel
and myself in 1938.[5] We described how in one segment of the re-
education of the American Indian, the Sioux Indians' historical
identity of the buffalo hunter stands counterposed to the occupational and class identity of his re-educator, the American civil
service employee. We pointed out that the identities of these
groups rest on extreme differences in geographic and historical
perspectives (collective ego-space-time) and on radical differences in economic goals and means (collective life plan).

In the remnants of the Sioux Indians' identity, the prehistoric
past is a powerful psychological reality. The conquered tribe has
never ceased to behave as if guided by a life plan consisting of
passive resistance to a present which fails to reintegrate the identity remnants of the economic past; and of dreams of restoration
in which the future would lead back into the past, time would
again become ahistoric, hunting grounds unlimited, and the
buffalo supply inexhaustible—a restoration which would permit
again the boundlessly centrifugal life of hunting nomads. Their
federal educators, on the other hand, preach values with centripetal and localized goals: homestead, fireplace, bank account
—all of which receive their meaning from a life plan in which
the past is overcome and in which the full measure of fulfillment
in the present is sacrificed to an ever-higher standard of living in
the future. The road to this future is not outer restoration but
inner reform.

Obviously every item of human experience as lived by a member of one of these groups and as shared or debated by members
of both groups, must be defined according to its place on the co-
ordinates of these now coexisting plans. In the primitive plan,
men have a direct relation to the sources and means of production. Their tools are extensions of the human body. Children in
these groups participate in technical and in magic pursuits; to

them, body and environment, childhood and culture may be full of dangers, but they are all one world. The inventory of social prototypes is small and static. In our world, machines, far from remaining an extension of the body, destine whole human organizations to be extensions of machinery; magic serves intermediate links only; and childhood becomes a separate segment of life with its own folklore. The expansiveness of civilization, together with its stratification and specialization, demanded that children base their ego models on shifting, sectional, and contradictory prototypes.

No wonder that Indian children, forced to live by both these plans, often seem blocked in their expectations and paralyzed in their ambitions. For the growing child must derive a vitalizing sense of reality from the awareness that his individual way of mastering experience, his ego synthesis, is a successful variant of a group identity and is in accord with its space-time and life plan. A child who has just found himself able to walk, for example, seems not only driven to repeat and perfect the act of walking by the promise of libidinal pleasure in the sense of Freud's locomotor erotism, or by the need for mastery in the sense of Ives Hendrick's work principle; he also becomes aware of the new status and stature of "one who can walk," with whatever connotation this happens to have in the co-ordinates of his culture's life plan—be it "one who will swiftly run after fleeing prey," "one who will go far," "one who will be upright," or "one who might go too far." To be "one who can walk" becomes one of the many steps in child development which through the coincidence of physical mastery and cultural meaning, of functional pleasure and social recognition, contribute to a realistic *self-esteem*. By no means only a narcissistic extension of infantile omnipotence, this self-esteem gradually grows into a conviction that the ego is capable of integrating effective steps toward a tangible collective future, that it is developing into a well-organized ego within a social reality. This sense I have tentatively called *ego identity*. We must now attempt to circumscribe the area embraced by this concept as a subjective experience and as a dynamic fact, as a group-psychological phenomenon and as a subject for clinical investigation.

But here it is necessary to differentiate between personal identity and ego identity. The conscious feeling of having a personal identity is based on two simultaneous observations: the perception of the selfsameness and continuity of one's existence in time and space and the perception of the fact that others recognize one's sameness and continuity. What I have called ego identity, however, concerns more than the mere *fact* of existence; it is, as it were, the ego *quality* of this existence. Ego identity then, in its subjective aspect, is the awareness of the fact that there is a self-sameness and continuity to the ego's synthesizing methods, the *style of one's individuality*, and that this style coincides with the sameness and continuity of one's *meaning for significant others* in the immediate community.

c

To return to the id: while it was a step of inestimable import when Freud applied concepts of physical energy to psychology, the exclusive emphasis on the theoretical model by which *instinctual energy* is transferred, displaced, and transformed in analogy to the preservation of energy in a closed system no longer suffices to help us manage the data which we observe when looking at man in his historical and cultural setting.

We must find the nexus of social images and of organismic forces—and this not merely in the sense that here images and forces are, as the saying goes, "interrelated." More than this: the mutual complementation of group identity and ego identity, of ethos and ego, puts a greater energy potential at the disposal of both ego synthesis and social organization. I have tried to approach this first by comparing traumata in childhood which, as clinical observation tells us, are universal to man, with anthropological observations concerning the form such traumata take in a given tribe. Such an experience may be the loss of the mother's breast. A "typical" trauma experienced by all the members of the Sioux tribe in early childhood "happens" when the nursing mothers punish the teething infants for biting the breast which up to then had been so generously offered. The children are said to react to this uniformly with rage. The tribe's ontogenetic "expulsion from paradise," then, causes a "fixation" which we found to be of decisive relevance in the Sioux's group identity and in his individual development. When the hero of the Sioux sun dance, at the height of the religious ceremonial, drives little sticks through his breast, ties the sticks to a rope, the rope to a pole, and in a peculiar trance dances backward until the rope tightens and the sticks split his breast so that the gushing blood runs freely down his body, we find both instinctual and social meaning in his extreme behavior. He is manfully atoning for the sin which cost him the paradise of habitual closeness to the mother's breast, but as a ceremonial hero he is also dramatizing a tragic involvement common to all.[6]

It makes similar sense when a Yurok man, having been with a woman, proceeds to heat himself by the fire of the sweathouse until he is supple and wet enough to squeeze through a very small oval opening in the wall, and then jumps into the cold river. Having thus given rebirth to himself, he is free from the dangerous bondage of women and pure and strong enough to net the sacred salmon. Here, also, male self-esteem and inner security are restored by ritual atonement. The same Indians, on the other hand, after having achieved the yearly engineering feat of bridging the river with a dam that collects a whole winter's supply of salmon, will indulge in promiscuous intercourse and experience the manic relief of orgiastic excess, which, once a year, throws atonement to the winds. In all these ritual acts we see "id" and "superego" put into conflictful oppositions such as those we have learned to recognize in the "private rituals," i.e., in the impulsive and compulsive symptoms of our patients.

But if we try to define the state of relative equilibrium between these dramatic extremes, if we ask what characterizes an Indian when he does not do much more than just calmly be an Indian bent on the daily chores of the year's cycle, our description lacks a fitting frame of reference. We look for small indications of the fact that man, anywhere, any time, betrays in minute emotional and ideational changes an ever-present conflict manifested in changes of mood from one that is decidedly low through what Freud referred to as "a certain in-between stage" to heightened well-being. But is this in-between stage dynamically so unimportant that it can be defined by pointing out what it is not; by stating that neither a manic nor a depressive trend is, at the time, clearly noticeable; that a momentary lull exists on the battlefield of the ego; that the superego is temporarily non-belligerent and that the id has agreed to an armistice?

d

The necessity for defining the relative equilibrium between various "states of mind" became acute in the need to appraise morale in war. I had an opportunity to make a few observations on one of the more extreme milieus of human endeavor, namely, life on submarines.[7]

On submarines the emotional plasticity and social resourcefulness of the crew are put to a high test. The heroic expectations and phallic-locomotor fantasies with which a young adult volunteer approaches submarine service are, on the whole, not verified in the small chores and in the constricted space of his daily experience on board and in the relatively blind, deaf, and dumb role demanded of him in action. The extreme interdependence with the crew and the mutual responsibility for comfort and life under prolonged conditions of extreme hardship soon supersede the original fantasies. Crew and captain establish a symbiosis not governed by official regulations alone. With astonishing tact and native wisdom, silent arrangements are made by which the captain becomes sensory system, brains, and conscience for the whole submerged organism of minutely tuned machinery and humanity, and by which the crew members mobilize in themselves compensatory mechanisms (for example, in the collective use of the generously provided food), permitting the crew to stand monotony and yet to be ready for instant action. Such automatic mutual adaptations to extreme milieus at first seem to make "psychoanalytical sense" where an apparent regression to a primal horde, and to a kind of oral lethargy, can be traced. In psychiatric discussions it is in fact not infrequently suspected on the evidence of mere analogies—that whole units, crews, and occupational groups are primarily motivated by latent homosexual or psychopathic tendencies; and it is true that individuals suspected of overt homosexuality have on occasion been treated with utmost derision and cruelty by submarine crews. Yet again, if we ask why men choose such a life, why they stick to it in spite of incredible monotony and occasional nightmarish danger, and above all why they function in good health, in high spirits, and with occasional heroism, we do not have a satisfactory dynamic answer.

What the submarine man on the job, the Indian at work, and the growing child have in common with all men who feel at one with what they are doing when and where they are doing it is akin to that "in-between state" which we wish our children would preserve as they grow older, and which we want our patients to gain when the synthesizing function of the ego is restored. Whenever this state is achieved, play becomes more inventive, health more radiant, sexuality freer, and work more meaningful. We are in need, then, of concepts which throw light on the *mutual complementation* of ego synthesis and social organization, the cultivation of which on ever higher levels is the aim of all therapeutic endeavor, social and individual.

II. EGO PATHOLOGY AND HISTORICAL CHANGE

a

A child has many opportunities to identify himself, more or less experimentally, with real or fictitious people of either sex and with habits, traits, occupations, and ideas. Certain crises force him to make radical selections. However, the historical era in which he lives offers only a limited number of socially meaningful models for workable combinations of identification fragments. Their usefulness depends on the way in which they simultaneously meet the requirements of the organism's maturational stage, the ego's style of synthesis, and the demands of the culture.

The desperate intensity of many a child's neurotic or delinquent symptom may express the necessity to defend a budding ego identity against thoughtless "guidance" or punishment. What to the observer may look like an especially powerful manifestation of naked instinctual expression is often only a desperate plea for permission to synthesize and sublimate in the only way possible. We therefore can expect our young patients to respond only to therapeutic measures which will help them to complete or to rearrange the prerequisites for an identity already under formation. Therapy and guidance may attempt to substitute more desirable identifications for undesirable ones, but the original direction of the identity formation remains unalterable.

I am thinking here of an ex-German soldier who emigrated to this country because he could not accept Nazism or was unacceptable to it. His little son had hardly had time to absorb Nazi indoctrination before he came to this country, where, like most children, he took to Americanization like a duck to water. Gradually, however, he developed a neurotic rebellion against all authority. What he said about the "older generation," and how he said it, was clearly taken from Nazi writings which he had never read and his behavior was an unconscious one-boy Hitler youth rebellion. A superficial analysis indicated that the boy in identifying with the slogans of Hitler youth identified himself with his father's aggressors.

At this point, the boy's parents decided to send him to a military school. I expected him to rebel violently. Instead, a marked change came over him the moment he was handed a uniform with the promise of gold bars, stars, and rank. It was as if these military symbols effected a sudden and decisive change in his inner economy. The boy was now an unconscious Hitler youth wrapped up in an American prototype: the military schoolboy. The father, a mere civilian, now was neither dangerous nor important.

Somewhere, however, it had been this same father and related father surrogates who with unconscious gestures [8] (especially when speaking of military exploits during the First World War) had helped establish in this boy the military prototype which is a part of many a European's group identity, and for the German has the special significance of being one of the few all-German and highly professionalized identities. As a historical focus of many part-identifications the military identity thus continues to be dominant unconsciously even in those who are excluded from its consummation by political developments.[9]

The more subtle methods by which children are induced to accept historical or actual people as prototypes of good and evil consist of minute displays of emotions such as affection, pride, anger, guilt, anxiety, and sexual tension. They themselves, rather than merely the words used, the meanings intended, or the philosophy implied, transmit to the human child the outlines of what really counts in his world, i.e., the variables of his group's space-time and the perspectives of its life plan. Equally elusive are the minute socioeconomic and cultural panics which involve the family, causing individual regressions to infantile atonements and a reactionary return to more primitive moral codes. When such panics coincide in time and dynamic quality with one of the child's psychosexual crises, they play a significant role in the "choice" of symptoms, for every neurosis reflects shared panic, isolated anxiety, and somatic tension all at once. But this also means, as in the example cited, that a symptom may combine individual with historical regression. In our guilt-culture, as a consequence, there occur not only individual regressions to early guilt feelings and atonements, but also reactionary returns to the content and form of historically earlier and stricter principles of behavior. Where a group's socioeconomic status is in danger, the implicit moral code becomes more restricted, more magic, more exclusive, and more intolerant, as though an outer danger had to be treated as an inner one. And it is clinically significant to realize that what our patients persistently describe as their childhood milieu often is the condensation of a few selected periods in which too many simultaneous changes resulted in a panicky atmosphere, "loaded" with a variety of conflicting affects.

In the case of a five-year-old boy who produced convulsions after a number of coincidental experiences of violent aggression and sudden death, the very idea of violence had received its problematic meaning from the family history. The father was an Eastern European Jew whom the mild, meek grandparents had taken as a five-year-old to New York's East Side, where he could survive only by superimposing on his earlier identity components that of a guy who hits first. This image he had painstakingly built into our small patient's budding identity, not without indicating how much it had cost him. Having survived with reasonable economic success, however, he then opened a store on the main street of a small Yankee town and moved into a residential neighborhood where he had to revoke his initial demands for toughness. Instead, he pleadingly and threateningly tried to impress on his now cocky and inquisitive little boy the fact that a shopkeeper's son must treat the gentiles gently. This revaluation of identity components occurred in the boy's phallic-locomotor stage at a time when he needed clear directions and new opportunities of expression—and incidentally at an age analogous to that at which his father had been the victim of migration. The family panic ("Let's be gentle or else we will lose ground"), the individual anxiety ("How can I be gentle when I must be tough to feel safe?"), the Oedipal problem of diverting aggression from the father to an out-group, and the somatic tension caused by undirected rage—these were all specific to one another, causing a short circuit instead of the mutual regulation which should dominate simultaneous changes in organism, environment, and ego. His epileptic reaction became manifest.[10]

b

I will now turn to a description of the way in which historical prototypes reappear in the transferences and resistances encountered in the treatment of adults. The following excerpt illustrates the relationship of an infantile identity crisis to the patient's adult life style.

A dancer, of considerable good looks although extremely small stature, developed the annoying symptom of having to hold her torso so rigidly upright that her dancing became awkward and ungainly. The analysis proved her hysterical erectness to be representative of an unconscious penis envy which had been provoked in childhood and had become intrinsic to her exhibitionism. The patient was the only daughter of a second-generation German-American, a successful businessman given to a certain exhibitionistic individualism which included a great pride in his powerful physique. He insisted on an erect posture (probably no longer consciously Prussian) on the part of his blond sons, but did not require the same from his dark-haired daughter; in fact, he did not seem to consider the over-all posture of the female body important. This inequality of treatment reinforced the patient's wish to compete with her brothers and to exhibit an "improved" posture in her dancing which became a caricature of Prussian ancestors whom she had never seen.

The historical meaning of such a sympton is clarified by the analysis of the resistances with which it is defended. The patient, who in her conscious and "positive" thoughts always drew a parallel between the father's and the analyst's tall, "Nordic" physiques, to her great dismay found herself dreaming of the analyst as a small, dirty, crumpled-up Jew. With this image of inferior race and weak masculinity, she apparently attempted to disqualify him from the right to explore the secret of her symptom. But it also illuminated the danger to her fragile ego identity of an unruly pair of historical prototypes—an ideal prototype (German, tall, phallic) and an evil prototype (Jewish, dwarfish, castrated). The patient's final ego identity had attempted to subsume and to sublimate this dangerous alternative in the role of the radically modern and erect dancer—a creative solution which, however, still harbored too much of an exhibitionistic protest against the inferiority of her female body. Her father's male exhibitionism, as well as his German prejudices, had been inculcated into the patient throught the sensual testimony of childhood and thus had retained a dangerous degree of disturbing power in her unconscious.

Analyses of this kind permit us, I think, to generalize that the unconscious evil identity, that which the ego is most afraid to resemble, is often composed of the images of the violated (castrated) body, the ethnic out-group, and the exploited minority. Although it manifests itself in a great variety of syndromes, this association is all-pervasive, in men and women, in majorities and minorities, and in all classes of a given national or cultural unit. For the ego, in the course of its synthesizing efforts, attempts to subsume the most powerful ideal and evil prototypes (the final contestants, as it were) and with them the whole existing imagery of superior and inferior, good and bad, masculine and feminine, free and slave, potent and impotent, beautiful and ugly, black and white, tall and small, in one simple alternative in order to make one battle and one strategy out of a bewildering number of skirmishes. In this connection, the latent image of the more homogeneous past exerts its reactionary influence in specific resistances. We must study it, so that we may understand the historical origin of the accentuated alternative for which the patient's ego is searching.

The unconscious associations of ethnic prototypes of good and evil with moral and sexual ones are, we may add, a necessary part of any group formation. In studying them, psychoanalysis perfects its therapeutic methods and, at the same time, contributes to the knowledge of the unconscious concomitants of group prejudice. But in the inventory of our patients' ideal and evil prototypes we probably also meet face to face the clinical facts on which Jung based his theory of inherited prototypes ("archetypes").

Jung's controversial theory reminds us in passing of the fundamental fact that conceptual controversies can throw light on the problem of the observer's identity problems, especially in the initial stages of original observation. Jung, it seems, could find a sense of identity in psychoanalytic work only by a juxtaposition of his ancestors' religious and mystical space-time with whatever he sensed in Freud's Jewish ancestry. His scientific rebellion thus also led to some ideological regression and eventually to (weakly denied) reactionary political acts. This phenomenon had its counterpart in the reaction to his findings within the psychoanalytic movement. As though in fear of endangering a common group identity based on an identification with Freud's personal greatness, psychoanalytic observers chose to ignore not only Jung's excesses but also the kind of universal fact he had, indeed, observed.

Such concepts as the "anima" and the "animus," i.e., the imagery representative of a man's feminine and a woman's masculine "side," seem at any rate recognizable in my woman patient's caricatured images of masculinity and femininity and in her more genuine imagery as well. The synthesizing function of the ego constantly works on subsuming in fewer and fewer images and personified *Gestalten* the fragments and loose ends of all infantile identifications. In doing so it not only uses existing historical prototypes; it also employs mechanisms of condensation and pictorial representation which characterize the products of collective imagery. In Jung's "persona" a weak ego seems to sell out to a compelling social prototype. A fake ego identity is established which suppresses rather than synthesizes those experiences and functions which endanger the "front." A dominant prototype of masculinity, for example, forces a man to exclude from his ego identity all that which characterizes the evil image of the lesser sex, the castrate. This may leave much of his receptive and maternal propensity dissimulated, undeveloped, and guilt-ridden, making a shell of mannishness out of what is left.

c

Therapeutic as well as reformist efforts verify the sad truth that in any system based on suppression, exclusion, and exploitation, the suppressed, excluded, and exploited unconsciously accept the evil image they are made to represent by those who are dominant.

I once had as a patient a tall, intelligent ranch owner who was influential in western agriculture. Nobody but his wife knew that he was born a Jew and raised in a Jewish neighborhood in a large city. His life, while outwardly expansive and successful, was made uncomfortable by a network of compulsions and phobias which, in analysis, proved to have reproduced and superimposed on his free movements in western valleys the outline of the street in which he grew up. His friends and adversaries, his elders and his inferiors all unknowingly played the roles of the German boys or the Irish gangs who had made the little Jewish boy miserable on his daily walk to school, which led him from an isolated and more refined Jewish street through the hostile remnants of tenements and gang warfare to the shortlived haven of the democratic classroom. This man's analysis provided a sad commentary on the fact that Streicher's presentation of an evil Jewish identity is no worse than that harbored by many a Jew who—with paradoxical results—may still be trying to live it down in an area where his past could be relatively unimportant in view of what he is.

The patient in question sincerely felt that the only true savior for the Jews would be a plastic surgeon. In the body ego of such cases of morbid ego identity, those body parts which are supposed to be of strategic importance in the characterization of the race (in this case, the nose; in that of the dancer, the backbone) play a role similar to that of the afflicted limb in a cripple and that of the genitals in neurotics in general. The body part in question has a different ego tonus; it is felt to be larger and heavier, or smaller and disembodied, and in both cases it feels dissociated from the whole body, while seeming to dominate the attention of others. In cases of morbid ego identity and in cripples, dreams occur where the dreamer unsuccessfully tries to hide the painfully spotlighted body part, and others in which he accidentally loses it.

What may be called an individual's ego space-time thus preserves the social topology of his childhood surroundings as well as the outline of his body image. To study both it is essential to correlate a patient's childhood history with the history of his family's sedentary residence in prototypal regions in the East, in the South, or on the western and northern frontiers, as these areas were gradually incorporated into the American version of the Anglo-Saxon cultural identity; his family's migration from, through, and to areas which, at various periods, may have represented the extreme sedentary or the extreme migratory pole of the developing American character; the family's religious conversions or diversions, with their class implications; abortive attempts at becoming standardized on a class level and the loss or abandonment of that level; and most of all, that individual or family segment which, whatever they were doing and wherever they were doing it, provided the last strong sense of cultural identity.

A compulsive patient's deceased grandfather was a businessman who built a mansion in a downtown district of an eastern metropolis. His will demanded that the mansion should stand and remain the family's castle even though skyscrapers and apartment houses mushroomed all around it. The mansion became a somewhat sinister symbol of conservatism, telling the world that the X's needed neither to move nor to sell, neither to expand nor to rise. The conveniences of modern travel were accepted only as comfortably insulated pathways between the mansion and its extensions: the club, the summer home, the private school, Harvard, etc. The grandfather's picture still hangs over the fireplace, a little bulb eternally lighting the rosiness of the cheeks in his generally powerful and contented countenance. His "individualistic" ways in business and his almost primeval power over the fate of his children are known but not questioned; rather they are overcompensated for by a sensitive show of respect, scrupulousness, and thrift. The grandsons of such men know that in order to find an identity of their own they have to break out of the mansion and join the mad striving which has engulfed the neighborhood. Some do, successfully; others take the mansion with them as an internalized pattern, a basic ego space, which determines their defense mechanism of proud and pained withdrawal and their symptoms of obsessiveness and sexual anesthesia. Their psychoanalyses last inordinately long, partially because the analyst's four walls become the new mansion and the analyst's comtemplative silence and theoretical approach become a new edition of the mansion's ritualistic isolation. The patient's politely "positive" transference, however, ends when the reticence of the analyst seems to resemble the restrained father rather than the ruthless grandfather. The father image, and with it the transference, appears to be split up. The image of the weak, mild father of the present is isolated from the Oedipal father image, which is fused with that of the powerful grandfather. As the analysis approaches this double image, fantasies appear which make plain the grandfather's overwhelming importance for the patient's real ego identity. They betray the violent sense of power, the fury of superiority which makes it hard for these overtly inhibited people to enter economic competition except on terms of prearranged superior privileges. These men, of the once highest strata, join those from the very lowest in being the truly disinherited in American life. From where they are there is no admission to free competition unless they have the strength to start all over again. If not, they may resist cure because it implies a change in ego identity, an ego resynthesis in terms of changed economic history.

The only way of breaking through this deep resignation is serious attention to memories which show that the child has experienced the grandfather really as a simple and warm man who fulfilled his public role not by force of some primeval power, but because history favored his capabilities.

d

Consider a boy whose grandparents came West, "where seldom is heard a discouraging word." This grandfather, a powerful and powerfully driven man, looked for new and challenging engineering tasks in widely separated regions. When the initial challenges were met, he handed the task over to others and moved on. His wife saw him only for an occasional impregnation. According to a typical family pattern, his sons could not keep pace with him and were left as respectable settlers by the wayside. To express their change of life style in fitting phrases, one would have to say that from an existence characterized by the slogan "let's get the hell out of here," they turned to one expressing the determination "let's stay—and keep the bastards out." Not atypically, the grandfather's only daughter (the patient's mother) alone remained identified with him. This very identification, however, did not permit her to take a husband equal to her strong father. She married a weak man and settled down. She brought her boy up to be God-fearing and industrious. He became reckless and shifting at times, depressed at others; at times an overgrown juvenile delinquent, at others a more enjoyable westerner with convivial alcoholic moods.

What his worried mother did not know is that she herself all through his childhood had belittled the sedentary father and decried the lack of mobility, geographic and social, of her marital existence. Idealizing the grandfather's exploits, she had yet also reacted with panicky punitiveness to any display of adventurous friskiness in the boy which might disturb the now well-defined neighborhood.

Or let us consider a problem from another region. A woman from the Middle West, rather unusually feminine and sensitive, uses a visit with relatives in the East to consult a psychoanalyst concerning a general feeling of affective constriction and an all-pervasive mild anxiety. During an exploratory analysis she seems almost lifeless. After some weeks, she occasionally produces a sudden flood of associations, all concerning horrid impressions of sex or death. Many of these memories emerge not from unconscious depths, but from an isolated corner of her consciousness where all those frightening matters were boarded off which on occasion had broken through the orderly factualness of the upper-middle-class surroundings of her childhood. This isolation of life segments is similar to that met with in compulsive neurotics anywhere. In this case it was part of a sanctioned way of life, an ethos, which in our patient had become truly uncomfortable only at a time when she was being courted by a European and was trying to envisage life in a cosmopolitan atmosphere.

She felt attracted but at the same time inhibited; her imagination was vividly provoked but restrained by anxiety. Her bowels reflected this conflict with disturbing alternations between constipation and diarrhea. The final impression gained was one of a general inhibition rather than of a basic impoverishment of imagination in matters either sexual or social.

The patient's dreams gradually revealed a hidden source of untapped freedom. While she still seemed pained and lifeless in her free associations, her dream life became humorous and imaginative in an almost autonomous way. She dreamed of entering a quiet church congregation in a flaming red dress and of throwing stones through respectable windows. But her most colorful dreams put her into Civil War days—on the Confederate side. The climax was a dream in which she sat on a toilet, set off by low partitions in the middle of a tremendous ballroom, and waved to elegantly dressed couples of Confederate officers and southern ladies who swirled around her to the sounds of powerful brass.

These dreams helped to unearth and highlight an isolated part of her childhood, namely, the gentle warmth awarded her by her grandfather, a Confederate veteran whose world was a fairy tale of the past. But for all its formalism, the grandfather's patriarchal masculinity and gentle affection had been experienced through the child's hungry senses and had proved more immediately reassuring to her searching ego than either her father's or mother's promises of standardized success. With the grandfather's death the patient's affects went dead because they were part of an abortive ego-identity formation which failed to receive nourishment either in the form of affection or of social rewards.

The psychoanalytic treatment of women with a prominent identity element of the southern lady (an identity which pervades more than one class or race) seems complicated by special resistances. To be sure, our patients are usually dislodged southerners, their ladyhood a defense, almost a symptom. Their wish for treatment finds its limits in three ideas which are all connected with the particular provisions in southern culture for safeguarding caste and race identity by imposing the prototype of the lady on the small girl.

There is, first, a pseudoparanoid suspicion that life is a series of critical tests in which vicious gossips attempt to stack up minor weaknesses and blemishes against the southern woman toward an inexorable final judgment, namely, to be—or not to be—a lady. Second, there is the all-pervading conviction that men, if not restrained by the formalities of a tacitly approved double standard which grants them lesser and darker sex objects at the price of overt respect for ladies, will prove to be no gentlemen and that they will at the very least try to blacken the lady's name and with it her claim to a socially superior husband and the prospect of having her children marry upward. But there is also the equally ambivalent implication that any man who does not proceed to shed his gentleman's inhibitions when the opportunity of sexual conquest offers itself is a weakling who only deserves to be mercilessly provoked. The usual feelings of guilt and inferiority thus all exist within the co-ordinates of a life plan dominated by the conscious hope for higher social status, and made morbid by its ambivalent counterpart, the hidden hope for the man who will dissolve the woman's need to be a lady in a moment of reckless passion. In all this there is a basic inability to conceive of any area in life where the standards and the words of a man and a woman could honestly coincide and be lifted above a certain primeval antagonism. Needless to say, such unconscious standards cause severe suffering in sincere and enlightened women, but only the verbalization of these internalized stereotypes, concomitantly with the analysis of the patient's transfer to the analyst of her whole conflictful imagery of men, makes psychoanalysis possible.

Psychoanalysts, of course, are consulted primarily by those who cannot stand the tension between alternatives, contrasts, and polarities which governs the American style of today: the unceasing necessity to remain tentative in order to be free for bigger and better opportunities. In their transferences and in

their resistances patients repeat abortive attempts at synchroniz-
ing fast-changing and sharply contrasting remnants of national,
regional, and class identities during critical stages of their child-
hoods. The analyst is woven into the patient's unconscious life
plan. He is idealized, especially if he is European-born, and compared with the patient's more homogeneous ancestors, or he is
resisted as the brainy enemy of a potentially successful American
identity.

The patient, however, can gain the courage to face the discontinuities of life in this country and the polarities of its struggle for an economic and cultural identity not as an imposed hostile reality, but as a potential promise for a more universal
human identity. This, as we have seen, finds its limits where individuals were either fundamentally impoverished in their childhood sensuality or are stalled by the "system" in their freedom
to use opportunities.

e

In work with veterans discharged from the armed forces as
psychoneurotics before the end of hostilities, we became familiar
with the recurring symptoms of partial loss of ego synthesis.
Many of these men, indeed, regressed to the "stage of unlearned
function." [11] The boundaries of their egos had lost their shock-
absorbing delineation. Anxiety and anger were provoked by
anything too sudden or too intense, a sudden sensory impression
from outside, an impulse, or a memory. A constantly "startled"
sensory system was attacked by external stimuli as well as by
somatic sensations: heat flashes, palpitation, cutting headaches.
Insomnia hindered the nightly restoration of sensory screening
by sleep and that of emotional rebinding by dreaming. Amnesia,
neurotic pseudologia, and confusion showed the partial loss of
time-binding and of spatial orientation. What definable symptoms and remnants of "peacetime neuroses" there were had a
fragmentary and false quality, as if the ego could not even accomplish an organized neurosis.

In some cases this ego impairment seemed to have had its origin in violent events, in others in the gradual grind of a million annoyances. Obviously the men were worn out by too many changes, in too many respects at once. *Somatic tension* and *social panic* and *ego anxiety* were always present. Above all, the men felt that they "did not know any more who they were": there was a distinct loss of ego identity. The sense of sameness and continuity and the belief in one's social role were gone. In this field of clinical observation I first found the assumption of a central loss of a sense of identity both inescapable and immediately clarifying.

A sense of identity was most enhanced in the armed forces among the recipients of promising commissions and members of teams in highly mechanized units. Yet men whose ego identity did thrive in military service sometimes broke down after discharge, when it appeared that the war had provoked them into more ambitious self-images than their more restricted peacetime identities could afford to sustain. For many others, however, the restraint and discipline of army life itself provided few ideal prototypes. For the American group identity supports an individual's ego identity as long as he can preserve a certain element of deliberate tentativeness, as long as he can convince himself that the next step is up to him and that no matter where he is staying or going he always has the choice of leaving or turning in the opposite direction. In this country the migrant does not want to be told to move on nor the sedentary man to stay where he is, for the life style of each contains the opposite element as an alternative which he wishes to consider for his most private and individual decisions. To quite a few soldiers, then, the military identity represented the despicable prototype of the sucker, of one who lets himself be sidetracked and stalled while others are free to pursue what could have been his chance and his girl. But in America to be a sucker means to be a social and sexual castrate. If you are a sucker, not even a mother's pity will be with you.

In the often profuse utterances of psychoneurotic veterans memories and anticipations consistently reappeared which per-

mitted them to blame circumstances for their failures as soldiers
and as men, and thus helped them to deny a sense of personal
inferiority. Their ego identities had fallen apart into bodily, sexual, social, occupational fragments, each having to overcome
again the danger of its evil prototype. Their traumatized egos
fought and fled from such images as the crying baby, the bleeding female, the submissive nigger, the sexual sissy, the economic
sucker, the mental moron—all prototypes the mere allusion to
which could bring these men close to homicidal or suicidal rage
followed by varying degrees of irritability or apathy. Their exaggerated attempts to blame their dilemma on circumstances and
individuals gave their childhood histories a more sordid character and themselves the appearance of more malignant psychopathy than was clinically justified. And an exaggerated diagnosis, once entered into the record, can only aggravate the vicious cycle of blame and self-blame. Rehabilitation work could
become effective and economical only if the clinical investigation focused on the patient's shattered life plan and if advice
tended to strengthen the resynthesis of the elements on which the
patient's ego identity was based.[12]

In addition to the several hundred thousand men who lost and
only gradually or partially regained their ego identity in the war
and to the tens of thousands whose acute loss of ego identity was
falsely diagnosed and treated as psychopathy, an untold number
experienced to the core the threat of a traumatic loss of ego
identity as a result of radical historical change.

The fact, however, that these men, their physicians, and their
contemporaries in increasing numbers turned to the bitter truths
of psychoanalytic psychiatry is in itself a historical development
which calls for critical appraisal. It expresses an increased acceptance of psychoanalytic insights in so far as they concern the
meaning of anxiety and disease in the *individual case history*. Yet
this partial acceptance of painful unconscious determinants of
human failure and this emphasis on individual treatment even
where the patient seemed anything but introspective and verbal

can also be seen as a widespread resistance against the awareness
of a failure of social mechanisms under radically changing historical determinants.

Historical change has reached a coercive universality and a
global acceleration which is experienced as a threat to the traditional American identity. It seems to devaluate the vigorous conviction that this nation can afford mistakes; that this nation, by
definition, is always so far ahead of the rest of the world in inexhaustible reserves, in vision of planning, in freedom of action,
and in tempo of progress that there is unlimited space and endless time in which to develop, test, and complete her social experiments. The difficulties met in the attempt to integrate this old
image of insulated spaciousness with the new image of explosive
global closeness are deeply disquieting. They are characteris-
tically first met with the application of traditional methods to a
new space-time.

The psychotherapist, in disregarding the contribution of such
developments to neurotic discomfort, is apt not only to miss
much of the specific dynamics in contemporary life cycles; he is
apt also to deflect individual energy from the collective tasks at
hand. A large-scale decrease of mental discomfort can be envisaged only by equal clinical attention to conditions as well as
to cases, to the emerging design for the future as well as to the
fixation on the past, to the unsafe surface and to the grumbling
depths.

In this connection it is worth noting that the popular use of
the word "ego" in this country has, if course, little to do with
the psychoanalytic concept of the same name; it commonly de-
notes unqualified, if perhaps unjustified, self-esteem. Bolstering,
bantering, boisterousness, and other "ego-inflating" behavior is,
of course, part of the American folkways. As such, it pervades
speech and gesture and enters into all interpersonal relations.
Without it, a therapeutic relationship in this country would remain outlandish and nonspecific. Another problem altogether is
the systematic exploitation of the national practice of "bolster-

ing" for the sake of making people "feel better," or of submerging their anxiety and tension so as to make them function better.

A weak ego does not gain substantial strength from being persistently bolstered. A strong ego, secured in its identity by a strong society, does not need and in fact is immune to any deliberate attempt at artificial inflation. Its tendency is toward the testing of what feels real, the mastery of that which works, the understanding of that which proves necessary, the enjoyment of the vital, and the overcoming of the morbid. At the same time it tends toward the creation of a strong mutual reinforcement with others in a group ego, which will transmit its purpose to the next generation.

The effectiveness of the psychoanalytic contribution to this development is guaranteed solely by the persistent humanist intention, beyond the mere adjustment of patients to limiting conditions, to apply clinical experience to the end of making man aware of human potentialities which are clouded by archaic fear. However, there are also the historical determinants of psychoanalytic concept formation; and more: if in the field of human motivation the same terms have been used over a period of half a century, they cannot but reflect the *ideologies of their day of origin* and absorb the *connotations of contemporary social changes*. Ideological connotation is the inevitable historical equation in the use of conceptual tools which concern the ego, man's organ of reality testing.

III. EGO THEORY AND SOCIAL PROCESSES

a

Freud originally stated that the sources of human self-esteem are

1. the residue of childish narcissism, i.e., the child's natural self-love;
2. such infantile omnipotence as is corroborated by experience giving the child the feeling that he fulfills his own ego ideal;
3. gratification of object libido, i.e., the love for others.

But if a healthy residue of *infantile narcissism* is to survive, the maternal environment must create and sustain it with a love which assures the child that it is good to be alive in the social co-ordinates in which he happens to find himself. "Natural" narcissism, which is said to fight so valiantly against the inroads of a frustrating environment, is in fact verified by the sensual enrichment and the encouragement of skills provided by this same environment. Widespread severe impoverishment of infantile narcissism, on the other hand, must be considered a breakdown of that collective synthesis which gives every newborn baby and his motherly surroundings a superindividual status as a trust of the community. And in the later absorption of this narcissism into more mature self-esteem, it is again of decisive importance whether or not the adolescent can expect an opportunity to employ what he has learned in childhood and to acquire thereby a feeling of continued communal meaning.

If experience is to corroborate a sound part of the infantile *sense of omnipotence*, then child-training methods must not only foster sensual health and progressive mastery, but also offer tangible social recognition as the fruits of health and mastery. For unlike the childish sense of omnipotence which is fed by make-believe and adult deception, the self-esteem which contributes to a sense of identity is based on the rudiments of skills and social techniques which assure a gradual coincidence of play and skillful performance, of ego ideal and social role, and thereby promise a tangible future.

If "*object libido*" is to be satisfied, then genital love and orgastic potency must be assured a cultural style of economic safety and emotional security, for only such a synthesis gives unified meaning to the full functional cycle of genitality, which includes conception, childbearing, and child rearing. Infatuation may gather incestuous childhood loves in a present "object"; genital activity may help two individuals to use one another as anchors against regression; but mutual genital love faces toward the future and the community. It works toward a division of labor in that life task which only two of the opposite sex can fulfill together: the synthesis of production, procreation, and re-creation in the primary social unit of some family system.

If the ego identity of lovers and mates is complementary in some essentials, it can be fused in marriage to the benefit of the offspring's ego development. From the point of view of such joint identities the "incestuous" attachment to parent images cannot be considered as necessarily pathogenic, as writers in psychopathology seem to infer. On the contrary, such a choice is part of an ethnic mechanism in that it creates a continuity between the family one grew up in and the family one establishes. It thus perpetuates tradition, i.e., the sum of all that had been learned by preceding generations, in a social analogy to the preservation of the gains of evolution in the mating within the species. Neurotic fixation on parents, however, and rigid inner defenses against incestuous wishes signify the failure, not the nature, of the affinity of generations.

However, as has been pointed out, many of the mechanisms of adjustment which once made for psychosocial evolution, tribal integration, and national or class coherence are at loose ends in a world of universally expanding identities. Education for an ego identity which receives strength from changing historical conditions demands a conscious acceptance of historical heterogeneity on the part of adults, combined with an enlightened effort to provide human childhood everywhere with a new fund of meaningful continuity.

Clinical histories help in research, if they avoid such stereotypes as "the patient had a domineering mother," stereotypes which have historical determinants and themselves acquire habitual connotations. Psychoanalytic thinking could well contribute to new methods of studying not only children, but also the spontaneous ways in which segments of modern society strive under vastly changing technological conditions to make a workable continuity out of child training and historical development. For whoever wants to cure or guide must understand, conceptualize, and use spontaneous trends of identity formation.

b

In studying his subject, the psychoanalyst, so Anna Freud points out, should occupy an observation point "equidistant from the id, the ego, and the superego"—so that he may be aware of their functional interdependence and so that as he observes a change in one of these sections of the mind he may not lose sight of related changes in the others.[13] What is here conceptualized as a compartmentalization of inner man reflects vast processes in which man is involved at all times.

In conclusion, then, we may reformulate the ego's task (and, maybe, the ego) by recognizing it as one of three indispensable and ceaseless processes by which man's existence becomes and remains continuous in time and organized in form. The first of these—first because studied originally through Freud's transfer of biological and physiological modes of thought to psychology —is the *biological process*, by which an organism comes to be a hierarchic organization of organ systems living out its life cycle. The second is the *social process*, by which organisms come to be organized in groups which are geographically, historically, and culturally defined. What may be called the *ego process* is the organizational principle by which the individual maintains himself as a coherent personality with a sameness and continuity both in his self-experience and in his actuality for others.

While these processes have yielded to study by different disciplines, alternately concentrating on the biological, the social, or the psychological, it must be obvious that the "physiology" of living, i.e., the unbroken interaction of all parts, is governed by a *relativity* which makes each process dependent on the other. This means that any changes observed in one will cause and again be influenced by changes in the others. True, each of these processes has its own warning signals: pain, anxiety, and panic. They warn of the danger of organic dysfunction, of impairment of ego mastery, and of loss of group identity; but each signal announces a threat to all.

In psychopathology we observe and study the apparent autonomy of one of these processes as it receives undue accentuation because of the loss of mutual regulation and general balance. Thus psychoanalysis first studied, as if it could be isolated, man's enslavement by the id, i.e., by the excessive demands on ego and society of frustrated organisms upset above all in their instinctuality. Next the focus of study shifted to man's enslavement by seemingly autonomous ego (and superego) strivings— defensive mechanisms which, in order to "contain" an upset libido economy, impoverish the ego's power of experiencing and planning. Perhaps psychoanalysis will complete its basic studies of neurosis by investigating more explicitly man's enslavement by historical conditions which claim autonomy by precedent and exploit archaic mechanisms within him, to deny him physical vitality and ego strength.[14]

The goal of psychoanalytic treatment itself has been defined as a simultaneous increase in the mobility of the id (that is, in the adaptability of our instinctual drives to opportunities for satisfaction as well as to necessary delays and frustrations), in the tolerance of the superego (which will condemn special acts but not the whole doer), and in the synthesizing power of the ego.[15] To the last point we add the suggestion that the analysis of the ego include the individual's ego identity in relation to the historical changes which dominated his childhood, his adolescent crisis, and his mature adjustment. For the individual's mastery over his neurosis begins where he is put in a position to accept the historical necessity which made him what he is. The individual feels free when he can choose to identify with his own ego identity and when he learns to apply that which is given to that which must be done. Only thus can he derive ego strength (for his generation and the next) from the coincidence of his one and only life cycle with a particular segment of human history.

2. ON TOTALITARIANISM

In a discussion of the historical phenomenon of totalitarianism, a psychoanalyst may ask what kind of unconscious motivation may lend itself to the invention, the initiation, and the widespread acceptance of totalitarian methods. More specifically, in what way do childhood and youth predispose man for totalitarianism? This is difficult, as are all tasks not facilitated or sanctioned by methodological tradition. And works on history, society, and morality usually contain little reference in the text, and none in the index, to the simple fact that all individuals were once children. To most scholars, childhood seems to belong to the field of social work rather than to that of social science, to the solicitudes of do-gooders rather than to those of thinkers. Yet among all creatures man is characterized by a long biological childhood, and civilization tends to make psychological childhood ever longer, because man must have time to learn how to learn: all his high specialization and all his intricate capabilities of co-ordination and reflection are, in fact, contingent upon his prolonged dependence. And only as a dependent does man develop conscience, that dependence on himself which makes him, in turn, dependable; and only when thoroughly dependable with regard to a number of fundamental values can he become independent and teach and develop tradition. But this dependability carries within it the ambiguity of its roots in a slow developmental process which leads from extreme helplessness to a high sense of freedom and mastery, and this within social systems all of which restrict freedom drastically and permit some men to exploit others ruthlessly.

Modern anthropology, often following suggestions derived from psychiatry, is studying the ways in which societies "intuitively" develop child-training systems designed not only to keep the small individual alive and well but also to ensure, through him and in him, a continuation of tradition and a preservation of his society's uniqueness. The contribution of man's extended childhood to the development of his technical capabilities and to his capacity for sympathy and faith is well known, but often too exclusively known. For it is becoming equally clear that the polarity adult-child is the first in the inventory of existential oppositions (male-female being the second) which makes man exploitable and induces him to exploit. The child's inborn procliv-

ity for feeling powerless, deserted, ashamed, and guilty in relation to those on whom he depends is systematically utilized for
his training, often to the point of exploitation. The result is that
even rational man remains irrationally preoccupied with anxieties and suspicions which center in such questions as who is
bigger or better and who can do what to whom. It is therefore
necessary to acquire deeper insight into the earliest consequences
of the psychological exploitation of childhood. By this I mean
the misuse of a divided function in such a way that one of the
partners is impaired in the development of his potentialities, with
the result that impotent rage is stored up where energy should
be free for productive development.

To those who accept all this it must seem reasonable enough
that childhood should be represented in a study of totalitarianism so that we may begin to do away with the "oversight" concerning the fateful importance of childhood. Yet it must be said
that this oversight does not seem to be an accidental one, and
therefore cannot be so easily corrected. Psychoanalysis has
amply demonstrated the fact that all men develop an amnesia
concerning crucial childhood experiences. There is good reason
to suspect that this individual amnesia is paralleled by a universal blind spot in the interpretation of man's condition, a tendency to overlook the fateful function of childhood in the fabric
of society. Maybe moral man and rational man, having fought so
hard to make man's civilized image absolute and irreversible, refuse to see how each man must begin with the beginning and
thus, ever again, acquire the potential for undoing human accomplishments with infantile compulsions and irrational impul-
sions. It is as if this refusal reflected a deep-seated superstition
that rational and practical man would lose his single-minded
stamina if he ever turned back to meet the Medusa of childhood
anxiety face to face again. Here a formidable "equation" imposes
itself on all attempts to put the fact of childhood in its proper
perspective. Yet if man would understand this fact, maybe he
could manage to become less destructively childish in some respects and remain more creatively childlike in others.

Truly new insights, however, are hard to formulate in a balanced way. It is probably a result of the long-undisputed existence of the universal blind spot discussed here that the sudden emergence in our time of insights into the importance of childhood have tended to develop another, compensatory loss of perspective: I mean the tendency on the part of the psychologists and psychopathologists to explain societal phenomena such as totalitarianism by equating them with particular infantile or juvenile stages ("adolescent"), with specific mental illness ("paranoid"), or with particular "character structures" (the "authoritarian personality"). From the *personological* approach, suggestive generalizations have emerged in regard to certain analogies between patterns of child rearing, ways of conceptualizing the world, and inclinations toward political creeds. This approach, however, has contributed little to the all-important question, namely, under what conditions does the energy invested in given patterns of thought and action (for example, authoritarian) become available for relevant political indoctrination and for effective mass action? The *psychopathological* approach in turn has weakened its case by diagnostic name-calling, designating peoples and people actively or passively involved in totalitarian revolutions as either pathological or immature human beings and attempting by this means to explain their political behavior. But man can be many things on many levels, and history rarely permits him that unification of defined creed, conscious attitude, and pragmatic action which we in the Protestant world have come to demand of a "mature" or at any rate a "logical" human being.

What follows, then, is not an attempt at fixing the origin or cause of totalitarianism in the fact of childhood or in particular forms of childhood training. Nor shall I treat it as a transient affliction or localized epidemic; I begin with the assumption that totalitarianism is based on universal human potentialities and is thus related to all aspects of human nature, wholesome and pathological, adult and infantile, individual and societal. Totalitarianism has probably often been a near reality in history, but had

to wait for "its" historical moment. This moment is determined
by the advance of technology in communication and organization and by the varieties of conditions which gave rise to the fanatic idea of the total state, favor its realization in well-timed
revolutionary acts, and, furthermore, maintain it through the realities of power and terror. Only such historical perspective can
give the proper measure of the different degrees and kinds of ideological involvement on the part of the many types that make
up a totalitarian state: fanatic apostles and shrewd revolutionaries; lonely leaders and oligarchic cliques; sincere believers and
sadistic exploiters; obedient bureaucrats and efficient managers,
soldiers, engineers; willing followers, apathetic toilers, and paralyzed opponents; unnerved victims and bewildered would-be
victims. My training and experience permit me to attempt a contribution to only one of the more basic and yet often less tangible factors in all these forms of participation, namely, the psychological prerequisites for an inspiring or paralyzing sense of
the legitimacy of totalitarianism.

I now return to my initial question concerning that something
in the nature of childhood which may throw light on man's inclination, under certain conditions, to be available for what the
Germans call *Umschaltung* and *Gleichschaltung*, that sudden
total realignment and, as it were, coalignment which accompany
a conversionlike conviction that the state may and must have absolute power over the minds as well as the lives and the fortunes
of its citizens.

As a clinician, however, I must start elsewhere: from examples
of total *inner* change. We discern in normal and abnormal individual histories, and in occasional transitory states not commonly considered psychopathological, sudden transitions from a
balanced "wholeness" of experience and judgment to states of
feeling, thinking, and acting "totally." The most dramatic clinical examples of such total restructuring of experience are to be
found on the borderline of severe pathology. As one young man
said to me, smilingly, in looking back on his tendency to withdraw: "I was a majority of One"—by which he meant that, hav-

ing chosen to be totally alone, he was the universe. A young woman spoke, in the same vein, of her "right to oneliness." Yet such solipsism is neither restricted to pathology nor to adult life. Already early in childhood a child's healthy alternation between waking or sleeping, for example, may suddenly turn into a total avoidance of sleep or an over-all sleepiness; a child's happy alternation between sociability and aloneness may turn into an anxious or furious insistence on his mother's total presence or a blank refusal to show awareness of her proximity. Many a mother is deeply disturbed when she notices, at her return from a sudden but not so lengthy absence, that her small child has blandly "forgotten" her. Total dependence or total independence may, temporarily or lastingly, become states which are not amenable to normal degrees of alternation; or total goodness or badness may suddenly appear as states seemingly beyond the reach of parents who may actually prefer a child who is reasonably good but by all means also a little bad. Such total restructuring may occur as a transitory phase at significant stages of infantile development; it may accompany the outbreak of a mental disturbance; or it may remain a latent potentiality in the adult.

As for the total dependence on an object or another person, we are all familiar with the small child's fetishes which, sometimes in the form of unhygienically bedraggled dolls, become the subject of parental disdain or worry and yet remain the child's total and exclusive token of security and comfort. Later, violent loves and hates and sudden conversions and aversions share with the child's fetishism and fears such factors as the exclusive focusing of a set of friendly or unfriendly affects on one person or idea; the primitivization of all affects thus focused; and a utopian or cataclysmic expectation of a total gain or a total loss to come from this source.

Finally we may point to a well-known example of a sudden total split of what was once wholly united: the change that comes over married couples who have decided on a divorce. The sudden transformation of what seemed a wholesome twoness into two exclusive totalities can be rather awesome, as one soon finds out if he tries to remain on friendly terms with both.

While such realignments may seem to appear suddenly, they develop slowly. Only uncommonly aware and brave people know about themselves what psychoanalysis reveals in others, and particularly in patients—namely, how strong and systematic are man's proclivities and potentialities for total realignments, often barely hidden behind exaggerated likes, predilections, and convictions, and how much energy is employed in inner defenses against a threatening total reorientation in which white may turn into black and vice versa. Only the affect released in sudden commitments and conversions and in sudden aversions testifies to the quantity of energy "bound" in such defenses. Equally revealing is the much described and much deplored, yet therapeutically useful, tendency of even the most enlightened and best-informed patients of psychiatry to develop a "transference" and to become, as it were, violently dependent on their therapists—and this with alternately positive or negative feelings: a sobering demonstration of the universal inner tendency for totalization which ill fits the contempt of many intellectuals for fellow humans dependent on cosmologies and deities, monarchies and ideologies. At any rate, we have learned to understand such realignments as readjustments on a more primitive level, made necessary by increased anxieties, especially of infantile origin, and called forth by acute life crises. To mark them as pathological or as "bad" helps neither to understand nor to overcome them: to chart a purposeful course of action toward them, one must understand their inner rationale, their psycho-logic.

In giving these examples, I have used the terms "wholeness" and "totality." Both mean entireness, yet I intended to underscore their differences. Wholeness seems to connote an assembly of parts, even quite diversifed parts, that enter into fruitful association and organization. This concept is most strikingly expressed in such terms as wholeheartedness, whole mindedness, wholesomeness, and the like. As a Gestalt, then, wholeness emphasizes a sound, organic, progressive mutuality between diversified functions and parts within an entirety, the boundaries of which are open and fluid. Totality, on the contrary, evokes a Gestalt in which an absolute boundry is emphasized: given a certain arbitrary delineation, nothing that belongs inside must be left outside, nothing that must be outside can be tolerated inside. A totality is as absolutely inclusive as it is utterly exclusive—whether or not the category-to-be-made-absolute is a logical one, and whether or not the constituent parts really have an affinity for one another.

We must postulate, then, a psychological need for a totality without further choice or alteration, even if it implies the abandonment of a much-desired wholeness. To say it in one sentence: When the human being, because of accidental or developmental shifts, loses an essential wholeness, he restructures himself and the world by taking recourse to what we may call *totalism*. As pointed out, it would be wise to abstain from considering this a merely regressive or infantile mechanism. It is an alternate, if more primitive, way of dealing with experience, and thus has, at least in transitory states, certain adjustment and survival value. It belongs to normal psychology. Any possible psychiatric inquiry is restricted to these questions: Can the transient means of emergency adjustment be prevented from becoming fixed ends? Can totalism reverse itself when the emergency is over? Can its elements be resynthesized in a wholeness which was previously possible?

In the individual it is the ego's task to promote the mastery of experience and the guidance of action in such a way that a certain wholeness synthesis is, ever again, created between the diverse and conflicting stages and aspects of life—between immediate impressions and associated memories, between impelling wishes and compelling demands, between the most private and the most public aspects of existence. To do its job, the ego develops modes of synthesis as well as screening methods and mechanisms of defense. As it matures through the constant interaction of maturational forces and environmental influences, a certain duality develops between higher levels of integration, which permits a greater tolerance of tension and of diversity, and lower levels of order where totalities and conformities must help to preserve a sense of security. The study of those fusions and defusions which—on the individual level—make for a successful wholeness or an attempted totality thus belongs to the realm of psychoanalytic ego psychology. Here I can do no more than point to this field of study.[16]

The ego's beginnings are difficult to assess, but as far as we know it emerges gradually out of a stage when "wholeness" is a matter of physiological equilibration, maintained through the mutuality between the baby's need to receive and the mother's need to give. The mother, of course, is not only a parturient creature but also a member of a family and society. She, in turn, must feel a certain wholesome relation between her biological role and the values of her community. Only thus can she communicate to the baby, in the unmistakable language of somatic interchange, that the baby may trust her, the world, and—himself. Only a relatively "whole" society can vouchsafe to the infant, through the mother, an inner conviction that all the diffuse somatic experiences and all the confusing social cues of early life can be accommodated in a sense of continuity and sameness which gradually unites the inner and outer world. The ontological source of faith and hope which thus emerges I have called a *sense of basic trust:* it is the first and basic wholeness, for it seems to imply that the inside and the outside can be experienced as an interrelated goodness. *Basic mistrust,* then, is the sum of all those diffuse experiences which are not somehow successfully balanced by the experience of integration. One cannot know what happens in a baby, but direct observation as well as overwhelming clinical evidence indicate that early mistrust is accompanied by an experience of "total" rage, with fantasies of the total domination or even destruction of the sources of pleasure and provision; and that such fantasies and rages live on in the individual and are revived in extreme states and situations.

In fact, every basic conflict of childhood lives on, in some form, in the adult. The earliest steps are preserved in the deepest layers. Every tired human being may regress temporarily to partial mistrust whenever the world of his expectations has been shaken to the core. Yet social institutions seem to provide the individual with continuing collective reassurances in regard to such anxieties as have accrued from his infantile past. There can be no question but that it is organized religion which systematizes and socializes the first and deepest conflict in life: it combines the dim images of each individual's first providers into collective images of primeval superhuman protectors; it makes comprehensible the vague discomfort of basic mistrust by giving it a metaphysical reality in the form of defined Evil; and it offers to man by way of rituals a periodic collective restitution of trust which in mature adults ripens to a combination of faith and realism. In prayer man assures a superhuman power that, in spite of everything, he has remained trustworthy, and asks for a sign that he now may also continue to trust his deity. In primitive life, which deals with one segment of nature and develops a collective magic, the Supernatural Providers of food and fortune are often treated as though they were angry if not malicious parents who needed to be appeased by prayer and self-torture.[17] Higher forms of religion and ritual equally clearly address themselves to the nostalgic remnant in each individual of his expulsion from the paradise of wholeness which once gave liberal provision, but which, alas, was lost, leaving forever an undefinable sense of evil division, potential malevolence, and deep nostalgia. Religion restores, at regular intervals and through rituals significantly connected with the important crises of the life cycle and the turning points of the yearly cycle, a new sense of wholeness, of things rebound.[18] But, as is the case with all such endeavors, that which was to be banished beyond the periphery is apt to reappear in the center. Much cruel, cold, and exclusive totalness has dominated some phases of the history of organized religion. One may well ask in what way the idea of a universe punitively or charitably embraced by One God and his dogma prepared mankind for the idea of One Total State as well as for that of One Whole Man-Kind: for there can be no doubt but that, in periods of transition, a total realignment can insure progress to greater wholeness, as well as to totalism.

Today no derision on the part of the careless unbeliever and no punitive fervor on the part of the dogmatist can deny the staggering fact that much of mankind finds itself without a living religion such as gave wholeness of existence to the tool man in his productive dealings with nature, and to the trading man in his gainful exchange of goods in an expanding world market. How deeply worried self-made man is in his need to feel safe in his man-made world can be seen from the deep inroad which an unconscious identification with the machine—comparable to the magic identification of primitive man with his principal prey —has made on the Western concept of human nature in general and on a kind of automatized and depersonalized child training in particular. The desperate need to function smoothly and cleanly, without friction, sputtering, or smoke, has attached itself to the ideas of personal happiness, of governmental perfection, and even of salvation. Sometimes one feels a strange totalism creeping up in those naïve initiators who expect a new wholeness to come from the process of technological development in and by itself, just as in times not so distant the millennium was to emerge from the unfailing wisdom of nature, from the mysterious self-balance of the market, or from the inner sanctity of wealth. Machines, of course, can be made more attractive and more comfortable as they become more practical; the question is where that deep sense of specific goodness will come from, which man needs in his relation to his principal source and technique of production in order to permit himself to be human in a reasonably familiar universe. Unanswered, this need will continue to increase a deep and widespread basic mistrust which, in areas overcome with all too sudden changes in historical and economic perspective, contributes to a willingness to accept a totalitarian and authoritarian delusion of wholeness, ready-made with one leader at the head of one party, one ideology giving a simple rationale to all nature and all history, one categorical enemy of production to be destroyed by one centralized agency of justice—and the steady diversion to outer enemies of the impotent rage stored up within.

It must be remembered here, however, that at least one of the systems which we call totalitarianism, Soviet communism, was born from an ideology which envisages beyond all revolutions a final wholeness of society, freed from the interference of an armed state and of the class structure which necessitated it. In this vision, the total revolution and the totalitarian superstate is only a state-to-end-all states: it will abolish itself by "becoming dormant," leaving in the final wholeness of a stateless democracy nothing to be administered except "things . . . and processes of production." I must leave it to others to discuss the question of the degree to which totalitarian means and methods may become too irreversibly rigid in the "aging" centers of such utopian undertaking. In the meantime, however, we must not lose sight of those newly emerging peoples (and their young people) on the periphery of both the Soviet world and ours who are in need of a total system of beliefs in this period of common technological change. I shall not outline here the implications of each of the successive childhood stages for the ideology of totalitarianism. The original alternative of a "whole" solution in the form of basic trust and a "total" solution in the form of basic mistrust, which we related to the matter of Faith, is followed on each step by analogous alternatives each, in turn, related to one of the basic human institutions.[19]

Only in passing do I wish to make reference to that aspect of infantile development which in the psychoanalytic literature on totalitarianism has received the greatest, if not an exclusive, emphasis: I mean the period around the age of five (often called the Oedipus stage) when the child gets ready to develop not only a more goal-directed and rebellious initiative, but also a more organized conscience. The wholesome and playful child of three or four often enjoys an unsurpassed sense of autonomous wholeness which outbalances an always threatening sense of doubt and shame and leads to great dreams of glory and achievement. It is then that the child suddenly faces episodes of phobic and secret guilt and evidences an early rigidity of conscience, which, now that the little human being has learned to enjoy the wholeness of being an antonomous being and to envisage excessive conquests, tries to divide him against himself.

The guardian of conscience is, according to Freud, the super-ego, which is superimposed on the ego like an inner governor, or, one might say, an inner governor-general, who represents the outer authorities, limiting the goals as well as the means of initiative. One could develop this analogy. While at one time answerable to a foreign king, this governor-general now makes himself independent, using native troops (and their methods) to combat native insurrection. The superego thus comes to reflect not only the sternness of the demands and limitations originally imposed by the parents, but also the relative crudeness of the infantile stage during which they were imposed. Thus human conscience, even while serving conscious ideals, retains a certain unconscious and infantile primitiveness. Only a combination in parents of true tolerance and firmness can guide an infantile process which otherwise falls prey to the cruelly "categoric" attitude employed by a strict conscience which first turns against the self, but in one way or another later focuses on the supression of others.

This inner split, then, is the second great inducement (separation from the mother was the first) to "total" solutions in life which are based on the simple and yet so fateful proposition that nothing is more unbearable than the vague tension of guiltiness. For this reason, then, some individuals sometimes try to overcome all moral vagueness by becoming totally good or totally bad—solutions which betray their ambivalent nature in that the totally "good" may learn to become torturers *ad majorem Dei gloriam*, while the totally "bad" may develop decided loyalties to leaders and cliques. It is obvious that authoritarian propaganda addresses itself to this conflict by inviting men, collectively and unashamedly, to project total badness on whatever inner or outer "enemy" can be appointed by state decree and propaganda as totally subhuman and verminlike, while the converted may feel totally good as a member of a nation, a race, or a class blessed by history.

The end of childhood seems to me the third, and more immediately political, crisis of wholeness. Young people must become whole people in their own right, and this during a developmental stage characterized by a diversity of changes in physical growth, genital maturation, and social awareness. The wholeness to be achieved at this stage I have called a *sense of inner identity*. The young person, in order to experience wholeness, must feel a progressive continuity between that which he has come to be during the long years of childhood and that which he promises to become in the anticipated future; between that which he conceives himself to be and that which he perceives others to see in him and to expect of him. Individually speaking, identity includes, but is more than, the sum of all the successive identifications of those earlier years when the child wanted to be, and often was forced to become, like the people he depended on. Identity is a unique product, which now meets a crisis to be solved only in new identifications with age mates and with leader figures outside of the family. The search for a new and yet reliable identity can perhaps best be seen in the persistent adolescent endeavor to define, overdefine, and redefine themselves and each other in often ruthless comparison, while a search for reliable alignments can be recognized in the restless testing of the newest in possibilities and the oldest in values. Where the resulting self-definition, for personal or for collective reasons, becomes too difficult, a *sense of role confusion* results: the young person counterpoints rather than synthesizes his sexual, ethnic, occupational, and typological alternatives and is often driven to decide definitely and totally for one side or the other.

Here society has the function of guiding and narrowing the individual's choices. Primitive societies have always taken this function most seriously; their puberty rites replace a horror of undefinedness, dramatized by rituals, with a defined sacrifice and a sacred badge. Advancing civilization has found other more spiritual means of "confirming" the right life plan. Yet youth has always found ways of reviving more primitive "initiations" by forming exclusive cliques, gangs, or fraternities. In America, where youth on the whole is free of primitive traditionalism, of punitive paternalism, and of standardization through state measures, a spontaneous self-standardization has nevertheless developed which makes seemingly senseless and constantly changing styles of clothing and ways of gesturing and speaking absolutely mandatory for "insiders." For the most part this is good-natured business, full of mutual support of an "other-directed" kind, but it is occasionally cruel to nonconformists and of course quite unmindful of the tradition of individualism which it pretends to extol.

Let me once more refer to individual pathology. The necessity of finding, at least temporarily, a total stamp of standard at this time is so great that youth sometimes prefers to be nothing, and that totally, rather than remain a contradictory bundle of identity fragments. Even in individual disturbances usually called prepsychotic or psychopathic or otherwise diagnosed in line with adult psychopathology, an almost willful *Umschaltung* to a negative identity (and its roots in past and present) can be studied. On a somewhat larger scale, an analogous turn toward a negative identity prevails in the delinquent (addictive, homosexual) youth of our larger cities, where conditions of economic, ethnic, and religious marginality provide poor bases for any kind of positive identity. If such "negative identities" are accepted as a youth's "natural" and final identity by teachers, judges, and psychiatrists, he not infrequently invests his pride as well as his need for total orientation in becoming exactly what the careless community expects him to become. Similarly, many young Americans from marginal and authoritarian backgrounds find temporary refuge in radical groups in which an otherwise unmanageable rebellion-and-confusion receives the stamp of universal righteousness within a black-and-white ideology. Some, of course, "mean it," but many are merely drifting into such association.

It must be realized, then, that only a firm sense of inner identity marks the end of the adolescent process and is a condition for further and truly individual maturation. In counterbalancing the inner remnants of the original inequalities of childhood, and in thus weakening the dominance of the superego, a positive sense of identity permits the individual to forgo irrational self-repudiation, the total prejudice against themselves which characterizes severe neurotics and psychotics, as well as fanatic hate of otherness. Such identity, however, depends on the support which the young individual receives from the collective sense of identity characterizing the social groups significant to him: his class, his nation, his culture.[20] Here it is important to remember that each group identity cultivates its own sense of freedom, which is the reason why one people rarely understands what makes another people feel free. Where historical and technological development, however, severely encroach upon deeply rooted or strongly emerging identities (i.e., agrarian, feudal, patrician) on a large scale, youth feels endangered, individually and collectively, whereupon it becomes ready to support doctrines offering a total immersion in a synthetic identity (extreme nationalism, racism, or class consciousness) and a collective condemnation of a totally stereotyped enemy of the new identity. The fear of loss of identity which fosters such indoctrination contributes significantly to that mixture of righteousness and criminality which, under totalitarian conditions, becomes available for organized terror and for the establishment of major industries of extermination. And since conditions undermining a sense of identity also fixate older individuals on adolescent alternatives, a great number of adults fall in line or are paralyzed in their resistance. My final suggestion, then, is that the study of this third major crisis of wholeness, at the very end of childhood and youth, reveals the strongest potentiality for totalism and, therefore, is of great significance in the emergence of new collective identities in our time. Totalitarian propaganda everywhere concentrates on the claim that youth is left high and dry by the ebbing wave of the past. A better understanding of this may help us to offer alternatives of enlightenment instead of our present inclination to disdain or to forbid in feeble attempts to out-totalize the totalitarians.

To have the courage of one's diversity is a sign of wholeness in individuals and in civilization. But wholeness, too, must have defined boundaries. In the present state of our civilization, it is not yet possible to foresee whether or not a more *universal identity* promises to embrace all the diversities and dissonances, relativities and mortal dangers which emerge with technological and scientific progress.

C H A P T E R
III

The Life Cycle:
Epigenesis of Identity

AMONG THE INDISPENSABLE CO-ordinates of identity is that of the life cycle, for we assume that not until adolescence does the individual develop the prerequisites in physiological growth, mental maturation, and social responsibility to experience and pass through the crisis of identity. We may, in fact, speak of the identity crisis as the psychosocial aspect of adolescing. Nor could this stage be passed without identity having found a form which will decisively determine later life.

Let us, once more, start out from Freud's far-reaching discovery that neurotic conflict is not very different in content from the "normative" conflicts which every child must live through in his childhood, and the residues of which every adult carries with him in the recesses of his personality. For man, in order to remain psychologically alive, constantly re-resolves these conflicts just as his body unceasingly combats the encroachment of physical deterioration. However, since I cannot accept the conclusion that just to be alive, or not to be sick, means to be healthy, or, as I would prefer to say in matters of personality, *vital*, I must have recourse to a few concepts which are not part of the official terminology of my field.

I shall present human growth from the point of view of the

conflicts, inner and outer, which the vital personality weathers, re-emerging from each crisis with an increased sense of inner unity, with an increase of good judgment, and an increase in the capacity "to do well" according to his own standards and to the standards of those who are significant to him. The use of the words "to do well" of course points up the whole question of cultural relativity. Those who are significant to a man may think he is doing well when he "does some good" or when he "does well" in the sense of acquiring possessions; when he is doing well in the sense of learning new skills and new knowledge or when he is not much more than just getting along; when he learns to conform all around or to rebel significantly; when he is merely free from neurotic symptoms or manages to contain within his vitality all manner of profound conflict.

There are many formulations of what constitutes a "healthy" personality in an adult. But if we take up only one—in this case, Marie Jahoda's definition, according to which a healthy personality *actively masters* his environment, shows a certain *unity of personality*, and is able to *perceive* the world and himself *correctly* [1]—it is clear that all of these criteria are relative to the child's cognitive and social development. In fact, we may say that childhood is defined by their initial absence and by their gradual development in complex steps of increasing differentiation. How, then, does a vital personality grow or, as it were, accrue from the successive stages of the increasing capacity to adapt to life's necessities—with some vital enthusiasm to spare?

Whenever we try to understand growth, it is well to remember the *epigenetic principle* which is derived from the growth of organisms *in utero*. Somewhat generalized, this principle states that anything that grows has a ground plan, and that out of this ground plan the parts arise, each part having its time of special ascendancy, until all parts have arisen to form a functioning whole. This, obviously, is true for fetal development where each part of the organism has its critical time of ascendance or danger of defect. At birth the baby leaves the chemical exchange of the womb for the social exchange system of his society, where his gradually increasing capacities meet the opportunities and limitations of his culture. How the maturing organism continues to unfold, not by developing new organs but by means of a prescribed sequence of locomotor, sensory, and social capacities, is described in the child-developement literature. As pointed out, psychoanalysis has given us an understanding of the more idiosyncratic experiences, and especially the inner conflicts, which constitute the manner in which an individual becomes a distinct personality. But here, too, it is important to realize that in the sequence of his most personal experiences the healthy child, given a reasonable amount of proper guidance, can be trusted to obey inner laws of development, laws which create a succession of potentialities for significant interaction with those persons who tend and respond to him and those institutions which are ready for him. While such interaction varies from culture to culture, it must remain within "the proper rate and the proper sequence" which governs all epigenesis. Personality, therefore, can be said to develop according to steps predetermined in the human organism's readiness to be driven toward, to be aware of, and to interact with a widening radius of significant individuals and institutions.

It is for this reason that, in the presentation of stages in the development of the personality, we employ an epigenetic diagram analogous to the one employed in *Childhood and Society* for an analysis of Freud's psychosexual stages.[2] It is, in fact, an implicit purpose of this presentation to bridge the theory of infantile sexuality (without repeating it here in detail) and our knowledge of the child's physical and social growth.

The diagram is presented on p. 94. The double-lined squares signify both a sequence of stages and a gradual development of component parts; in other words, the diagram formalizes a progression through time of a differentiation of parts. This indicates (1) that each item of the vital personality to be discussed is systematically related to all others, and that they all depend on the proper development in the proper sequence of each item; and (2) that each item exists in some form before "its" decisive

	1	2	3	4	5	6	7	8
VIII								INTEGRITY vs. DESPAIR
VII							GENERATIVITY vs. STAGNATION	
VI						INTIMACY vs. ISOLATION		
V	Temporal Perspective vs. Time Confusion	Self-Certainty vs. Self-Consciousness	Role Experimentation vs. Role Fixation	Apprenticeship vs. Work Paralysis	IDENTITY vs. IDENTITY CONFUSION	Sexual Polarization vs. Bisexual Confusion	Leader- and Followership vs. Authority Confusion	Ideological Commitment vs. Confusion of Values
IV				INDUSTRY vs. INFERIORITY	Task Identification vs. Sense of Futility			
III			INITIATIVE vs. GUILT		Anticipation of Roles vs. Role Inhibition			
II		AUTONOMY vs. SHAME, DOUBT			Will to Be Oneself vs. Self-Doubt			
I	TRUST vs. MISTRUST				Mutual Recognition vs. Autistic Isolation			

and critical time normally arrives.

If I say, for example, that a sense of basic trust is the first component of mental vitality to develop in life, a sense of autonomous will the second, and a sense of initiative the third, the diagram expresses a number of fundamental relations that exist among the three components, as well as a few fundamental facts for each.

Each comes to its ascendance, meets its crisis, and finds its lasting solution in ways to be described here, toward the end of the stages mentioned. All of them exist in the beginning in some form, although we do not make a point of this fact, and we shall not confuse things by calling these components different names at earlier or later stages. A baby may show something like "autonomy" from the beginning, for example, in the particular way in which he angrily tries to wriggle his hand free when tightly held. However, under normal conditions, it is not until the second year that he begins to experience the whole critical alternative between being an autonomous creature and being a dependent one, and it is not until then that he is ready for a specifically new encounter with his environment. The environment, in turn, now feels called upon to convey to him its particular ideas and concepts of autonomy in ways decisively contributing to his personal character, his relative efficiency, and the strength of his vitality.

It is this encounter, together with the resulting crisis, which is to be described for each stage. Each stage becomes a crisis because incipient growth and awareness in a new part function go together with a shift in instinctual energy and yet also cause a specific vulnerability in that part. One of the most difficult questions to decide, therefore, is whether or not a child at a given stage is weak or strong. Perhaps it would be best to say that he is always vulnerable in some respects and completely oblivious and insensitive in others, but that at the same time he is unbelievably persistent in the same respects in which he is vulnerable. It must be added that the baby's weakness gives him power; out of his very dependence and weakness he makes signs to which his environment, if it is guided well by a responsiveness combining "instinctive" and traditional patterns, is peculiarly sensitive. A baby's presence exerts a consistent and persistent domination over the outer and inner lives of every member of a household. Because these members must reorient themselves to accommodate his presence, they must also grow as individuals and as a group. It is as true to say that babies control and bring up their families as it is to say the converse. A family can bring up a baby only by being brought up by him. His growth consists of a series of challenges to them to serve his newly developing potentialities for social interaction.

Each successive step, then, is a potential crisis because of a radical change in perspective. Crisis is used here in a developmental sense to connote not a threat of catastrophe, but a turning point, a crucial period of increased vulnerability and heightened potential, and therefore, the ontogenetic source of generational strength and maladjustment. The most radical change of all, from intrauterine to extrauterine life, comes at the very beginning of life. But in postnatal existence, too, such radical adjustments of perspective as lying relaxed, sitting firmly, and running fast must all be accomplished in their own good time. With them, the interpersonal perspective also changes rapidly and often radically, as is testified by the proximity in time of such opposites as "not letting mother out of sight" and "wanting to be independent." Thus, different capacities use different opportunities to become full-grown components of the ever-new configuration that is the growing personality.

1. INFANCY AND THE MUTUALITY OF RECOGNITION

For the most fundamental prerequisite of mental vitality, I have already nominated a *sense of basic trust*, which is a pervasive attitude toward oneself and the world derived from the experiences of the first year of life. By "trust" I mean an essential trustfulness of others as well as a fundamental sense of one's own trustworthiness.

In describing a development of a series of alternative basic attitudes, including identity, we take recourse to the term "a sense of." It must be immediately obvious, however, that such "senses" as a sense of health or vitality, or a sense of the lack of either, pervades the surface and the depth, including what we experience as consciousness or what remains barely conscious or is altogether unconscious. As a conscious experience, trust is accessible to introspection. But it is also a way of behaving, observable by others; and it is, finally, an inner state verifiable only by testing and psychoanalytic interpretation. All three of these dimensions are to be inferred when we loosely speak of "a sense of."

As is usual in psychoanalysis, we learned first of the "basic" nature of trust from adult psychopathology. In adults a radical impairment of basic trust and a prevalence of *basic mistrust* is expressed in a particular form of severe estrangement which characterizes individuals who withdraw into themselves when at odds with themselves and with others. Such withdrawal is most strikingly displayed by individuals who regress into psychotic states in which they sometimes close up, refusing food and comfort and becoming oblivious to companionship. What is most radically missing in them can be seen from the fact that as we attempt to assist them with psychotherapy, we must try to "reach" them with the specific intent of convincing them that they can trust us to trust them and that they can trust themselves.

Familiarity with such radical regressions as well as with the deepest and most infantile propensities in our not-so-sick patients has taught us to regard basic trust as the cornerstone of a vital personality. Let us see what justifies our placing the crisis and the ascendancy of this component at the beginning of life.

As the newborn infant is separated from his symbiosis with the mother's body, his inborn and more or less co-ordinated ability to take in by mouth meets the mother's more or less co-ordinated ability and intention to feed him and to welcome him. At this point he lives through, and loves with, his mouth, and the mother lives through, and loves with, her breasts or whatever parts of her countenance and body convey eagerness to provide what he needs.

For the mother this is a late and complicated accomplishment, highly dependent on her development as a woman, on her unconscious attitude toward the child, on the way she has lived through pregnancy and delivery, on her and her community's attitude toward the act of nursing and caring—and on the response of the newborn. To him the mouth is the focus of a general first approach to life—the incorporative approach. In psychoanalysis this stage is usually referred to as the oral stage. Yet it is clear that in addition to the overwhelming need for food, a baby is, or soon becomes, receptive in many other respects. As he is willing and able to suck on appropriate objects and to swallow whatever appropriate fluids they emit, he is soon also willing and able to "take in" with his eyes whatever enters his visual field. His senses, too, seem to "take in" what feels good. In this sense, then, one can speak of an *incorporative stage*, in which he is, relatively speaking, receptive to what he is being offered. Yet babies are sensitive and vulnerable too. In order to insure that their first experiences in this world will not only keep them alive but will also help them to co-ordinate their sensitive breathing and their metabolic and circulatory rhythms, we must see to it that we deliver to their senses stimuli as well as food in the proper intensity and at the right time; otherwise their willingness to accept may change radically into diffuse defense or into lethargy.

Now, while it is quite clear what must happen to keep a baby alive—the minimum supply necessary—and what must not happen, lest he be physically damaged or chronically upset—the maximum of early frustration tolerable—there is a certain leeway in regard to what *may* happen, and different cultures make extensive use of the prerogatives to decide what they consider workable and insist upon calling necessary. Some people think that a baby, lest he scratch his own eyes out, must necessarily be swaddled completely for most of the day and throughout the

The Life Cycle: Epigenesis of Identity

greater part of the first year, and that he should be rocked or fed whenever he whimpers. Others think that he should feel the freedom of his kicking limbs as early as possible, but also that, as a matter of course, he should be forced to cry "please" for his meals until he literally gets blue in the face. All of this, more or less consciously, seems related to the culture's general aim and system. I have known some old American Indians who bitterly decried the way in which we once let our small babies cry because we believed that it would "make their lungs strong." No wonder, these Indians said, that the white man, after such an initial reception, seems to be so intent on getting to "heaven." But the same Indians spoke proudly of the way their infants, breast fed into the second year, became blue in the face with fury when they were thumped on the head for "biting" their mother's nipples; here the Indians, in turn, believed that it would "make good hunters of them."

There is, then, some intrinsic wisdom, some unconscious planning, and much superstition in the seemingly arbitrary varieties of child training. But there is also a logic—however instinctive and prescientific—in the assumption that what is "good for the child," what *may* happen to him, depends on what he is supposed to become and where.

At any rate, it is already in his earliest encounters that the human infant meets up with the principal modalities of his culture. The simplest and the earliest modality is *to get*, not in the sense of "go and get" but in that of receiving and accepting what is given. This is easy when it works and yet any disturbance shows how complicated the process really is. The groping and unstable newborn's organism learns this modality only as he learns to regulate his readiness to "get" with the methods of a mother who, in turn, will permit him to co-ordinate his means of getting as she develops and co-ordinates her means of giving. But in thus getting what is given, and in learning to get somebody to do for him what he wishes to have done, the baby also develops the necessary groundwork "to get to be" the giver—that is, to identify with her and eventually to become a giving person.

In some especially sensitive individuals, or in individuals whose early frustration was never compensated for, a weakness in such early mutual regulation can be at the root of a disturbance in their relationship to the world in general, and especially to significant people. But, of course, there are ways of maintaining mutuality through the satiation of other than oral receptors: the baby's pleasure in being held, warmed, smiled at, talked to, rocked, and so forth. Besides such "horizontal" compensation (compensation during the same stage of development) there are many "longitudinal" compensations in life which emerge from later stages of the life cycle.[3]

During the "second oral" stage the capacities to pursue and take pleasure in a more active and more directed incorporative approach ripen. Teeth develop and with them the pleasure of biting on hard things, biting through things, and biting off things. This active-incorporative mode characterizes a variety of other activities, as did the first incorporative mode. The eyes, first seemingly passive in accepting impressions as they come along, have now learned to focus on, isolate, and "grasp" objects from the vaguer background and follow them. The organs of hearing similarly have learned to discern significant sounds, localize them, and guide appropriate changes in position, such as lifting and turning the head or lifting and turning the upper body. The arms have learned to reach out determinedly and the hands to grasp firmly. We are, then, more interested in the overall configuration of developing approaches to the world than we are in the first appearance of isolated abilities which are so well documented in the child-development literature. One can think of a stage as the time when a given capacity first appears (or appears in testable form) or as that period when a number of related items are so well established and integrated that the next step in development can safely be initiated.

During the second stage, interpersonal patterns are established which are united in the social modality of *taking* and *holding on* to things—things which are more or less freely offered and given and things which have more or less a tendency to slip away. As the baby learns to change positions, to roll over, and very gradually to establish himself on the throne of his sedentary kingdom, he must perfect the mechanisms of grasping, appropriating, and holding as well as chewing all that is within his reach.

The crisis of the second oral stage is difficult to assess and more difficult to verify. It seems to consist of the coincidence in time of three developments: (1) a more "violent" drive to incorporate, appropriate, and observe more actively, a tension associated with the discomfort of "teething" and other changes in the oral machinery; (2) the infant's increasing awareness of himself as a distinct person; and (3) the mother's gradual turning away from the baby toward pursuits which she had given up during late pregnancy and postnatal care. These pursuits include her full return to conjugal intimacy and perhaps to a new pregnancy.

Where breast feeding lasts into the biting stage, and, generally speaking, this has been the rule, it is now necessary to learn how to continue sucking without biting, so that the mother will not withdraw the nipple in pain or anger. Our clinical work indicates that this stage in the individual's early history provides him with some sense of basic loss, leaving the general impression that once upon a time one's unity with a maternal matrix was destroyed. Weaning, therefore, should not mean sudden loss of both the breast and the mother's reassuring presence, unless, of course, other women can be depended upon to sound and feel much like the mother. A drastic loss of accustomed mother love without proper substitution at this time can lead, under otherwise aggravating conditions, to acute infantile depression [4] or to a mild but chronic state of mourning which may give a depressive undertone to the remainder of one's life. But even under more favorable circumstances, this stage seems to introduce into the psychic life a sense of division and a dim but universal nostalgia for a lost paradise.

It is against the combination of these impressions of having been deprived, of having been divided, and of having been abandoned, all of which leave a residue of basic mistrust, that basic trust must establish and maintain itself.

What we here call "trust" coincides with what Therese Bene-dek has called "confidence." If I prefer the word "trust," it is because there is more naïveté and more mutuality in it: an infant can be said to be trusting, but it would be assuming too much to say that he has confidence. The general state of trust, further-more, implies not only that one has learned to rely on the same-ness and continuity of the outer providers but also that one may trust oneself and the capacity of one's own organs to cope with urges; that one is able to consider oneself trustworthy enough so that the providers will not need to be on guard or to leave.

In the psychiatric literature we find frequent references to an "oral character," which is an emphasis on traits representative of the unsolved conflicts of this stage. Wherever oral pessimism be-comes dominant and exclusive, infantile fears such as that of "being left empty" or simply of "being left," and also of being "starved of stimulation," can be discerned in the depressive forms of "being empty" and of "being no good." Such fears, in turn, can give orality that particular avaricious quality which in psychoanalysis is called oral sadism, that is, a cruel need to get and to take in ways harmful to others or to oneself. But there is an optimistic oral character, too, one who has learned to make giving and receiving the most important thing in life. And there is "orality" as a normal substratum in all individuals, a lasting residuum of this first period of dependency on powerful provid-ers. It normally expresses itself in our dependencies and nostal-gias, and in our all too hopeful and all too hopeless states. The integration of the oral stage with all the following ones results, in adulthood, in a combination of faith and realism.

The pathology and irrationality of oral trends depend entirely on the degree to which they are integrated with the rest of the personality and the degree to which they fit into the general cul-tural pattern and use approved interpersonal techniques for their expression.

Here, as elsewhere, we must therefore consider as a topic for discussion the expression of infantile urges in cultural patterns which one may or may not consider a pathological deviation in the total economic or moral system of a culture or nation. One could speak, for example, of the invigorating belief in "chance," that traditional prerogative of American trust in one's own resourcefulness and in Fate's store of good intentions. This belief, at times, can be seen to degenerate in large-scale gambling, or in "taking chances" in the form of an arbitrary and often suicidal provocation of Fate or in the insistence that one has not only the right to an equal chance, but also the privilege of being preferred over all other "investors." In a similar way, all the pleasant reassurances which can be derived, especially in company, from old and new taste sensations, inhaling and sipping, munching and swallowing and digesting can turn into mass addictions neither expressive of nor conducive to the kind of basic trust we have in mind. Here we are obviously touching on phenomena calling for an epidemiological approach to the problem of the more or less malignant elaboration of infantile modalities in cultural excesses, as well as in mild forms of addiction, self-delusion, and avaricious appropriation, which are expressive of a certain weakness in oral reassurance.

It must be said, however, that the amount of trust derived from earliest infantile experience does not seem to depend on absolute quantities of food or demonstrations of love, but rather on the quality of the maternal relationship. Mothers create a sense of trust in their children by that kind of administration which in its quality combines sensitive care of the baby's individual needs and a firm sense of personal trustworthiness within the trusted framework of their community's life style. This forms the very basis in the child for a component of the sense of identity which will later combine a sense of being "all right," of being oneself, and of becoming what other people trust one will become. Parents must not only have certain ways of guiding by prohibition and permission, they must also be able to represent to the child a deep, almost somatic conviction that there is a meaning in what they are doing. In this sense a traditional system of child care can be said to be a factor making for trust, even where certain items of that tradition, taken singly, may seem arbitrary or unnecessarily cruel—or lenient. Here much depends on whether such items are inflicted on the child by the parent in the firm traditional belief that this is the only way to do things or whether the parent misuses his administration of the baby and the child in order to work off anger, alleviate fear, or win an argument, either with the child himself or with somebody else—mother-in-law, doctor, or priest.

In times of change—and what other times are there, in our memory?—one generation differs so much from another that items of tradition often become disturbances. Conflicts between mother's ways and one's own self-made style, conflicts between the expert's advice and mother's ways, and conflicts between the expert's authority and one's own style may disturb a young mother's trust in herself. Furthermore, all the mass transformations in American life (immigration, migration, and Americanization; industrialization, urbanization, mechanization, and others) are apt to disturb young mothers in those tasks which are so simple yet so far-reaching. No wonder, then, that the first section of the first chapter of Benjamin Spock's book is entitled "Trust Yourself." [5]

IN A DISCUSSION of development, it is unavoidable that one must begin with the beginning. This is unfortunate because we know so little of the earliest and deepest strata of the human mind. But I would claim that we have now touched upon the major directions from which any of the emerging components of human vitality can be studied—from the beginning of life to the identity crisis and beyond. We will not be able to be equally expansive in regard to the other stages, although this chapter as a whole should complete an "inventory" such as we have now outlined for the first stage of life. In addition to the measurable aspects of growth, our implicit scheme should cover: (1) The *expanding libidinal needs* of the developing being and, with them, new possibilities of satisfaction, of frustration, and of "sublimation." (2) *The widening social radius*, i.e., the number and kinds of people to whom he can respond meaningfully on the basis of (3) his ever more highly differentiated *capacities*. (4) The *developmental crisis* evoked by the necessity to manage new encounters within a given time allowance. (5) A new *sense of estrangement* awakened along with the awareness of new dependences and new familiarities (e.g., in early infancy, the sense of abandonment). (6) A specifically new *psychosocial strength* (here a favorable ratio of trust over mistrust) which is a foundation for all future strengths.

This is a forbidding array of items [6] and is too demanding for what is our immediate task, namely, a descriptive account of the early experiences which facilitate or endanger the future identity.

What would we consider to be the earliest and most undifferentiated "sense of identity"? I would suggest that it arises out of the encounter of maternal person and small infant, an encounter which is one of mutual trustworthiness and mutual recognition. This, in all its infantile simplicity, is the first experience of what in later reoccurances in love and admiration can only be called a sense of "hallowed presence," the need for which remains basic in man. Its absence or impairment can dangerously limit the capacity to feel "identical" when adolescent growth makes it incumbent on the person to abandon his childhood and to trust adulthood and, with it, the search for self-chosen loves and incentives.

At this point, I must add to the list already given one further dimension, the seventh—namely, the contribution of each stage to one major human endeavor which in adulthood takes over the guardianship of the particular strength originating in this stage and the ritual appeasement of its particular estrangement.

Each successive stage and crisis has a special relation to one of the basic institutionalized endeavors of man for the simple reason that the human life cycle and human institutions have evolved together. The relation between them is twofold: each generation brings to these institutions the remnants of infantile needs and youthful fervor and receives from them—as long as they, indeed, manage to maintain their institutional vitality—a specific reinforcement of childlike vitality. If I name religion as the institution which throughout man's history has striven to verify basic trust, I disavow any intention to call religion as such childish or religious behavior as such regressive, although it is obvious that large-scale infantilization is not foreign to the practice and the intent of organized religion. As we overcome our universal amnesia for the frightening aspects of childhood, we may well also acknowledge gratefully the fact that, in principle, the glory of childhood also survives in adult life. Trust, then, becomes the capacity for *faith*—a vital need for which man must find some institutional confirmation. Religion, it seems, is the oldest and has been the most lasting institution to serve the ritual restoration of a sense of trust in the form of faith while offering a tangible formula for a sense of evil against which it promises to arm and defend man. Childlike strength as well as a potential for infantilization are suggested in the fact that all religious practice includes periodic childlike surrender to the Power that creates and re-creates, dispensing earthly fortune as well as spiritual well-being; the demonstration of smallness and dependence by reduced posture and humble gesture; the confession in prayer and song of misdeeds, misthoughts, and evil intentions and the fervent appeal for inner reunification by divine guidance. At best, all of this is highly stylized and thus becomes suprapersonal; [7] individual trust becomes a common faith, individual mistrust a commonly formulated evil, while the individual's plea for restoration becomes part of the ritual practice of many and a sign of trustworthiness in the community.

When religion loses its acutal power of presence, then, it would seem, an age must find other forms of joint reverence for life which derive vitality from a shared world image. For only a reasonably coherent world provides the faith which is transmitted by the mothers to the infants in a way conducive to the vital strength of *hope*, that is, the enduring predisposition to believe in the attainability of primal wishes in spite of the anarchic urges and rages of dependency. The shortest formulation of the identity gain of earliest childhood may well be: I am what hope I have and give.[8]

2. EARLY CHILDHOOD AND THE WILL TO BE ONESELF

Psychoanalysis has enriched the vocabulary with the word "anality" to designate the particular pleasureableness and willfulness which are often attached to the eliminative organs in early childhood. The whole procedure of evacuating the bowels and the bladder is, of course, enhanced from the beginning by a premium of satisfaction over a major job "well done." At first this premium must make up for quite frequent discomfort and tension suffered as the bowels learn to do their daily work. Two developments gradually give anal experiences the necessary "volume": the arrival of better-formed stool and the general coordination of the muscle system which permits the development of voluntary release as well as of retention. This new dimension of approach to things, however, is not restricted to the sphincters. A general ability, indeed, a violent need, develops to alternate withholding and expelling at will and, in general, to keep tightly and to throw away willfully whatever is held.

The over-all significance of this second stage of early childhood lies in the rapid gains in muscular maturation, in verbalization, and in discrimination and the consequent ability—and doubly felt inability—to co-ordinate a number of highly conflicting action patterns characterized by the tendencies of "holding on" and "letting go." In this and in many other ways, the still highly dependent child begins to experience his *autonomous will*. At this time sinister forces are leashed and unleashed, especially in the guerilla warfare of unequal wills, for the child is often unequal to his own violent will and parent and child are often unequal to one another.

As far as anality proper is concerned, everything depends on whether the cultural environment wants to make something of it. There are primitive and agrarian cultures where the parents ignore anal behavior and leave it to the older children to lead the toddler out to the bushes so that his compliance in this matter may coincide with his wish to imitate the bigger ones. Our Western civilization (as well as others—for example, Japan), and especially certain classes within it, have chosen to take the matter more seriously. It is here that the machine age has provided the ideal of a mechanically trained, faultlessly functioning, and always clean, punctual, and deodorized body. In addition, it has been more or less superstitiously assumed that early and rigorous training is absolutely necessary for the kind of personality which will function efficiently in a mechanized world in which time is money. Thus a child becomes a machine which must be set and tuned even as before it was an animal which must be broken—while, in fact, will power can develop only by steps. At any rate our clinical work suggests that the neurotics of our time include the *compulsive type*, who is stingy, retentive, and meticulous in matters of affection, time, and money as well as in the management of his bowels. Also, bowel and bladder training has become the most obviously disturbing item of child training in wide circles of our society.

What, then, makes the anal problem potentially important and difficult?

The anal zone lends itself more than any other to the expression of stubborn insistence on conflicting impulses because, for one thing, it is the model zone for two contradictory modes which must become alternating, namely, retention and elimination. Furthermore, the sphincters are only part of the muscle system with its general ambiguity of rigidity and relaxation, of flexion and extension. This whole stage, then, becomes a *battle for autonomy*. For as he gets ready to stand on his feet more firmly, the infant also learns to delineate his world as "I" and "you," and "me" and "mine." Every mother knows how astonishingly pliable a child may be at this stage, if and when he has made the decision that he wants to do what he is supposed to do. It is impossible, however, to find a reliable formula for making him want to do just that. Every mother knows how lovingly a child at this stage will snuggle close to her and how ruthlessly he will suddenly try to push her away. At the same time the child is apt both to hoard things and to discard them, to cling to treasured objects and to throw them out of the windows of houses and vehicles. All of these seemingly contradictory tendencies, then, we include under the formula of the *retentive-eliminative modes*. All basic modalities, in fact, lend themselves to both hostile and benign expectations and attitudes. Thus, "to hold" can become a destructive and cruel retaining or restraining, and it can become a pattern of care: "to have and to hold." To "let go," too, can turn into an inimical letting loose of destructive forces, or it can become a relaxed "to let pass" and "to let be." Culturally speaking, these modalities are neither good nor bad; their value depends on how they are built into the patterns of affirmation and rejection demanded in the culture.

The matter of mutual regulation between adult and child now faces its severest test. If outer control by too rigid or too early training persists in robbing the child of his attempt gradually to control his bowels and other functions willingly and by his free choice, he will again be faced with a double rebellion and a double defeat. Powerless against his own anal instinctuality and sometimes afraid of his own bowel movements and powerless outside, he will be forced to seek satisfaction and control either by regression or by fake progression. In other words, he will return to an earlier, oral control; that is, he will suck his thumb and become doubly demanding; or he will become hostile and willful, often using his feces (as he will later the corresponding dirty words) as aggressive ammunition; or he will pretend an autonomy and an ability to do without anybody's help which he has by no means really gained.

This stage, therefore, becomes decisive for the ratio between loving good will and hateful self-insistence, between co-operation and willfulness, and between self-expression and compulsive self-restraint or meek compliance. A sense of self-control without loss of self-esteem is the ontogenetic source of a sense of *free will*. From an unavoidable sense of loss of self-control and of parental overcontrol comes a lasting propensity for *doubt* and *shame.*

For the growth of autonomy a firmly developed early trust is necessary. The infant must have come to be sure that his faith in himself and in the world will not be jeopardized by the violent wish to have his choice, to appropriate demandingly, and to eliminate stubbornly. Only parental firmness can protect him against the consequences of his as yet untrained discrimination and circumspection. But his environment must also back him up in his wish to "stand on his own feet," while also protecting him against the now newly emerging pair of estrangements, namely, that sense of having exposed himself permaturely and foolishly which we call shame or that secondary mistrust, that "double take," which we call doubt—doubt in himself and doubt in the firmness and perspicacity of his trainers.

Shame is an infantile emotion insufficiently studied because in our civilization it is so early and easily absorbed by guilt. Shame supposes that one is completely exposed and conscious of being looked at—in a word, self-conscious. One is visible and not ready to be visible; that is why in dreams of shame we are stared at in a condition of incomplete dress, in night attire, "with one's pants down." Shame is early expressed in an impulse to bury one's face or to sink, right then and there, into the ground. This potentiality is abundantly utilized in the educational method of "shaming" used so exclusively by some primitive peoples, where it supplants the often more destructive sense of guilt to be discussed later. The destructiveness of shaming is balanced in some civilizations by devices for "saving face." Shaming exploits the increased sense of being small, which paradoxically develops as the child stands up and as his awareness permits him to note the relative measures of size and power.

Too much shaming does not result in a sense of propriety but in a secret determination to try to get away with things when unseen, if, indeed, it does not result in deliberate shamelessness. There is an impressive American ballad in which a murderer to be hanged on the gallows before the eyes of the community, instead of feeling mortally afraid or totally shamed, begins to be-rate the onlookers, ending every salvo of defiance with the words, "God damn your eyes." Many a small child, when shamed beyond endurance, may be in a mood (although not in possession of either the courage or the words) to express defiance in similar terms. What I mean by this sinister reference is that there is a limit to a child's and an adult's individual endurance in the face of demands which force him to consider himself, his body, his needs, and his wishes as evil and dirty, and to believe in the infallibility of those who pass such judgment. Occasionally, he may turn things around, become secretly oblivious to the opinion of others, and consider as evil only the fact that they exist: his chance will come when they are gone or when he can leave them.

The psychiatric danger of this stage is, as it is at all other stages, the potential aggravation of the normative estrangement to the point where it will cause neurotic or psychotic tendencies. The sensitive child may turn all his urge to discriminate against himself and thus develop a *precocious conscience*. Instead of willfully appropriating things in order to test them by repetitive play, he will become obsessed by his own repetitiveness and will want to have everything "just so," and only in a given sequence and tempo. By such infantile obsessiveness and procrastination, or by becoming a stickler for ritualistic repetitions, the child then learns to gain power over his parents in areas where he could not find large-scale mutual regulation with them. Such hollow victory, then, is the infantile model for an adult compulsion neurosis.

In adolescence, for example, a compulsive person may attempt to free himself with maneuvers expressing the wish to "get away with" things and yet find himself unable to get away even with the wish. For while such a young person learns evasion from others, his precocious conscience does not let him really get away with anything, and he goes through his identity crisis habitually ashamed, apologetic, and afraid to be seen; or else, in an "overcompensatory" manner, he evinces a defiant kind of autonomy which may find sanction and ritual in the shameless defiance of gangs. This will be discussed in more detail in Chapter VI.

Doubt is the brother of shame. Whereas shame is dependent on the consciousness of being upright and exposed, doubt has much to do with a consciousness of having a front and a back —and especially a "behind." For this reverse area of the body, with its aggressive and libidinal focus in the sphincters and buttocks, cannot be seen by the child, and yet it can be dominated by the will of others. The "behind" is the small being's dark continent, an area of the body which can be magically dominated and effectively invaded by those who would attack one's power of autonomy and who would designate as evil those products of the bowels which were felt to be all right when they were being passed. This basic sense of doubt in whatever one has left behind is the model for the habitual "double take" or other later and more verbal forms of compulsive doubting. It finds its adult expression in paranoiac fears concerning hidden persecutors and secret persecutions threatening from behind (and from within the behind). Again, in adolescence, this may be expressed in a transitory total self-doubt, a feeling that all that is now "behind" in time—the childhood family as well as the earlier manifestations of one's personality—simply do not add up to the prerequisites for a new beginning. All of this may then be denied in a willful display of dirtiness and messiness, with all the implications of "dirty" swearing at the world and at oneself.

As was the case with the "oral" personality, the compulsive or "anal" personality has its normal aspects and its abnormal exaggerations. If eventually integrated with compensatory traits, some *impulsiveness* releases expression even as some *compulsiveness* is useful in matters in which order, punctuality, and cleanliness are of the essence. The question is always whether we remain the masters of the modalities by which things become more manageable or whether the rules master the ruler.

It takes stamina as well as flexibility to train a child's will so as to help him to overcome too much willfulness, develop some "good will," and (while learning to obey in some essential ways)

maintain an autonomous sense of free will. As far as psychoanalysis is concerned, it has focused primarily on excessively
early toilet training and on unreasonable shaming as causes of
the child's estrangement from his own body. It has attempted at
least to formulate what should *not* be done to children, and
there are, of course, any number of avoidances which can be
learned from the study of the life cycle. Many such formulations, however, are apt to arouse superstitious inhibitions in
those who are inclined to make anxious rules out of vague warn-
ings. We are gradually learning what exactly not to do to what
kind of children at what age; but then we must still learn what
to do, spontaneously and joyfully. The expert, to quote Frank
Fremont-Smith, can only "set the frame of reference within
which choice is permissible and desirable." In the last analysis, as
comparative studies in child training have convinced us, the kind
and degree of a sense of autonomy which parents are able to
grant their small children depends on the dignity and sense of
personal independence they derive from their own lives. We
have already suggested that the infant's sense of trust is a reflection of parental faith; similarly, the sense of autonomy is a reflection of the parents' dignity as autonomous beings. For no
matter what we do in detail, the child will primarily feel what it
is we live by as loving, co-operative, and firm beings, and what
makes us hateful, anxious, and divided in ourselves.

What social institution, then, guards the lasting gains of the
second stage of life? Man's basic need for a delineation of his autonomy seems to have an institutional safeguard in the principle
of *law and order*, which in everyday life as well as in the courts
of law apportions to each his privileges and his limitations, his
obligations and his rights. Only a sense of rightfully delimited
autonomy in the parents fosters a handling of the small individual which expresses a suprapersonal indignation rather than an
arbitrary rightousness. It is important to dwell on this point because much of the lasting sense of doubt, and of the indignity of
punishment and restriction common to many children, is a consequence of the parents' frustrations in marriage, in work, and in

citizenship. Where large numbers of people have been prepared in childhood to expect from life a high degree of personal autonomy, pride, and opportunity, and then in later life find themselves ruled by impersonal organizations and machineries too intricate to understand, the result may be deep chronic disappointment that makes them unwilling to grant each other—or their children—a measure of autonomy. They may be possessed, instead, by irrational fears of losing what is left of their autonomy or of being sabotaged, restricted, and constricted in their free will by anonymous enemies and at the same time, paradoxically enough, of not being controlled enough, of not being *told* what to do.

We have, again at length, characterized the struggles and triumphs of a childhood stage. In what way does this stage contribute to the identity crisis, either by supporting the formation of identity or by contributing a particular kind of estrangement to its confusion? The stage of autonomy, of course, deserves particular attention, for in it is played out the first emancipation, namely, from the mother. There are clinical reasons (to be discussed in the chapter on identity confusion) to believe that the adolescent turning away from the whole childhood milieu in many ways repeats this first emancipation. For this reason the most rebellious youths can also regress partially (and sometimes wholly) to a demanding and plaintive search for a guidance which their cynical independence seems to disavow. Apart from such "clinical" evidence, however, the over-all contribution to an eventual identity formation is the very courage to be an independent individual who can choose and guide his own future.

We said that the earliest stage leaves a residue in the growing being which, on many hierarchic levels and especially in the individual's sense of identity, will echo something of the conviction "I am what hope I have and give." The analogous residue of the stage of autonomy appears to be "I am what I can will freely." [9]

3. CHILDHOOD AND THE ANTICIPATION
OF ROLES

Being firmly convinced that he is a person on his own, the child must now find out what kind of a person he may become. He is, of course, deeply and exclusively "identified" with his parents, who most of the time appear to him to be powerful and beautiful, although often quite unreasonable, disagreeable, and even dangerous. Three developments support this stage, while also serving to bring about its crisis: (1) the child learns to move around more freely and more violently and therefore establishes a wider and, to him, unlimited radius of goals; (2) his sense of language becomes perfected to the point where he understands and can ask incessantly about innumerable things, often hearing just enough to misunderstand them thoroughly; and (3) both language and locomotion permit him to expand his imagination to so many roles that he cannot avoid frightening himself with what he himself has dreamed and thought up. Nevertheless, out of all this he must emerge with a *sense of initiative* as a basis for a realistic sense of ambition and purpose.

What, then, are the criteria for an unbroken sense of initiative? The criteria for the development of all the "senses" discussed here are the same: a crisis beset with some new estrangement is resolved in such a way that the child suddenly seems to be "more himself," more loving, more relaxed, and brighter in his judgment—in other words, vital in a new way. Most of all, he seems to be more activated and activating; he is in the free possession of a certain surplus of energy which permits him to forget many failures rather quickly and to approach new areas that seem desirable, even if they also seem dangerous, with undiminished zest and some increased sense of direction.

We are now approaching the end of the third year, when walking is getting to be a thing of ease, of vigor. The books tell us that a child can walk much before this, but walking and running become an item in his sphere of mastery when gravity is felt to be within, when he can forget that he is doing the walking and instead find out what he can do with it. Only then do his legs become part of him instead of being an ambulatory appendix. Only then will he find out with advantage what he now *may* do, along with what he *can* do, and now he is ready to visualize himself as being as big as the perambulating grownups. He begins to make comparisons and is apt to develop untiring curiosity about differences in size and kind in general, and about sexual and age differences in particular. He tries to comprehend possible future roles or, at any rate, to understand what roles are worth imagining. More immediately, he can now associate with those of his own age. Under the guidance of older children or special women guardians, he gradually enters into the infantile politics of nursery school, street corner, and barnyard. His learning now is eminently intrusive and vigorous; it leads away from his own limitations and into future possibilities.

The *intrusive mode*, dominating much of the behavior of this stage, characterizes a variety of configurationally "similar" activities and fantasies. These include (1) the intrusion into space by vigorous locomotion; (2) the intrusion into the unknown by consuming curiosity; (3) the intrusion into other people's ears and minds by the aggressive voice; (4) the intrusion upon or into other bodies by physical attack; (5) and, often most frighteningly, the thought of the phallus intruding the female body.

This, therefore, is called the *phallic stage* in the theory of infantile sexuality. It is the stage of infantile curiosity, of genital excitability, and of a varying preoccupation and overconcern with sexual matters, such as the apparent loss of the penis in girls. This "genitality" is, of course, rudimentary, a mere promise of things to come; often it is not even particularly noticeable. If not specifically provoked into precocious manifestation by especially seductive practices or by pointed prohibitions and threats of "cutting it off" or special customs such as sex play in groups of children, it is apt to lead to no more than a series of peculiarly fascinating experiences which soon become frightening and pointless enough to be repressed. This leads to the ascendancy of that human specialty which Freud called the "latency" period, that is, the long delay separating infantile sexuality (which in animals merges into maturity) and physical sexual maturation. It is accompanied by the recognition of the fact that in spite of all efforts to imagine oneself as being, in principle, as capable as mother and father, not even in the distant future is one ever going to be father in sexual relationship to mother, or mother in sexual relationship to father. The very deep emotional consequences of this insight and the magic fears associated with it make up what Freud has called the Oedipus complex. It is based on the logic of development which decrees that boys attach their first genital affection to the maternal adults who have otherwise given comfort to their bodies and that they develop their first sexual rivalry against the persons who are the sexual owners of those maternal persons. The little girl, in turn, becomes attached to her father and other important men and jealous of her mother, a development which may cause her much anxiety, for it seems to block her retreat to that selfsame mother, while it makes her mother's disapproval much more magically dangerous because it is secretly "deserved."

Girls often undergo a sobering change at this stage, because they observe sooner or later that although their locomotor, mental, and social intrusiveness is as vigorous as that of the boys', thus permitting them to become perfectly good tomboys, they lack one item, the penis, and, with it, important prerogatives in most cultures and classes. While the boy has this visible, erectable, and comprehensible organ to which he can attach dreams of adult bigness, the girl's clitoris only poorly sustains dreams of sexual equality, and she does not even have breasts as analogously tangible tokens of her future. The idea of her eventual *inception* of the intruding phallus is as yet too frightening, and her maternal drives are relegated to play fantasy or baby tending. On the other hand, where mothers dominate households the boy can develop a sense of inadequacy because he learns at this stage that while he can do well outside in play and work, he will never boss the house, his mother, or his older sisters. His mother and sisters may, in fact, get even with him for their doubts in themselves by making him feel that a boy is really a somewhat repulsive creature.

Where the necessities of economic life and the simplicity of its social plan make the male and female roles and their specific powers and rewards comprehensible, these early misgivings about sexual differences are, of course, more easily integrated into the culture's design for the differentiation of sexual roles. Both girl and boy are, therefore, extraordinarily appreciative of any convincing promise of the fact that someday they will be as good as mother or father—perhaps better; and they are grateful for sexual enlightenment, a little at a time and patiently repeated at intervals.

The ambulatory stage, that of play and infantile genitality, adds to the inventory of basic social modalities in both sexes that of "making," first in the childlike sense of "being on the make." There are no simpler, stronger words to match basic social modalities than those of Basic English. The words suggest enjoyment of competition, insistence on goal, pleasure of conquest. In the boy the emphasis remains on "making" by head-on attack; in the girl it may turn to "catching" either by aggressive snatching or by making herself attractive and endearing. The child thus develops the prerequisites for masculine or feminine initiative and, above all, some sexual self-images which will become essential ingredients in the positive and negative aspects of his future identity. On the way, however, the vastly increased imagination and, as it were, the intoxication of increased locomotor powers lead to secret fantasies of gigantic and terrifying proportions. A deep *sense of guilt* is awakened—a strange sense, for it seems forever to imply that the individual has committed crimes and deeds that were, after all, not only not committed but would have been biologically quite impossible. While the struggle for autonomy at its worst had concentrated on keeping rivals out, and was therefore more an expression of *jealous rage* most often directed against encroachments by younger siblings, initiative brings with it *anticipatory rivalry* with those who were there first and who may therefore occupy with their superior equipment the field toward which one's initiative is at first directed. Jealousy and rivalry, those often embittered and yet essentially futile attempts at demarcating a sphere of unquestioned privilege, now come to a climax in a final contest for a favored position with one of the parents: the inevitable and necessary failure leads to guilt and anxiety. The child indulges in fantasies of being a giant or a tiger, but in his dreams he runs in terror for dear life. This, then, is the stage of fear for life and limb, of the *"castration complex"*—the intensified fear of losing, or on the part of the girl the conviction that she has lost, the male genital as punishment for secret fantasies and deeds.

The great governor of initiative is *conscience*. The child, we said, now not only feels afraid of being found out, but he also hears the "inner voice" of self-observation, self-guidance, and self-punishment, which divides him radically within himself: a new and powerful estrangement. This is the ontogenetic cornerstone of morality. But from the point of view of human vitality, we must point out that if this great achievement is overburdened by all too eager adults, it can be bad for the spirit and for morality itself. For the conscience of the child can be primitive, cruel, and uncompromising, as may be observed in instances where children learn to constrict themselves to the point of over-all inhibition; where they develop an obedience more literal than the one the parent wishes to exact; or where they develop deep regressions and lasting resentments because the parents themselves do not seem to live up to the conscience which they have fostered in the child. One of the deepest conflicts in life is caused by hate for a parent who served initially as the model and the executor of the conscience, but who was later found trying to "get away with" the very transgressions which the child could no longer tolerate in himself. Thus the child comes to feel that the whole matter is not one of universal goodness but of arbitrary power. The suspiciousness and evasiveness which is added to the all-or-nothing quality of the superego makes moralistic man a great potential danger to himself and to his fellow men. Morality can become synonymous with vindictiveness and with the suppression of others.

All of this may seem strange to readers who have not suspected the potential powerhouse of destructive drives which can be aroused and temporarily buried at this stage, only to contribute later to the inner arsenal of a destructiveness so ready to be used when opportunity provokes it. By using the words "potential," "provoke," and "opportunity," I mean to emphasize that there is little in these inner developments which cannot be harnessed to constructive and peaceful initiative if we learn to understand the conflicts and anxieties of childhood and the importance of childhood for mankind. But if we should choose to overlook or belittle the phenomena of childhood, along with the best and the worst of our childhood dreams, we shall have failed to recognize one of the eternal sources of human anxiety and strife. For again, the pathological consequences of this stage may not show until much later, when conflicts over initiative may find expression in *hysterical denial* or in a *self-restriction* which keeps an individual from living up to his inner capacities or to the powers of his imagination and feeling, if not in relative sexual impotence or frigidity. All of this, in turn, may be "overcompensated" in a great show of tireless initiative, in a quality of "go-at-itiveness" at any cost. Many adults feel that their worth as people consists entirely in what they are "going at" in the future and not in what they are in the present. The strain consequently developed in their bodies, which are always "on the go," with the engine racing even at moments of rest, is a powerful contribution to the much-discussed psychosomatic diseases of our time. It is as if the culture had made a man overadvertise himself and so identify with his own advertisement that only disease can designate the limit.

A comparative view of child training, however, suggests a fact most important for identity development, namely, that adults by their own example and by the stories they tell of the big life and of what to them is the great past, offer children of this age an eagerly absorbed *ethos of action* in the form of ideal types and techniques fascinating enough to replace the heroes of picture book and fairy tale. For this reason also the play age relies on the existence of some form of basic family, which teaches the child by patient example where play ends and irreversible purpose begins and where "don'ts" are superseded by sanctioned avenues of vigorous action. For the children now look for new identifications which seem to promise a field of initiative with less of the conflict and guilt which attach to the hopeless rivalry of the home. Also, in connection with comprehensible games and work activities, a companionship may develop between father and son, and between mother and daughter, an experience of essential equality in worth, in spite of the inequality in developmental schedule. Such companionship is a lasting treasure not only for parent and child, but for the community, as it is a counterforce to those hidden hatreds based on differences in mere size or age. Only thus are guilt feelings integrated in a strong but not severe conscience, only thus is language certified as a shared actuality. The "Oedipal" stage thus eventually results not only in a moral sense constricting the horizon of the permissible; it also sets the direction toward the possible and the tangible which attaches infantile dreams to the varied goals of technology and culture.

We may now see what induced Freud to place the Oedipus complex at the core of man's conflicted existence, and this not only according to psychiatric evidence but also to the testimony of great fiction, drama, and history. For the fact that man began as a playing child leaves a residue of play-acting and role playing even in what he considers his highest purposes. These he projects on the glorified past as well as on a larger and always more perfect historical future; these he will dramatize in the ceremonial present with uniformed players in ritual arrangements which sanction aggressive initiative even as they assuage guilt by submission to a higher authority.

Among the group psychological consequences of the initiative stage, then, there is also a latent and often rageful readiness in the best and the most industrious to follow any leader who can make goals of conquest seem both impersonal and glorious enough to excite an intrinsically phallic enthusiam in men (and a compliance in women) and thus to relieve their irrational guilt. It is obvious, then, that man's aggressive ideals are to a large extent anchored in the stage of initiative, a fact of importance for the conflict of identity formation—and confusion.

The indispensable contribution of the initiative stage to later identity development, then, obviously is that of freeing the child's initiative and sense of purpose for adult tasks which promise (but cannot guarantee) a fulfillment of one's range of capacities. This is prepared in the firmly established, steadily growing conviction, undaunted by guilt, that "I am what I can imagine I will be." It is equally obvious, however, that a widespread disappointment of this conviction by a discrepancy between infantile ideals and adolescent reality can only lead to an unleashing of the guilt-and-violence cycle so characteristic of man and yet so dangerous to his very existence.

4. SCHOOL AGE AND TASK IDENTIFICATION

Such is the wisdom of the ground plan that at no time is the child more ready to learn quickly and avidly, to become big in the sense of sharing obligation, discipline, and performance than at the end of the period of expansive imagination. He is also eager to make things together, to share in constructing and planning, instead of trying to coerce other children or provoke restriction. Children now also attach themselves to teachers and the parents of other children, and they want to watch and imitate people representing occupations which they can grasp—firemen and policemen, gardeners, plumbers, and garbage men. If they are lucky they live at least part of their lives near barnyards or on safe streets around busy people and around many other children of all ages so that they can observe and participate as their capacities and their initiative grow in tentative spurts. But when they reach school age, children in all cultures receive some systematic instruction, although it is by no means always in the kind of school which literate people must organize around teachers who have learned how to teach literacy. In preliterate people much is learned from adults who become teachers by acclamation rather than by appointment, and much is learned from older children, but the knowledge gained is related to the basic skills of simple technologies which can be understood the moment the child gets ready to handle the utensils, the tools, and the weapons (or facsimiles thereof) used by the big people. He enters the technology of his tribe very gradually but also very directly. More literate people, with more specialized careers, must prepare the child by teaching him things which first of all make him literate. He is then given the widest possible basic education for the greatest number of possible careers. The greater the specialization, the more indistinct the goal of initiative becomes, the more complicated the social reality, and the vaguer the father's and mother's role in it. Between childhood and adulthood, then, our children go to school, and school skill seems to many to be a world all by itself, with its own goals and limitations, its achievements and disappointments.

At nursery-school age, playfulness reaches into the world shared with others. At first these others are treated as things; they are inspected, run into, or forced to "be horsie." Such learning is necessary in order to discover what potential play content can be admitted only to fantasy or only to play by and with oneself; what content can be successfully represented only in the world of toys and small things; and what content can be shared with others and even forced upon them. It is not restricted to the technical mastery of toys and things, but also includes an infantile way of mastering social experience by experimenting, planning, and sharing.

While all children at times need to be left alone in solitary play or, later, in the company of books and radio, motion pictures and television, and while all children need their hours and days of make-believe in games, they all, sooner or later, become dissatisfied and disgruntled without a sense of being able to make things and make them well and even perfectly: it is this that I have called the *sense of industry*. Without this, even the best-entertained child soon acts exploited. It is as if he knows and his society knows that now that he is psychologically already a rudimentary parent, he must begin to be something of a worker and potential provider before becoming a biological parent. With the oncoming latency period, then, the advancing child forgets, or rather quietly "sublimates"—that is, applies to concrete pursuits and approved goals—the drives which have made him dream and play. He now learns to win recognition by producing things. He develops perseverance and adjusts himself to the inorganic laws of the tool world and can become an eager and absorbed unit of a productive situation.

The danger at this stage is the development of an estrangement from himself and from his tasks—the well-known *sense of inferiority*. This may be caused by an insufficient solution of the preceding conflict: the child may still want his mommy more than knowledge; he may still prefer to be the baby at home rather than the big child in school; he still compares himself with his father, and the comparison arouses a sense of guilt as well as a sense of inferiority. Family life may not have prepared him for school life, or school life may fail to sustain the promises of earlier stages in that nothing that he has learned to do well so far seems to count with his fellows or his teacher. And then again, he may be potentially able to excel in ways which are dormant and which, if not evoked now, may develop late or never.

It is at this point that wider society becomes significant to the child by admitting him to roles preparatory to the actuality of technology and economy. Where he finds out immediately, however, that the color of his skin or the background of his parents rather than his wish and will to learn are the factors that decide his worth as a pupil or apprentice, the human propensity for feeling unworthy may be fatefully aggravated as a determinant of character development.

Good teachers who feel trusted and respected by the community know how to alternate play and work, games and study. They know how to recognize special efforts, how to encourage special gifts. They also know how to give a child time and how to handle those children to whom school, for a while, is not important and is considered something to endure rather than enjoy, or even the child to whom, for a while, other children are much more important than the teacher. But good parents also feel a need to make their children trust their teachers, and therefore to have teachers who can be trusted. For nothing less is at stake than the development and maintenance in children of a positive identification with those who know things and know how to do things. Again and again in interviews with especially gifted and inspired people, one is told spontaneously and with a special glow that *one* teacher can be credited with having kindled the flame of hidden talent. Against this stands the overwhelming evidence of vast neglect.

The fact that the majority of teachers in our elementary schools are women must be considered here in passing, because it can lead to a conflict with the nonintellectual boy's masculine identification, as if knowledge were feminine, action masculine. Bernard Shaw's statement that those who can, do, while those who cannot, teach, still has frequent validity for both parents and children. The selection and training of teachers, then, is vital for the avoidance of the dangers which can befall the individual at this stage. The development of a sense of inferiority, the feeling that one will never be "any good," is a danger which can be minimized by a teacher who knows how to emphasize what a child *can* do and who recognizes a psychiatric problem when she sees one. Obviously, here lies the best opportunity for preventing the particular identity confusion which goes back to incapacity or a flagrant lack of opportunity to learn. On the other hand, the child's budding sense of identity can remain prematurely fixed on being nothing but a good little worker or a good little helper, which may by no means be all he might become. Finally, there is the danger, probably the most common one, that throughout the long years of going to school a child will never acquire the enjoyment of work and pride in doing at least one kind of thing really well.

Regarding the period of a developing sense of industry, I have referred to outer and inner hindrances in the use of new capacities but not to aggravations of new human drives, nor to submerged rages resulting from their frustration. This stage differs from the earlier ones in that it is not a swing from an inner upheaval to a new mastery. Freud calls it the latency stage because violent drives are normally dormant. But it is only a lull before the storm of puberty, when all the earlier drives re-emerge in new combinations.

On the other hand, this is socially a most decisive stage. Since industry involves doing things beside and with others, a first sense of division of labor and of differential opportunity—that is, a sense of the *technological ethos* of a culture—develops at this time. Therefore, the configurations of culture and the manipulations basic to the *prevailing technology* must reach meaningfully into school life, supporting in every child a feeling of competence—that is, the free exercise of dexterity and intelligence in the completion of serious tasks unimpaired by an infantile sense of inferiority. This is the lasting basis for co-operative participation in productive adult life.

Two poles in American grammar school education may serve to illustrate the contribution of the school age to the problem of identity. There is the traditional extreme of making early school life an extension of grim adulthood by emphasizing self-restraint and a strict sense of duty in doing what one is told to do, as opposed to the modern extreme of making it an extension of the natural tendency in childhood to find out by playing, to learn what one must do by doing what one likes to do. Both methods work for some children in some ways, but impose on others a special adjustment. The first trend, if carried to the extreme, exploits a tendency on the part of the preschool and grammar school child to become entirely dependent on prescribed duties. He thus may learn much that is absolutely necessary and he may develop an unshakable sense of duty. But he may never unlearn an unnecessary and costly self-restraint with which he may later make his own life and other people's lives miserable, and in fact spoil, in turn, his own children's natural desire to learn and to work. The second trend, when carried to an extreme, leads not only to the well-known popular objection that children do not learn anything any more but also to such feelings in children as those expressed in the by now famous question of a metropolitan child: "Teacher, *must* we do today what we *want* to do?" Nothing could better express the fact that children at this age do like to be mildly but firmly coerced into the adventure of finding out that one can learn to accomplish things which one would never have thought of by oneself, things which owe their attractiveness to the very fact that they are not the product of play and fantasy but the product of reality, practicality, and logic; things which thus provide a token sense of participation in the real world of adults. Between these extremes we have the many schools which have no styles at all except grim attendance to the fact that school must be. Social inequality and backwardness of method still create a hazardous gap between many children and the technology which needs them not only so that they may serve technological aims, but, more imperatively, so that technology may serve humanity.

But there is another danger to identity development. If the overly conforming child accepts work as the only criterion of worthwhileness, sacrificing imagination and playfulness too readily, he may become ready to submit to what Marx called "craft-idiocy," i.e., become a slave of his technology and of its dominant role typology. Here we are already in the midst of identity problems, for with the establishment of a firm initial relationship to the world of skills and tools and to those who teach and share them, and with the advent of puberty, childhood proper comes to an end. And since man is not only the learning but also the teaching and above all the working animal, the immediate contribution of the school age to a sense of identity can be expressed in the words "I am what I can learn to make work." It is immediately obvious that for the vast majority of men, in all times, this has been not only the beginning but also the limitation of their identity; or better: the majority of men have always consolidated their identity needs around their technical and occupational capacities, leaving it to special groups (special by birth, by choice or election, and by giftedness) to establish and preserve those "higher" institutions without which man's daily work has always seemed an inadequate self-expression, if not a mere grind or even a kind of curse. It may be for that very reason that the identity problem in our time becomes both psychiatrically and historically relevant. For as man can leave some of the grind and curse to machines, he can visualize a greater freedom of identity for a larger segment of mankind.

5. ADOLESCENCE

As technological advances put more and more time between early school life and the young person's final access to specialized work, the stage of adolescing becomes an even more marked and conscious period and, as it has always been in some cultures in some periods, almost a way of life between childhood and adulthood. Thus in the later school years young people, beset with the physiological revolution of their genital maturation and the uncertainty of the adult roles ahead, seem much concerned with faddish attempts at establishing an adolescent subculture with what looks like a final rather than a transitory or, in fact, initial identity formation. They are sometimes morbidly, often curiously, preoccupied with what they appear to be in the eyes of others as compared with what they feel they are, and with the question of how to connect the roles and skills cultivated earlier with the ideal prototypes of the day. In their search for a new sense of continuity and sameness, which must now include sexual maturity, some adolescents have to come to grips again with crises of earlier years before they can install lasting idols and ideals as guardians of a final identity. They need, above all, a moratorium for the integration of the identity elements ascribed in the foregoing to the childhood stages: only that now a larger unit, vague in its outline and yet immediate in its demands, replaces the childhood milieu—"society." A review of these elements is also a list of adolescent problems.

If the earliest stage bequeathed to the identity crisis an important need for trust in oneself and in others, then clearly the adolescent looks most fervently for men and ideas to have *faith* in, which also means men and ideas in whose service it would seem worth while to prove oneself trustworthy. (This will be discussed further in the chapter on fidelity.) At the same time, however, the adolescent fears a foolish, all too trusting commitment, and will, paradoxically, express his need for faith in loud and cynical mistrust.

If the second stage established the necessity of being defined by what one can *will* freely, then the adolescent now looks for an opportunity to decide with free assent on one of the available or unavoidable avenues of duty and service, and at the same time is mortally afraid of being forced into activities in which he would feel exposed to ridicule or self-doubt. This, too, can lead to a paradox, namely, that he would rather act shamelessly in the eyes of his elders, out of free choice, than be forced into activities which would be shameful in his own eyes or in those of his peers.

If an unlimited *imagination* as to what one *might* become is the heritage of the play age, then the adolescent's willingness to put his trust in those peers and leading, or misleading, elders who will give imaginative, if not illusory, scope to his aspirations is only too obvious. By the same token, he objects violently to all "pedantic" limitations on his self-images and will be ready to settle by loud accusation all his guiltiness over the excessiveness of his ambition.

Finally, if the desire to make something work, and to make it work well, is the gain of the school age, then the choice of an occupation assumes a significance beyond the question of remuneration and status. It is for this reason that some adolescents prefer not to work at all for a while rather than be forced into an otherwise promising career which would offer success without the satisfaction of functioning with unique excellence.

In any given period in history, then, that part of youth will have the most affirmatively exciting time of it which finds itself in the wave of a technological, economic, or ideological trend seemingly promising all that youthful vitality could ask for.

Adolescence, therefore, is least "stormy" in that segment of youth which is gifted and well trained in the pursuit of expanding technological trends, and thus able to identify with new roles of competency and invention and to accept a more implicit ideological outlook. Where this is not given, the adolescent mind becomes a more explicitly ideological one, by which we mean one searching for some inspiring unification of tradition or anticipated techniques, ideas, and ideals. And, indeed, it is the ideological potential of a society which speaks most clearly to the adolescent who is so eager to be affirmed by peers, to be confirmed by teachers, and to be inspired by worth-while "ways of life." On the other hand, should a young person feel that the environment tries to deprive him too radically of all the forms of expression which permit him to develop and integrate the next step, he may resist with the wild strength encountered in animals who are suddenly forced to defend their lives. For, indeed, in the social jungle of human existence there is no feeling of being alive without a sense of identity.

Having come this far, I would like to give one example (and I consider it representative in structure) of the individual way in which a young person, given some leeway, may utilize a traditional way of life for dealing with a remnant of negative identity. I had known Jill before her puberty, when she was rather obese and showed many "oral" traits of voracity and dependency while she also was a tomboy and bitterly envious of her brothers and in rivalry with them. But she was intelligent and always had an air about her (as did her mother) which seemed to promise that things would turn out all right. And, indeed, she straightened out and up, became very attractive, an easy leader in any group, and, to many, a model of young girlhood. As a clinician, I watched and wondered what she would do with that voraciousness and with the rivalry which she had displayed earlier. Could it be that such things are simply absorbed in fortuitous growth?

Then one autumn in her late teens, Jill did not return to college from the ranch out West where she had spent the summer. She had asked her parents to let her stay. Simply out of liberality and confidence, they granted her this moratorium and returned East.

That winter Jill specialized in taking care of newborn colts, and would get up at any time during a winter night to bottle feed the most needy animals. Having apparently acquired a certain satisfaction within herself, as well as astonished recognition from the cowboys, she returned home and reassumed her place. I felt that she had found and hung on to an opportunity to do actively and for others what she had always yearned to have done for her, as she had once demonstrated by overeating: she had learned to feed needy young mouths. But she did so in a context which, in turning passive into active, also turned a former symptom into a social act.

One might say that she turned "maternal" but it was a maternalism such as cowboys must and do display; and, of course, she did it all in jeans. This brought recognition "from man to man" as well as from man to woman, and beyond that the confirmation of her optimism, that is, her feeling that something could be done that felt like her, was useful and worth while, and was in line with an ideological trend where it still made immediate practical sense.

Such self-chosen "therapies" depend, of course, on the leeway given in the right spirit at the right time, and this depends on a great variety of circumstances. I intend to publish similar fragments from the lives of children in greater detail at some future date; let this example stand for the countless observations in everyday life, where the resourcefulness of young people proves itself when the conditions are right.

The estrangement of this stage is *identity confusion*, which will be elaborated in clinical and biographic detail in the next chapter. For the moment, we will accept Biff's formulation in Arthur Miller's *Death of a Salesman:* "I just can't take hold, Mom, I can't take hold of some kind of a life." Where such a dilemma is based on a strong previous doubt of one's ethnic and sexual identity, or where role confusion joins a hopelessness of long standing, delinquent and "borderline" psychotic episodes

are not uncommon. Youth after youth, bewildered by the incapacity to assume a role forced on him by the inexorable standardization of American adolescence, runs away in one form or
another, dropping out of school, leaving jobs, staying out all
night, or withdrawing into bizarre and inaccessible moods. Once
"delinquent," his greatest need and often his only salvation is the
refusal on the part of older friends, advisers, and judiciary per-
sonnel to type him further by pat diagnoses and social judgments which ignore the special dynamic conditions of adolescence. It is here, as we shall see in greater detail, that the concept
of identity confusion is of practical clinical value, for if they
are diagnosed and treated correctly, seemingly psychotic and
criminal incidents do not have the same fatal significance which
they may have at other ages.

In general it is the inability to settle on an occupational identity which most disturbs young people. To keep themselves together they temporarily overidentify with the heroes of cliques
and crowds to the point of an apparently complete loss of individuality. Yet in this stage not even "falling in love" is entirely,
or even primarily, a sexual matter. To a considerable extent adolescent love is an attempt to arrive at a definition of one's identity by projecting one's diffused self-image on another and by
seeing it thus reflected and gradually clarified. This is why so
much of young love is conversation. On the other hand, clarification can also be sought by destructive means. Young people
can become remarkably clannish, intolerant, and cruel in their
exclusion of others who are "different," in skin color or cultural
background, in tastes and gifts, and often in entirely petty as-
ects of dress and gesture arbitrarily selected as the signs of an in-
grouper or out-grouper. It is important to understand in principle (which does not mean to condone in all of its manifestations) that such intolerance may be, for a while, a necessary defense against a sense of identity loss. This is unavoidable at a time
of life when the body changes its proportions radically, when
genital puberty floods body and imagination with all manner of
impulses, when intimacy with the other sex approaches and is,

on occasion, forced on the young person, and when the immediate future confronts one with too many conflicting possibilities and choices. Adolescents not only help one another temporarily through such discomfort by forming cliques and stereotyping themselves, their ideals, and their enemies; they also insistently test each other's capacity for sustaining loyalties in the midst of inevitable conflicts of values.

The readiness for such testing helps to explain (as pointed out in Chapter II) the appeal of simple and cruel totalitarian doctrines among the youth of such countries and classes as have lost or are losing their group identities—feudal, agrarian, tribal, or national. The democracies are faced with the job of winning these grim youths by convincingly demonstrating to them—by living it—that a democratic identity can be strong and yet tolerant, judicious and still determined. But industrial democracy poses special problems in that it insists on self-made identities ready to grasp many chances and ready to adjust to the changing necessities of booms and busts, of peace and war, of migration and determined sedentary life. Democracy, therefore, must present its adolescents with ideals which can be shared by young people of many backgrounds, and which emphasize autonomy in the form of independence and initiative in the form of constructive work. These promises, however, are not easy to fulfill in increasingly complex and centralized systems of industrial, economic, and political organization, systems which increasingly neglect the "self-made" ideology still flaunted in oratory. This is hard on many young Americans because their whole upbringing has made the development of a self-reliant personality dependent on a certain degree of choice, a sustained hope for an individual chance, and a firm commitment to the freedom of self-realization.

We are speaking here not merely of high privileges and lofty ideals but of psychological necessities. For the social institution which is the guardian of identity *is* what we have called *ideology*. One may see in ideology also the imagery of an aristocracy in its widest possible sense, which connotes that within a defined world image and a given course of history the best people will come to rule and rule will develop the best in people. In order not to become cynically or apathetically lost, young people must somehow be able to convince themselves that those who succeed in their anticipated adult world thereby shoulder the obligation of being best. For it is through their ideology that social systems enter into the fiber of the next generation and attempt to absorb into their lifeblood the rejuvenative power of youth. Adolescence is thus a vital regenerator in the process of social evolution, for youth can offer its loyalties and energies both to the conservation of that which continues to feel true and to the revolutionary correction of that which has lost its regenerative significance.

We can study the identity crisis also in the lives of creative individuals who could resolve it for themselves only by offering to their contemporaries a new model of resolution such as that expressed in works of art or in original deeds, and who furthermore are eager to tell us all about it in diaries, letters, and self-representations. And even as the neuroses of a given period reflect the ever-present inner chaos of man's existence in a new way, the creative crises point to the period's unique solutions.

We will in the next chapter present in greater detail what we have learned of these specialized individual crises. But there is a third manifestation of the remnants of infantilism and adolescence in man: it is the pooling of the individual crises in transitory upheavals amounting to collective "hysterias." Where there are voluble leaders their creative crises and the latent crises of their followers can be at least studied with the help of our assumptions—and of their writings. More elusive are spontaneous group developments not attributable to a leader. And it will, at any rate, not be helpful to call mass irrationalities by clinical names. It would be impossible to diagnose clinically how much hysteria is present in a young nun participating in an epidemic of convulsive spells or how much perverse "sadism" in a young Nazi commanded to participate in massive parades or in mass killings. So we can point only most tentatively to certain similarities between individual crises and group behavior in order to indicate that in a given period of history they are in an obscure contact with each other.

But before we submerge ourselves in the clinical and biographic evidence for what we call identity confusion, we will take a look beyond the identity crisis. The words "beyond identity," of course, could be understood in two ways, both essential for the problem. They could mean that there is more to man's core than identity, that there is in fact in each individual an "I," an observing center of awareness and of volition, which can transcend and must survive the *psychosocial identity* which is our concern in this book. In some ways, as we will see, a sometimes precocious self-transcendence seems to be felt strongly in a transient manner in youth, as if a pure identity had to be kept free from psychosocial encroachment. And yet no man (except a man aflame and dying like Keats, who could speak of identity in words which secured him immediate fame) can transcend himself in youth. We will speak later of the transcendence of identity. In the following "beyond identity" means life after adolescence and the uses of identity and, indeed, the return of some forms of identity crisis in the later stages of the life cycle.

6. BEYOND IDENTITY

The first of these is the crisis of *intimacy*. It is only when identity formation is well on its way that true intimacy—which is really a counterpointing as well as a fusing of identities—is possible. Sexual intimacy is only part of what I have in mind, for it is obvious that sexual intimacies often precede the capacity to develop a true and mutual psychosocial intimacy with another person, be it in friendship, in erotic encounters, or in joint inspiration. The youth who is not sure of his identity shies away from interpersonal intimacy or throws himself into acts of intimacy which are "promiscuous" without true fusion or real self-abandon.

Where a youth does not accomplish such intimate relationships with others—and, I would add, with his own inner resources—in late adolescence or early adulthood, he may settle for highly stereotyped interpersonal relations and come to retain a deep *sense of isolation*. If the times favor an impersonal kind of interpersonal pattern, a man can go far, very far, in life and yet harbor a severe character problem doubly painful because he will never feel really himself, although everyone says he is "somebody."

The counterpart of intimacy is *distantiation:* the readiness to repudiate, isolate, and, if necessary, destroy those forces and people whose essence seems dangerous to one's own. Thus, the lasting consequence of the need for distantiation is the readiness to fortify one's territory of intimacy and solidarity and to view all outsiders with a fanatic "overvaluation of small differences" between the familiar and the foreign. Such prejudices can be utilized and exploited in politics and in war and secure the loyal self-sacrifice and the readiness to kill from the strongest and the best. A remnant of adolescent danger is to be found where intimate, competitive, and combative relations are experienced with and against the selfsame people. But as the areas of adult responsibility are gradually delineated, as the competitive encounter, the erotic bond, and merciless enmity are differentiated from each other, they eventually become subject to that *ethical sense* which is the mark of the adult and which takes over from the ideological conviction of adolescence and the moralism of childhood.

Freud was once asked what he thought a normal person should be able to do well. The questioner probably expected a complicated, "deep" answer. But Freud simply said, *"Lieben und arbeiten"* ("to love and to work"). It pays to ponder on this simple formula; it grows deeper as you think about it. For when Freud said "love," he meant the generosity of intimacy as well as genital love; when he said love and work, he meant a general work productiveness which would not preoccupy the individual to the extent that he might lose his right or capacity to be a sexual and a loving being.

Psychoanalysis has emphasized *genitality* as one of the developmental conditions for full maturity. Genitality consists in the capacity to develop orgastic potency which is more than the discharge of sex products in the sense of Kinsey's "outlets." It combines the ripening of intimate sexual mutuality with full genital sensitivity and with a capacity for discharge of tension from the whole body. This is a rather concrete way of saying something about a process which we really do not yet quite understand. But the experience of the climactic mutuality of orgasm clearly provides a supreme example of the mutual regulation of complicated patterns and in some way appeases the hostilities and the potential rages caused by the daily evidence of the oppositeness of male and female, of fact and fancy, of love and hate, of work and play. Such experience makes sexuality less obsessive and sadistic control of the partner superfluous.

Before such genital maturity is reached, much of sexual life is of the self-seeking, identity-hungry kind; each partner is really trying only to reach himself. Or it remains a kind of genital combat in which each tries to defeat the other. All this remains as part of adult sexuality, but it is gradually absorbed as the differences between the sexes become a full polarization within a joint life style. For the previously established vital strengths have helped to make the two sexes first become similar in consciousness, language, and ethics in order to then permit them to be maturely different.

Man, in addition to erotic attraction, has developed a selectivity of "love" which serves the need for a new and shared identity. If the estrangement typical for this stage is *isolation*, that is, the incapacity to take chances with one's identity by sharing true intimacy, such inhibition is often reinforced by a fear of the outcome of intimacy: offspring—and care. Love as mutual devotion, however, overcomes the antagonisms inherent in sexual and functional polarization, and is the vital strength of young adulthood. It is the guardian of that elusive and yet all-pervasive power of cultural and personal style which binds into a "way of life" the affiliations of competition and co-operation, production and procreation.

If we should continue the game of "I am" formulations "beyond identity" we should have to change the tune. For now the increment of identity is based on the formula "*We* are what we love."

EVOLUTION has made man a teaching as well as a learning animal, for dependency and maturity are reciprocal: mature man needs to be needed, and maturity is guided by the nature of that which must be cared for. *Generativity*, then, is primarily the concern for establishing and guiding the next generation. There are of course, people who, from misfortune or because of special and genuine gifts in other directions, do not apply this drive to offspring of their own, but to other forms of altruistic concern and creativity which many absorb their kind of parental drive. And indeed, the concept of generativity is meant to include productivity and creativity, neither of which, however, can replace it as designations of a crisis in development. For the ability to lose oneself in the meeting of bodies and minds leads to a gradual expansion of ego-interests and to a libidinal investment in that which is being generated. Where such enrichment fails altogether, regression to an obsessive need for pseudointimacy takes place, often with a pervading *sense of stagnation*, boredom, and interpersonal impoverishment. Individuals, then, often begin to indulge themselves as if they were their own—or one another's —one and only child; and where conditions favor it, early invalidism, physical or psychological, becomes the vehicle of self-concern. On the other hand, the mere fact of having or even wanting children does not "achieve" generativity. Some young parents suffer, it seems, from a retardation in the ability to develop true care. The reasons are often to be found in early childhood impressions; in faulty identifications with parents; in excessive self-love based on a too strenuously self-made personality; and in the lack of some faith, some "belief in the species," which would make a child appear to be a welcome trust. The very nature of generativity, however, suggests that its most circumscribed pathology must now be sought in the next generation, that is, in the form of those unavoidable estrangements which we have listed for childhood and youth and which may appear in aggravated form as a result of a generative failure on the part of the parents.

As to the institutions which reinforce generativity and safeguard it, one can only say that *all* institutions by their very nature codify the ethics of generative succession. Generativity is itself a driving power in human organization. And the stages of childhood and adulthood are a system of generation and regeneration to which institutions such as shared households and divided labor strive to give continuity. Thus the basic strengths enumerated here and the essentials of an organized human community have evolved together as an attempt to establish a set of proven methods and a fund of traditional reassurance which enables each generation to meet the needs of the next in relative independence from personal differences and changing conditions.

IN THE aging person who has taken care of things and people and has adapted himself to the triumphs and disappointments of being, by necessity, the originator of others and the generator of things and ideas—only in him the fruit of the seven stages gradually ripens. I know no better word for it than *integrity*. Lacking a clear definition, I shall point to a few attributes of this stage of mind. It is the ego's accrued assurance of its proclivity for order and meaning—an emotional integration faithful to the image-bearers of the past and ready to take, and eventually to renounce, leadership in the present. It is the acceptance of one's one and only life cycle and of the people who have become significant to it as something that had to be and that, by necessity, permitted of no substitutions. It thus means a new and different love of one's parents, free of the wish that they should have been different, and an acceptance of the fact that one's life is one's own responsibility. It is a sense of comradeship with men and women of distant times and of different pursuits who have created orders and objects and sayings conveying human dignity and love. Although aware of the relativity of all the various life

styles which have given meaning to human striving, the posses-
sor of integrity is ready to defend the dignity of his own life
style against all physical and economic threats. For he knows
that an individual life is the accidental coincidence of but one
life cycle with but one segment of history, and that for him all
human integrity stands and falls with the one style of integrity
of which he partakes.

Clinical and anthropological evidence suggest that the lack or
loss of this accrued ego integration is signified by *disgust* and by
despair: fate is not accepted as the frame of life, death not as its
finite boundary. Despair expresses the feeling that time is short,
too short for the attempt to start another life and to try out alternate roads to integrity. Such a despair is often hidden behind
a show of disgust, a misanthropy, or a chronic contemptuous
displeasure with particular institutions and particular people—a
disgust and a displeasure which, where not allied with the vision
of a superior life, only signify the individual's contempt of himself.

A meaningful old age, then, preceding a possible terminal
senility, serves the need for that integrated heritage which gives
indispensable perspective to the life cycle. Strength here takes
the form of that detached yet active concern with life bounded
by death, which we call *wisdom* in its many connotations from
ripened "wits" to accumulated knowledge, mature judgment,
and inclusive understanding. Not that each man can evolve wisdom for himself. For most, a living *tradition* provides the essence
of it. But the end of the cycle also evokes "ultimate concerns"
for what chance man may have to transcend the limitations of
his identity and his often tragic or bitterly tragicomic engagement in his one and only life cycle within the sequence of generations. Yet great philosophical and religious systems dealing
with ultimate individuation seem to have remained responsibly
related to the cultures and civilizations of their times. Seeking
transcendence by renunciation, they yet remain ethically concerned with the "maintenance of the world." By the same token,
a civilization can be measured by the meaning which it gives to

the full cycle of life, for such meaning, or the lack of it, cannot fail to reach into the beginnings of the next generation, and thus into the chances of others to meet ultimate questions with some clarity and strength.

To WHATEVER abyss ultimate concerns may lead individual men, man as a psychosocial creature will face, toward the end of his life, a new edition of an identity crisis which we may state in the words "I am what survives of me." From the stages of life, then, such dispositions as faith, will power, purposefulness, competence, fidelity, love, care, wisdom—all criteria of vital individual strength—also flow into the life of institutions. Without them, institutions wilt; but without the spirit of institutions pervading the patterns of care and love, instruction and training, no strength could emerge from the sequence of generations.

Psychosocial strength, we conclude, depends on a total process which regulates individual life cycles, the sequence of generations, and the structure of society simultaneously: for all three have evolved together.

Identity Confusion in Life History and Case History

---

1. BIOGRAPHIC I: CREATIVE CONFUSION
I. G.B.S. (AGE 70) ON YOUNG SHAW (AGE 20)

WHEN GEORGE BERNARD SHAW was a famous man of seventy, he was called upon to review and preface the unsuccessful work of his early twenties, namely, two volumes of fiction that had not previously been published.[1] As one would expect, Shaw proceeded to make light of the production of his young adulthood, but not without offering the reader a detailed analysis of young Shaw. Were he not so deceptively witty in what he says about his younger years, his observations might well have been recognized as an analytical achievement which, in fact, hardly calls for additional interpretation. Yet it is Shaw's own mark of identity that he eases and teases his reader along a path of apparent superficialities and sudden depths. I dare to excerpt him here for my purposes only in the hope that I will make the reader curious enough to follow every step of his exposition.

G.B.S. (for this is the public identity which was one of his masterpieces) describes young Shaw as an "extremely disagreeable and undesirable" young man, "not at all reticent of diabolical opinion," while inwardly "suffering . . . from simple cowardice . . . and horribly ashamed of it." "The truth is," he concludes, "that all men are in a false position in society until they have realized their possibilities and imposed them on their neighbors. They are tormented by a continual shortcoming in themselves; yet they irritate others by a continual overweening. This discord can be resolved by acknowledged success or failures only: everyone is ill at ease until he has found his natural place, whether it be above or below his birthplace." But Shaw must always exempt himself from any universal law which he inadvertently pronounces, so he adds: "This finding of one's place may be very puzzling by the fact that there is no place in ordinary society for extraordinary individuals."

Shaw proceeds to describe a crisis at the age of twenty. This crisis was not caused by lack of success or the absence of a defined role, but by too much of both: "I made good in spite of myself, and found, to my dismay, that Business, instead of expelling me as the worthless imposter I was, was fastening upon me with no intention of letting me go. Behold me, therefore, in my twentieth year, with a business training, in an occupation which I detested as cordially as any sane person lets himself detest anything he cannot escape from. In March 1876 I broke loose." Breaking loose meant to leave family and friends, business and Ireland, and to avoid the danger of success unequal to "the enormity of my unconscious ambition." He granted himself a prolongation of the interval between youth and adulthood, which we will call a "psychosocial moratorium." He writes: "When I left my native city, I left this phase behind me, and associated no more with men of my age until, after about eight years of solitude in this respect, I was drawn into the Socialist revival of the early eighties, among Englishmen intensely serious and burning with indignation at very real and very fundamental evils that affected all the world." In the meantime, he seemed to avoid opportunities, sensing that "behind the conviction that they could lead to nothing that I wanted, lay the unspoken fear that they might lead to something I did not want." This occupational part of the moratorium was reinforced by an intellectual one: "I cannot learn anything that does not interest me. My memory is not indiscriminate; it rejects and selects; and its selections are not academic. . . . I congratulate myself on this; for I am firmly persuaded that every unnatural activity of the brain is as mischievous as any unnatural activity of the body. . . . Civilization is always wrecked by giving the governing classes what is called secondary education. . . ."

Shaw settled down to study and to write as he pleased, and it was then that the extraordinary workings of an extraordinary personality came to the fore. He managed to abandon the kind of work he had been doing without relinquishing the work habit:

My office training had left me with a habit of doing something regularly every day as a fundamental condition of industry as distinguished from idleness. I knew I was making no headway unless I was doing this, and that I should never produce a book in any other fashion. I bought supplies of white paper, demy size, by sixpence-worths at a time; folded it in quarto; and condemned myself to fill five pages of it a day, rain or shine, dull or inspired. I had so much of the schoolboy and the clerk still in me that if my five pages ended in the middle of a sentence I did not finish it until the next day. On the other hand, if I missed a day, I made up for it by doing a double task on the morrow. On this plan I produced five novels in five years. It was my professional apprenticeship. . . .

We may add that these five novels were not published for over fifty years, but Shaw had learned to write as he worked, and to wait as he wrote. How important such initial ritualization of his work life was for the young man's inner defenses may be seen from one of those casual (in fact, parenthetical) remarks with which the great wit almost coyly admits his psychological insights: "I have risen by sheer gravitation, too industrious by acquired habit to stop work (I work as my father drank)." He thus points to that combination of addictiveness and compulsiveness which we see as the basis of much pathology in late adolescence and of some accomplishments in young adulthood.

His father's "drink neurosis" Shaw describes in detail, finding in it one of the sources of his biting humor: "It had to be either a family tragedy or family joke." For his father was not "convivial, nor quarrelsome, nor boastful, but miserable, racked with shame and remorse." However, the father had a "humorous sense of anticlimax which I inherited from him and used with much effect when I became a writer of comedy. His anti-climaxes depended for their effect on our sense of the sacredness (of the subject matter). . . . It seems providential that I was driven to the essentials of religion by the reduction of every factitious or fictitious element in it to the most irreverent absurdity."

A more unconscious level of Shaw's Oedipal tragedy is represented with dreamlike symbolism in what looks like a "screen memory," that is, one condensed scene standing for others of a like kind:

A boy who has seen "the governor" with an imperfectly wrapped-up goose under one arm and a ham in the same condition under the other (both purchased under heaven knows what delusion of festivity) butting at the garden wall in the belief that he was pushing open the gate, and transforming his tall hat to a concertina in the process, and who, instead of being overwhelmed with shame and anxiety at the spectacle, has been so disabled by merriment (uproariously shared by the maternal uncle) that he has hardly been able to rush to the rescue of the hat and pilot its wearer to safety, is clearly not a boy who will make tragedies of trifles instead of making trifles of tragedies. If you cannot get rid of the family skeleton, you may as well make it dance.

It is obvious that the analysis of the psychosexual aspect of Shaw's personality could find a solid anchor point in the symbolism of paternal impotence in this memory.

Shaw explains his father's downfall with a brilliant analysis of the socioeconomic circumstance of his day. For the father was "second cousin to a baronet, and my mother the daughter of a country gentleman whose rule was, when in difficulties, mort-gage. That was my sort of poverty." His father was "the younger son of a younger son of a younger son" and he was "a downstart and the son of a downstart." Yet he concluded: "To say that my father could not afford to give me a university education is like saying that he could not afford to drink, or that I could not afford to become an author. Both statements are true;

but he drank and I became an author all the same."

His mother he remembers for the "one or two rare and de-lightful occasions when she buttered my bread for me. She buttered it thickly instead of merely wiping a knife on it." Most of the time, however, he says significantly, she merely "accepted me as a natural and customary phenomenon and took it for granted that I should go on occurring in that way." There must have been something reassuring in this kind of impersonality, for "technically speaking, I should say she was the worst mother conceivable, always, however, within the limits of the fact that she was incapable of unkindness to any child, animal, or flower, or indeed to any person or thing whatsoever. . . ." If this could not be considered either a selective devotion or an education, Shaw explains: "I was badly brought up because my mother was so well brought up. . . . In her righteous reaction against . . . the constraints and tyrannies, the scoldings and browbeatings and punishments she had suffered in her childhood . . . she reached a negative attitude in which having no substitute to propose, she carried domestic anarchy as far as in the nature of things it can be carried." All in all, Shaw's mother was "a thoroughly disgusted and disillusioned woman . . . suffering from a hopelessly disappointing husband and three uninteresting children grown too old to be petted like the animals and the birds she was so fond of, to say nothing of the humiliating inadequacy of my father's income."

Shaw had really three parents, the third being a man named Lee ("meteoric," "impetuous," "magnetic") who gave Shaw's mother lessons in singing, not without revamping the whole Shaw household as well as Bernard's ideals:

Although he supplanted my father as the dominant factor in the household, and appropriated all the activity and interest of my mother, he was so completely absorbed in his musical affairs that there was no friction and hardly any intimate personal contacts between the two men: certainly no unpleasantness. At first his ideas astonished us. He said that people should sleep with their windows open. The daring of this appealed to me; and I have done so ever since. He ate brown bread instead of white: a startling eccentricity.

Of the many identity elements which ensued from such a perplexing picture, let me select, condense, and name three for this occasion.

1. The Snob

"As compared with similar English families, we had a power of derisive dramatization that made the bones of the Shavian skeletons rattle more loudly." Shaw recognizes these as "family snobbery mitigated by the family sense of humor." On the other hand, "though my mother was not consciously a snob, the divinity which hedged an Irish lady of her period was not acceptable to the British suburban parents, all snobs, who were within her reach (as customers for private music lessons)." Shaw had "an enormous contempt for family snobbery" until he found that one of his ancestors was an Earl of Fife: "It was as good as being descended from Shakespeare, whom I had been unconsciously resolved to reincarnate from my cradle."

2. The Noisemaker

All through his childhood, Shaw seems to have been exposed to an oceanic assault of music making: the family played trombones and ophicleides, violoncellos, harps, and tambourines—and, most of all (or was it worst of all), they sang. Finally, however, he taught himself to play the piano, and this with intrusive noisiness.

When I look back on all the banging, whistling, roaring, and growling inflicted on nervous neighbours during this process of education, I am consumed with useless remorse. . . . I used to drive [my mother] nearly crazy by my favorite selections from Wagner's Ring, which to her was "all recitative," and horribly discordant at that. She never complained at the time, but confessed it after we separated, and said that she had sometimes gone away to cry. If I had committed a murder I do not think it would trouble my conscience very much; but this I cannot bear to think of.

That, in fact, he may have learned to get even with his musical tormentors, he does not profess to realize. Instead, he compromised by becoming a music critic, i.e., one who writes about the noise made by others. As a critic, he chose the nom de plume Corno di Bassetto—the name of an instrument which hardly anybody knew and which is so meek in tone that "not even the devil could make it sparkle." Yet Bassetto became a sparkling critic, and more: "I cannot deny that Bassetto was occasionally vulgar; but that does not matter if he makes you laugh. Vulgarity is a necessary part of a complete author's equipment; and the clown is sometimes the best part of the circus."

3. The Diabolical One

How the undoubtedly lonely little boy (whose mother listened only to the musical noisemakers) came to use his imagination to converse with a great imaginary companion, is described thus: "In my childhood I exercised my literary genius by composing my own prayers. . . . They were a literary performance for the entertainment and propitiation of the Almighty." In line with his family's irreverence in matters of religion, Shaw's piety had to find and rely on the rock-bottom of religiosity which, in him, early became a mixture of "intellectual integrity . . . synchronized with the dawning of moral passion." At the same time it seems that Shaw was (in some unspecified way) a little devil of a child. At any rate, he did not feel identical with himself when he was good: "Even when I was a good boy, I was so only theatrically, because, as actors say, I saw myself in the character." And indeed, at the completion of his identity struggle, i.e., "when Nature completed my countenance in 1880 or thereabouts (I had only the tenderest sprouting of hair on my face until I was 24), I found myself equipped with the upgrowing moustaches and eyebrows, and the sarcastic nostrils of the operatic fiend whose airs (by Gounod) I had sung as a child, and whose attitudes I had affected in my boyhood. Later on, as the generations moved past me, I . . . began to perceive that imaginative fiction is to life what the sketch is to the picture or the conception to the statue."

Thus G.B.S., more or less explicitly, traces his own roots. Yet it is well worth noting that what he finally became seems to him to have been as innate as the intended reincarnation of Shakespeare referred to above. His teacher, he says, "puzzled me with her attempts to teach me to read; for I can remember no time at which a page of print was not intelligible to me, and can only suppose that I was born literate." However, he thought of a number of professional choices: "As an alternative to being a Michelangelo I had dreams of being a Badeali (note, by the way, that of literature I had no dreams at all, any more than a duck has of swimming)."

He also calls himself "a born Communist" (which, we hasten to say, means a Fabian socialist), and he explains the peace that comes with the acceptance of what one seems to be made to be; the "born Communist . . . knows where he is, and where this society which has so intimidated him is. He is cured of his MAUVAISE HONTE . . ." Thus "the complete outsider" gradually became his kind of complete insider: "I was," he said, "outside society, outside politics, outside sport, outside the Church"—but this "only within the limits of British barbarism. . . . The moment music, painting, literature, or science came into question the positions were reversed: it was I who was the Insider."

As he traces all of these traits back into childhood, Shaw becomes aware of the fact that only a tour de force could have integrated them all:

If I am to be entirely communicative on this subject, I must add that the mere rawness which so soon rubs off was complicated by a deeper strangeness which has made me all my life a sojourner on this planet rather than a native of it. Whether it be that I was born mad or a little too sane, my kingdom was not of this world: I was at home only in the realm of my imagination, and at my ease only with the mighty dead. Therefore, I had to become an actor, and create for myself a fantastic personality fit and apt for dealing with men, and adaptable to the various parts I had to play as author, journalist, orator, politician, committee man, man of the world, and so forth.

"In this," Shaw concludes significantly, "I succeeded later on only too well." This statement is singularly illustrative of that faint disgust with which older men at times review the inexorable identity which they had come by in their youth—a disgust which in the lives of some can become mortal despair and inexplicable psychosomatic involvement.

The end of his crisis of younger years, Shaw sums up in these words: "I had the intellectual habit; and my natural combination of critical faculty with literary resource needed only a clear comprehension of life in the light of an intelligible theory: in short, a religion, to set it in triumphant operation." Here the old Cynic has circumscribed in one sentence what the identity formation of any human being must add up to. To translate this into terms more conducive to discussion in more complicated and therefore more respectable terms: Man, to take his place in society, must acquire a "conflict-free," habitual use of a dominant faculty, to be elaborated in an occupation; a limitless resource, a feedback, as it were, from the immediate exercise of this occupation, from the companionship it provides, and from its tradition; and finally, an intelligible theory of the processes of life which the old atheist, eager to shock to the last, calls a religion. The Fabian socialism to which he, in fact, turned is rather an ideology, a general term to which we shall adhere, for reasons which will become clear at the end of this chapter.

II. WILLIAM JAMES, HIS OWN ALIENIST

William James was preoccupied all his life with what was then called "morbid psychology." He himself suffered in his youth and into his manhood under severe emotional strain for which he vainly sought the help of a variety of nerve cures. His letters also attest to the fact that he was interested in his friends' crises and that he offered them a kind of passionate advice which betrayed his own struggle for sanity. In the peculiar milieu of Boston, furthermore, which enjoys such blatant contrasts between materialistic vigor and the immersion of spirit and mind, he was drawn into the argument over the matter of faith healing. And finally, he was one of the men who played host to the emerging psychiatric schools, among them that of Freud, who visited this country in 1907. While Freud himself impressed him as a man obsessed with fixed ideas (he could make nothing in his own case with Freud's dream theories, James said, as have many of the most and the least intelligent before and after him), he nevertheless expressed the hope that Freud and his pupils would carry on their studies.

In what follows I will quote a few of James's most outstanding formulations, not from his theoretical treatises but from his more personal confessions, in which he gives such vital expression to the experience of a prolonged identity crisis.

William James, as Matthiessen points out "came to maturity extremely slowly." [2] Even at twenty-six, he wrote to Wendell Holmes: "Much would I give for a constructive passion of some kind." This nostalgic complaint we find, again and again, among the young college men of today; only in James's life the doubt and delay were, according to Matthiessen, due to his father's fanatic insistence on *being*, which made it difficult for most of his children to find what, if anything, they could be *doing* (although at least two of them eventually proceeded to do extremely well). I point to this because today doubt and delay are so obviously often due to the circumstance that young men and women find themselves involved in a doing into which they were forced by a compulsion to excel fast, before enough of a sense of being was secured to give to naked ambition a style of individuality or a compelling communal spirit.

This is not the place to deal in detail with the personality or the parental habits of the father, Henry James, Sr., who by a combination of infirmity, inclination, and affluence was permitted to spend his days at home, making his family life a tyranny of liberalism and a school in utopianism in which every choice was made from the freest and most universal point of view and, above all, was to be discussed with Father. Nor can I follow here the interesting path by which James's later philosophy became at once a continuation and an abrogation of his father's creed.

What claims our attention here is the particularly prolonged identity crisis which drove William from art school to a "scientific school" to medical school, and from Cambridge (Mass.) to the Amazon to Europe and back to Cambridge. Having suffered severe neurotic discomfort in Europe, he spent his late twenties as a neurotic invalid in his father's home, until at the age of thirty he accepted the offer of President Eliot, who had early "spotted" him, to teach anatomy at Harvard. James's invalidism, however, was comparable to that of Darwin—that is, a restriction of activities and associations which left at any given time only a narrow path for interest and activity. And yet along that narrow path such men find, as if with a sleepwalker's sure-footedness, their final goal of intellectual and social concentration. In James's case the path led from artistic observation, through a naturalistic sense of classification and the physiologist's grasp of organic functioning, to the exile's multilingual perceptiveness, and finally through the sufferer's self-knowledge and empathy to psychology and philosophy. As James put it sovereignly: "I originally studied medicine in order to be a physiologist, but I drifted into psychology and philosophy from a sort of fatality. I never had any philosophic instruction, the first lecture on psychology I ever heard being the first I ever gave."

It was not until he wrote, during a period of middle-aged cardiac dismay, his *Varieties of Religious Experience*, that James gave an undoubted autobiographic account of a state "of the worst kind of melancholy," purportedly reported to him by a young "French sufferer."

Whilst in this state of philosophic pessimism and general depression of spirits about my prospects, I went one evening into a dressing-room in the twilight, to procure some article that was there; when suddenly there fell upon me without any warning, just as if it came out of the darkness, a horrible fear of my own existence. . . . It was like a revelation; and although the immediate feelings passed away, the experience has made me sympathetic with the morbid feelings of others ever since. . . . I dreaded to be left alone. I remember wondering how other people could live, how I myself had ever lived, so unconscious of that pit of insecurity beneath the surface of life. My mother in particular, a very cheerful person, seemed to me a perfect paradox in her unconsciousness of danger, which you may well believe I was very careful not to disturb by revelations of my own state of mind. I have always thought that this experience of melancholia of mine had a religious bearing. . . . I mean that the fear was so invasive and powerful, that, if I had not clung to scripture-texts like *The eternal God is my refuge*, etc. *Come unto me all ye that labor and are heavy-laden,* etc., *I am the Resurrection and the Life,* etc. I think I should have grown really insane.[3]

To this James added in a footnote a reference to a similar crisis of alienation (and psychiatrists were then called "alienists") which had been experienced and described by his father thus:

One day . . . towards the close of May, having eaten a comfortable dinner, I remained sitting at the table after the family had disappeared, idly gazing at the embers in the grate, thinking of nothing, and feeling only the exhilaration incident to a good digestion, when suddenly—in a lightning-flash as it were—fear came upon me and trembling, which made all my bones to shake.[4]

A comparison of the two attacks leaves open the question as to how much conformity with his father's inner life and life style, and how much liberation by way of a revelation may be seen in the experience. One thing is certain: each age has its own forms of alienation (forms often more culturebound than the sense of being "beside oneself" would suggest) and both the father's and the son's inner struggle concerned the identity of naked and stubborn selfhood so typical for extreme individualism, as against the surrender to some higher identity—be it outer and all-enveloping, or inner and all-pervasive. That the father, as he further reports, in his moment of distress reluctantly turned to his wife, while the son assures us that he did not wish to disturb his unaccountably cheerful mother, makes one wonder how much anxiety it took for the self-made men of that day to turn to the refuge of woman.

As Henry James, Sr., put it, reviving a bit of agrarian romanticism, "Time and again while living at this dismal watercure, and listening to its endless 'strife of tongues' about diet, and regimen, and disease, and politics, and parties, and persons, I have said to myself, The curse of mankind, that which keeps our manhood so little and so depraved, is its sense of self-hood, and the absurd, abominable opinionativeness it engenders. How sweet it would be to find oneself no longer man, but one of those innocent and ignorant sheep pasturing upon that placid hillside, and drinking in eternal dew and freshness from Nature's lavish bosom!" [5]

One important step on William James's road to maturity and some liberation from acute alienation is reported by him, the other by his father.

"I think that yesterday was a crisis in my life," James wrote to his father; "I finished the first part of Renouvier's second 'Essais' and see no reason why his definition of Free Will—'the sustaining of a thought because I choose to when I might have other thoughts'—need be the definition of an illusion. At any rate, I will assume for the present—until next year—that it is no illusion. My first act of free will shall be to believe in free will." [6] To this he adds a sentence which admirably expresses a principle dominant in today's ego psychology:

Hitherto, when I have felt like taking a free initiative, like daring to act originally, without carefully waiting for contemplation of the external world to determine all for me, suicide seemed the most manly form to put my daring into; now, I will go a step further with my will, not only act with it, but believe as well; believe in my individual reality and creative power. My belief, to be sure, can't be optimistic—but I will posit life (the real, the good) in the *self-governing resistance of the ego to the world*. Life shall [be built in] doing and suffering and creating. [7]

I am quoting this formulation of a self-governing as well as a resisting aspect of the ego to emphasize what has become the psychoanalytic meaning of it, that is, the inner synthesis which organizes experience and guides action.

And here is Henry James, Sr.'s report on his son's other great and liberating thought-experience:

[William] came in the other afternoon while I was sitting alone, and after walking the floor in an animated way for a moment, broke out: "Bless my soul, what a difference between me as I am now and as I was last spring at this time!" . . . He had a great effusion. I was afraid of interfering with it, or possibly checking it, but I ventured to ask what especially in his opinion had produced the change. He said several things . . . but more than anything else, his having given up the notion that all mental disorder requires to have a physical basis. This had become perfectly untrue to him. . . . He has been shaking off his respect for men of mere science as such, and is even more universal and impartial in his mental judgments than I have known him before . . .[8]

No doubt old Henry, Sr., suited his son's words a bit to his own style of thought, but this scene is typically James. Clearly, the first insight, concerning the self-determination of free will, is related to the second, that is the abandonment of physiological factors as fatalistic arguments against a neurotic person's continued self-determination. Together they are the basis of psychotherapy, which, no matter how it is described and conceptualized, aims at the restoration of the patient's power of choice.

2. GENETIC: IDENTIFICATION AND IDENTITY

The autobiographies of extraordinary (and extraordinarily self-perceptive) individuals are one source of insight into the development of identity. In order to describe the universal genetics of identity, one would wish to be able to trace its development through the life histories of "ordinary" individuals. Here I must rely on general impressions from daily life, on guidance work with mildly disturbed young people, and on my participation in one of the rare "longitudinal" studies [9]—a source which excludes the detailed publication of biographic data. In the following genetic sketch, some repetition of what has been said previously is unavoidable.

Adolescence is the last stage of childhood. The adolescent process, however, is conclusively complete only when the individual has subordinated his childhood identifications to a new kind of identification, achieved in absorbing sociability and in competitive apprenticeship with and among his age mates. These new identifications are no longer characterized by the playfulness of childhood and the experimental zest of youth: with dire urgency they force the young individual into choices and decisions which will, with increasing immediacy, lead to commitments "for life." The task to be performed here by the young person and by his society is formidable. It necessitates, in different individuals and in different societies, great variations in the duration, intensity, and ritualization of adolescence. Societies offer, as individuals require, more or less sanctioned intermediary periods between childhood and adulthood, often characterized by a combination of prolonged immaturity and provoked precocity.

In postulating a "latency period" which precedes puberty, psychoanalysis has given recognition to some kind of psychosexual moratorium in human development—a period of delay which permits the future mate and parent first to go to whatever "school" his culture provides and to learn the technical and social rudiments of a work situation. The libido theory, however, offers no adequate account of a second period of delay, namely, prolonged adolescence. Here the sexually matured individual is more or less retarded in his psychosexual capacity for intimacy and in the psychosocial readiness for parenthood. This period can be viewed as a *psychosocial moratorium* during which the young adult through free role experimentation may find a niche in some section of his society, a niche which is firmly defined and yet seems to be uniquely made for him.

If, in the following, we speak of the community's response to the young individual's need to be "recognized" by those around him, we mean something beyond a mere recognition of achievement; for it is of great relevance to the young individual's identity formation that he be responded to and be given function and status as a person whose gradual growth and transformation make sense to those who begin to make sense to him. It has not been sufficiently recognized in psychoanalysis that such recognition provides an entirely indispensable support to the ego in the specific tasks of adolescing, which are: to maintain the most important ego defenses against the vastly growing intensity of impulses (now invested in a matured genital apparatus and a powerful muscle system); to learn to consolidate the most important "conflict-free" achievements in line with work opportunities; and to resynthesize all childhood identifications in some unique way and yet in concordance with the roles offered by some wider section of society—be that section the neighborhood block, an anticipated occupational field, an association of kindred minds, or perhaps (as in Shaw's case) the "mighty dead."

A MORATORIUM is a period of delay granted to somebody who is not ready to meet an obligation or forced on somebody who should give himself time. By psychosocial moratorium, then, we mean a delay of adult commitments, and yet it is not only a delay. It is a period that is characterized by a selective permissiveness on the part of society and of provocative playfulness on the part of youth, and yet it also often leads to deep, if often transitory, commitment on the part of youth, and ends in a more or less ceremonial confirmation of commitment on the part of society. Such moratoria show highly individual variations, which are especially pronounced in very gifted people (gifted for better or for worse), and there are, of course, institutional variations linked with the ways of life of cultures and subcultures.

Each society and each culture institutionalizes a certain moratorium for the majority of its young people. For the most part, these moratoria coincide with apprenticeships and adventures that are in line with the society's values. The moratorium may be a time for horse stealing and vision-quests, a time for *Wanderschaft* or work "out West" or "down under," a time for "lost youth" or academic life, a time for self-sacrifice or for pranks—and today, often a time for patienthood or delinquency. For much of juvenile delinquency, especially in its organized form, must be considered to be an attempt at the creation of a psychosocial moratorium. In fact, I would assume that some delinquency has been a relatively institutionalized moratorium for a long time in parts of our society, and that it forces itself on our awareness now only because it proves too attractive and compelling for too many youngsters at once. In addition to all this, our society seems to be in the process of incorporating psychiatric treatment as one of the few permissible moratoria for young people who otherwise would be crushed by standardization and mechanization. This we must consider carefully, for the label or diagnosis one acquires during the psychosocial moratorium is of the utmost importance for the process of identity formation.

But the moratorium does not need to be consciously experienced as such. On the contrary, the young individual may feel deeply committed and may learn only much later that what he took so seriously was only a period of transition; many "recovered" delinquents probably feel quite estranged about the "foolishness" that has passed. It is clear, however, that any experimentation with identity images means also to play with the inner fire of emotions and drives and to risk the outer danger of ending up in a social "pocket" from which there is no return. Then the moratorium has failed; the individual is defined too early, and he has committed himself because circumstances or, indeed, authorities have committed him.

LINGUISTICALLY as well as psychologically, identity and identification have common roots. Is identity, then, the mere sum of earlier identifications, or is it merely an additional set of identifications?

The limited usefulness of the mechanism of identification becomes obvious at once if we consider the fact that none of the identifications of childhood (which in our patients stand out in such morbid elaboration and mutual contradiction) could, if merely added up, result in a functioning personality. True, we usually believe that the task of psychotherapy is the replacement of morbid and excessive identifications by more desirable ones. But as every cure attests, "more desirable" identifications at the same time tend to be quietly subordinated to a new, unique Gestalt which is more than the sum of its parts. The fact is that identification as a mechanism is of limited usefulness. Children at different stages of their development identify with those part aspects of people by which they themselves are most immediately affected, whether in reality or fantasy. Their identifications with parents, for example, center in certain overvalued and ill-understood body parts, capacities, and role appearances. These part aspects, furthermore, are favored not because of their social acceptability (they often are everything but the parents' most adjusted attributes) but by the nature of infantile fantasy which only gradually gives way to more realistic judgment.

In later childhood the individual is faced with a comprehensible hierarchy of roles, from the younger siblings to the grandparents and whoever else belongs to the wider family. All through childhood this gives him some kind of a set of expectations as to what he is going to be when he grows older, and very small children identify with a number of people in a number of respects and establish a kind of hierarchy of expectations which then seeks "verification" later in life. That is why cultural and historical change can prove so traumatic to identity formation: it can break up the inner consistency of a child's hierarchy of expectations.

IF WE consider introjection, identification, and identity formation to be the steps by which the ego grows in ever more mature interplay with the available models, the following psychosocial schedule suggests itself.

The mechanism of *introjection* (the primitive "incorporation" of another's image) depends for its integration on the satisfactory mutuality between the mothering adult(s) and the mothered child. Only the experience of such initial mutuality provides a safe pole of self-feeling from which the child can reach out for the other pole: his first love "objects."

The fate of childhood *identifications*, in turn, depends on the child's satisfactory interaction with trustworthy representatives of a meaningful hierarchy of roles as provided by the generations living together in some form of family.

Identity formation, finally, begins where the usefulness of identification ends. It arises from the selective repudiation and mutual assimilation of childhood identifications and their absorption in a new configuration, which, in turn, is dependent on the process by which a society (often through subsocieties) identifies the young individual, recognizing him as somebody who had to become the way he is and who, being the way he is, is taken for granted. The community, often not without some initial mistrust, gives such recognition with a display of surprise and pleasure in making the acquaintance of a newly emerging individual.

For the community in turn feels "recognized" by the individual who cares to ask for recognition; it can, by the same token, feel deeply—and vengefully—rejected by the individual who does not seem to care.

A community's ways of *identifying* the *individual*, then, meet more or less successfully the individual's ways of identifying himself with others. If the young person is "recognized" at a critical moment as one who arouses displeasure and discomfort, the community sometimes seems to suggest to the young person that he change in ways that to him do not add up to anything "identical with himself." To the community, the desirable change is nevertheless conceived of as a mere matter of good will or of will power ("he could if he wanted to") while resistance to such change is perceived as a matter of bad will or, indeed, of inferiority, hereditary or otherwise. Thus the community often underestimates to what extent a long, intricate childhood history has restricted a youth's further choice of identity change, and also to what extent the community could, if it only would, still help to determine a youth's destiny within these choices.

All through childhood tentative crystallizations of identity take place which make the individual feel and believe (to begin with the most conscious aspect of the matter) as if he approximately knew who he was—only to find that such self-certainty ever again falls prey to the discontinuities of development itself. An example would be the discontinuity between the demands made in a given milieu on a little boy and those made on a "big boy" who, in turn, may well wonder why he was first made to believe that to be little is admirable, only to be forced to exchange this more effortless status for the special obligations of one who is "big now." Such discontinuities can, at any time, amount to a crisis and demand a decisive and strategic repatterning of action, leading to compromises which can be compensated for only by a consistently accruing sense of the practicability and feasibility of such increasing commitment. The cute, or ferocious, or good small boy who becomes a studious, or gentlemanly, or tough big boy must be able—and must be enabled—to combine both sets of values in a recognized identity which permits him, in work and play and in official and intimate behavior, to be (and to let others be) a combination of a big boy and a little boy.

The community supports such development to the extent that it permits the child, at each step, to orient himself toward a complete "life plan" with a hierarchical order of roles as represented by individuals of different ages. Family, neighborhood, and school provide contact and experimental identification with younger and older children and with young and old adults. A child, in the multiplicity of successive and tentative identifications, thus begins early to build up expectations of what it will be like to be older and what it will feel like to have been younger—expectations which become part of an identity as they are, step by step, verified in decisive experiences of psychosocial "fittedness."

The final identity, then, as fixed at the end of adolescence, is superordinated to any single identification with individuals of the past: it includes all significant identifications, but it also alters them in order to make a unique and reasonably coherent whole of them.

THE critical phases of life have been described in psychoanalysis primarily in terms of instincts and defenses, i.e., as "typical danger situations." [10] Psychoanalysis has concerned itself more with the encroachment of psychosexual crises on psychosocial (and other) functions than with the specific crisis created by the maturation of each function. Take for example a child who is learning to speak: he is acquiring one of the prime functions supporting a sense of individual autonomy and one of the prime techniques for expanding the radius of give-and-take. The mere indication of an ability to give intentional sound-signs soon obligates the child to "say what he wants." It may force him to achieve by proper verbalization the attention which was afforded him previously in response to mere gestures of needfulness. Speech not only increasingly commits him to his own characteristic kind of voice and to the mode of speech he develops, it also defines him as one responded to by those around him with changed diction and attention. They in turn expect henceforth to be understood by him with fewer explanations or gestures. Furthermore, a spoken word is a pact. There is an irrevocably committing aspect to an utterance remembered by others, although the child may have to learn early that certain commitments (adult ones to a child) are subject to change without notice, while others (his to them) are not. This intrinsic relationship of speech not only to the world of communicable facts, but also to the social value of verbal commitment and uttered truth is strategic among the experiences which mark ego development. It is this psychosocial aspect of the matter which we must learn to relate to the by now better known psychosexual aspects represented, for example, in the autoerotic enjoyment of speech; the use of speech as an oral or otherwise erotic "contact"; or in such organ-mode emphases as eliminative or intrusive sounds or uses of speech. Thus the child may come to develop, in the use of voice and word, a particular combination of whining or singing, judging or arguing as part of a new element of the future identity, namely, the element "one who speaks and is spoken to in such-and-such a way." This element in turn will be related to other elements of the child's developing identity (he is clever and/or good-looking and/or tough) and will be compared with other people, alive or dead, judged as ideal or evil.

It is the ego's function to integrate the psychosexual and psychosocial aspects on a given level of development and at the same time to integrate the relation of newly added identity elements with those already in existence—that is, to bridge the inescapable discontinuities between different levels of personality development. For earlier crystallizations of identity can become subject to renewed conflict when changes in the quality and quantity of drive, expansions in mental equipment, and new and often conflicting social demands all make previous adjustments appear insufficient and, in fact, make previous opportunities and rewards suspect. Yet such developmental and normative crises differ from imposed, traumatic, and neurotic crises in that the very process of growth provides new energy even as society offers new and specific opportunities according to its dominant conception of the phases of life. From a genetic point of view, then, the process of identity formation emerges as an evolving configuration—a configuration which is gradually established by succesive ego syntheses and resyntheses throughout childhood. It is a configuration gradually integrating constitutional givens, idiosyncratic libidinal needs, favored capacities, significant identifications, effective defenses, successful sublimations, and consistent roles.

THE final assembly of all the converging identity elements at the end of childhood (and the abandonment of the divergent ones) [11] appears to be a formidable task: how can a stage as "abnormal" as adolescence be trusted to accomplish it? It is not always easy to recall that in spite of the similarity of adolescent "symptoms" and episodes to neurotic and psychotic symptoms and episodes, adolescence is not an affliction but a normative crisis, i.e., a normal phase of increased conflict characterized by a seeming fluctuation in ego strength as well as by a high growth potential. Neurotic and psychotic crises are defined by a certain self-perpetuating propensity, by an increasing waste of defensive energy, and by a deepened psychosocial isolation; while normative crises are relatively more reversible, or, better, traversable, and are chacterized by an abundance of available energy which, to be sure, revives dormant anxiety and arouses new conflict, but also supports new and expanded ego functions in the searching and playful engagement of new opportunities and associations. What under prejudiced scrutiny may appear to be the onset of a neurosis often is only an aggravated crisis which might prove to be self-liquidating and even, in fact, contributive to the process of identity formation.

It is true, of course, that the adolescent, during the final stage of his identity formation, is apt to suffer more deeply than he ever did before or ever will again from a confusion of roles. And it is also true that such confusion renders many an adolescent defenseless against the sudden impact of previously latent malignant disturbances. But it is important to emphasize that the diffused and vulnerable, aloof and uncommitted, yet demanding and opinionated personality of the not-too-neurotic adolescent contains many necessary elements of a semi-deliberate role experimentation of the "I dare you" and "I dare myself" variety. Much of this apparent confusion thus must be considered social play—the true genetic successor of childhood play. Similarly, the adolescent's ego development demands and permits playful, if daring, experimentation in fantasy and introspection. We are apt to be alarmed when the adolescent reveals a "closeness to consciousness" in his perception of dangerous fantasies (fantasies that had been suppressed at earlier stages and will be suppressed again later), especially if, in our zealous pursuit of our task of "making conscious" in the psychotherapeutic situation, we push someone who is already leaning out a little too far over the precipice of the unconscious. The adolescent's leaning out over any number of precipices is normally an experimentation with experiences which are thus becoming more amenable to ego control, provided they are not prematurely responded to with fatal seriousness by overeager or neurotic adults. The same must be said of the adolescent's "fluidity of defenses," which so often causes genuine concern on the part of the worried clinician. Much of this fluidity is anything but pathological, for adolescence is a crisis in which only fluid defense can overcome a sense of victimization by inner and outer demands and in which only trial and error can lead to the most felicitous avenues of action and self-expression.

In general, one may say that in regard to the social play of adolescents, prejudices similar to those which once concerned the nature of childhood play are not easily overcome. We alternately consider such behavior irrelevant, unnecessary, or irrational, and ascribe to it purely regressive and neurotic meanings. As in the past, when the study of children's spontaneous games was neglected in favor of that of solitary play,[12] so now the mutual "joinedness" of adolescent clique behavior fails to be properly assessed in our concern for the individual adolescent. Whether or not a given adolescent's newly acquired capacities are drawn back into infantile conflict depends to a significant extent on the quality of the opportunities and rewards available to him in his peer clique as well as on the more formal ways in which society at large invites a transition from social play to work experimentation and from rituals of transit to final commitments, all of which must be based on an implicit mutual contract between the individual and society.

Is THE sense of identity conscious? At times, of course, it seems only too conscious. For between the double prongs of vital inner need and inexorable outer demand, the as yet experimenting individual may become the victim of a transitory extreme identity consciousness, which is the common core of the many forms of "self-consciousness" typical for youth. Where the processes of identity formation are prolonged (a factor which can bring creative gain), such preoccupation with the "self-image" also prevails. We are thus most aware of our identity when we are just about to gain it and when we (with that startle which motion pictures call a "double take") are somewhat surprised to make its acquaintance; or, again, when we are just about to enter a crisis and feel the encroachment of identity confusion—a syndrome to be described presently.

An optimal sense of identity, on the other hand, is experienced merely as a sense of psychosocial well-being. Its most obvious concomitants are a feeling of being at home in one's body, a sense of "knowing where one is going," and an inner assuredness of anticipated recognition from those who count.

3. PATHOGRAPHIC: THE CLINICAL PICTURE OF SEVERE IDENTITY CONFUSION

Pathography remains the traditional source of psychoanalytic insight. In the following, I shall sketch a syndrome of disturbances in young people who can neither make use of the careers provided in their society nor create and maintain for themselves (as Shaw did) a unique moratorium all their own. They come, instead, to psychiatrists, priests, judges, and recruitment officers in order to be given an authorized if ever so uncomfortable place in which to wait things out. What follows is a first formulation of the more severe symptoms of identity confusion. It is based on clinical observations made in the fifties, on individuals diagnosed as preschizophrenics or, for the most part, as "borderline" cases in the Austen Riggs Center in the Berkshires and in the Western Psychiatric Institute in Pittsburgh. The clinically oriented reader will rightly feel that in my endeavor to understand identity confusion as a developmental disturbance, I neglect the diagnostic signs which would mark a malignant and more irreversible condition. Identity confusion, of course, is not a diagnostic entity, but I would think that a description of the developmental crisis in which a disturbance had its acute onset should become part of any diagnostic picture, and especially of any prognosis and any statement concerning the kind of therapy indicated. This whole chapter serves the purpose of indicating such an additional diagnostic direction, but it does not demonstrate in detail the way in which it could be made functional. The nonclinical reader, on the other hand, should be warned that any sympathetic and nonmedical description of mental states makes any reader believe that he—or somebody near to him—shares the condition described. And, indeed, it is easy (in the sense of usual) to have one or a number of the symptoms of identity confusion, but quite difficult to accomplish the more severe ensemble of them all which could be verified in the individual case only by a trained observer.

A state of acute identity confusion usually becomes manifest at a time when the young individual finds himself exposed to a combination of experiences which demand his simultaneous commitment to physical intimacy (not by any means always overtly sexual), to decisive occupational choice, to energetic competition, and to psychosocial self-definition. Whether or not the ensuing tension will lead to paralysis now depends primarily on the regressive pull exerted by a latent illness. This regressive pull often receives the greatest attention from workers in our field, partially because we are on more familiar ground wherever we can diagnose signs of regression and partially because it is the regression which calls for cure. Yet the disturbances under discussion cannot be comprehended without some insight into the specific conditions which may have forced a transitory adolescent regression on the individual as an attempt to postpone and to avoid, as it were, a psychosocial foreclosure. The social function of the state of paralysis which ensues is that of maintaining a state of minimal actual choice and commitment. But alas, illness, too, commits.

THE PROBLEM OF INTIMACY

That many of our patients break down at an age which is properly considered more preadult than postadolescent is explained by the fact that often only an attempt to engage in intimate fellowship and competition or in sexual intimacy fully reveals the latent weakness of identity.

True "engagement" with others is the result and the test of firm self-delineation. As the young individual seeks at least tentative forms of playful intimacy in friendship and competition, in sex play and love, in argument and gossip, he is apt to experience a peculiar strain, as if such tentative engagement might turn into an interpersonal fusion amounting to a loss of identity and requiring, therefore, a tense inner reservation, a caution in commitment. Where a youth does not resolve such strain, he may isolate himself and enter, at best, only stereotyped and formalized interpersonal relations; or he may, in repeated hectic attempts and dismal failures, seek intimacy with the most improbable partners. For where an assured sense of identity is missing, even friendships and affairs become desperate attempts at delineating the fuzzy outlines of identity by mutual narcissistic mirrorying: to fall in love then often means to fall into one's mirror image, hurting oneself and damaging the mirror. During lovemaking or in sexual fantasies a loosening of sexual identity threatens; it even becomes unclear whether sexual excitement is experienced by the individual or by his partner, and this applies in either heterosexual or homosexual encounters. The ego thus loses its flexible capacity for abandoning itself to sexual and affectual sensations in a fusion with another individual who is both partner to the sensation and guarantor of one's continuing identity: fusion with another becomes identity loss. A sudden collapse of all capacity for mutuality threatens, and a desperate wish ensues to start all over again, with a (quasideliberate) regression to a stage of basic bewilderment and rage such as only the very small child experiences.

It must be remembered that the counterpart of intimacy is distantiation, i.e., the readiness to repudiate, ignore, or destroy those forces and people whose essence seems dangerous to one's own. Intimacy with one set of people and ideas would not be really intimate without an efficient repudiation of another set. Thus, weakness or excess in repudiation is an intrinsic aspect of the inability to gain intimacy because of an incomplete identity: whoever is not sure of his "point of view" cannot repudiate judiciously.

Young persons often indicate in rather pathetic ways the feeling that only by merging with a "leader" can they be saved, the leader being an adult who is able and willing to offer himself as a safe object for experimental surrender and as a guide in the relearning of the very first steps toward an intimate mutuality and a legitimate repudiation. The late adolescent wants to be an apprentice or disciple, a follower, a sexual servant, or patient to such a person. When this fails, as it often must from its very intensity and absoluteness, the young individual recoils to a position of strenuous introspection and self-testing which, given particularly aggravating circumstances or a history of relatively strong autistic trends, can lead him into a paralyzing borderline state. Symptomatically, this state consists of a painfully heightened sense of isolation; a disintegraton of the sense of inner continuity and sameness; a sense of over-all ashamedness; an inability to derive a sense of accomplishment from any kind of activity. In these young patients, masturbation and nocturnal emissions, far from being an occasional release of excess pressure, only serve to aggravate tension. They become part of a vicious cycle in which omnipotent narcissism is momentarily heightened only to give way to a sense of physical and mental castration and emptiness. Thus, life is happening to the individual rather than being lived by his initiative; his mistrust leaves it to the world, to society, and indeed to psychiatry to prove that he does exist in a psychosocial sense, i.e., can count on an invitation to become himself.

DIFFUSION OF TIME PERSPECTIVE

In extreme instances of delayed and prolonged adolescence, an extreme form of a disturbance in the experience of time appears which, in its milder form, belongs to the psychopathology of everyday adolescence. It consists of a sense of great urgency and yet also of a loss of consideration for time as a dimension of living. The young person may feel simultaneously very young, and in fact babylike, and old beyond rejuvenation. Protests of missed greatness and of a premature and fatal loss of useful potentials are common among our patients, as they are among adolescents in cultures which consider such protestations romantic; the implied malignancy, however, consists of a decided disbelief in the possibility that time may bring change, and yet also of a violent fear that it might. This contradiction is often expressed in a general slowing up which makes the patient behave, within the routine of his activities and of his therapy, as if he were moving in molasses. It is hard for him to go to bed and face the transition into a state of sleep, and it is equally hard for him to get up and face the necessary restitution of wakefulness; it is hard to come to the therapeutic appointment, and hard to leave it. Such complaints as "I don't know," "I give up," and "I quit" are by no means mere habitual statements reflecting a mild depression; they are often expressions of the kind of despair discussed by Edward Bibring [13] as a wish on the part of the ego "to let itself die."

The assumption that life could actually be made to end with the end of adolescence or at tentatively planned later "dates of expiration" is by no means entirely unwelcome, and, in fact, can become the only condition on which a tentative new beginning can be based. Some of our patients even require the feeling that the therapist does not intend to commit them to a continuation of life if treatment should fail to prove it really worth while. Without such a conviction the moratorium would not be a real one. In the meantime, the "wish to die" is a really suicidal wish only in those rare cases where "to be a suicide" becomes an inescapable identity choice in itself. I am thinking here of a pretty young girl, the oldest of a number of daughters of a mill worker. Her mother had repeatedly expressed the thought that she would rather see her daughters dead than become prostitutes, and at the same time she suspected "prostitution" in the daughters' every move toward companionship with boys. The daughters were finally forced into a kind of conspiratorial sorority of their own, obviously designed to elude the mother, in order to experiment with ambiguous situations and yet probably also to give each other protection from men. They were finally caught in compromising circumstances. The authorities, too, took it for granted that they intended to prostitute themselves, and they were sent to a variety of institutions where they were forcefully impressed with the kind of "recognition" society had in store for them. No appeal was possible to a mother who, they felt, had left them no choice, and much of the good will and understanding of social workers was sabotaged by circumstances. At least for the oldest girl—for a number of reasons—no other future was possible except that of another chance in another world. She hanged herself after having dressed nicely and written a note which ended with the cryptic words "Why I achieve honor only to discard it . . ."

DIFFUSION OF INDUSTRY

Severe identity confusion is regularly accompanied by an acute upset in the sense of workmanship, either in the form of an inability to concentrate on required or suggested tasks or in a self-destructive preoccupation with some one-sided activity, i.e., excessive reading. The way in which such patients sometimes, under treatment, find the one activity in which they can re-employ their once lost sense of workmanship is a chapter in it-self. Here it is well to keep in mind the stage of development which precedes puberty and adolescence, namely, the elemen-tary school age, when the child is taught the prerequisites for participation in the particular technology of his culture and is given the opportunity and the life task of developing a sense of workmanship and work participation. As we saw, the school age significantly follows the Oedipal stage: the accomplishment of real, not merely playful, steps toward a place in the economic structure of society permits the child to reidentify with parents as workers and tradition bearers rather than as sexual and famil-ial beings, thus nurturing at least one concrete and more "neu-tral" possibility of becoming like them. The tangible goals of the elementary practice of skills are shared by and with age mates in places of instruction (sweathouse, prayer house, fishing hole, workshop, kitchen, schoolhouse) most of which, in turn, are geographically separated from the home, from the mother, and from infantile memories; here, however, there are wide differ-ences in the treatment of the sexes. Work goals, then, by no means only support or exploit the suppression of infantile in-stinctual aims; they also enhance the functioning of the ego, in that they offer a constructive activity with actual tools and ma-terials in a communal reality. The ego's tendency to turn passiv-ity into activity thus acquires a new field of manifestation, in many ways superior to the mere turning of passive into active in infantile fantasy and play, for now the inner need for activity, practice, and work completion is ready to meet the correspond-ing demands and opportunities in social reality.

Because of the immediate Oedipal antecedents of the begin-nings of a work identity, however, the attitude toward work in our young patients reverses gears toward Oedipal competitive-ness and sibling rivalry. Thus identity confusion is accompanied not only by an inability to concentrate, but by an excessive awareness of as well as an abhorrence of competitiveness. Although the patients in question usually are intelligent and able and have often shown themselves successful in office work, scholastic studies, and sports, they now lose the capacity for work, exercise, and sociability and thus lose the most important vehicle of social play and the most significant refuge from formless fantasy and vague anxiety. Instead, infantile goals and fantasies are dangerously endowed with the energy emanating from matured sexual equipment and vicious aggressive power. One parent, again, becomes the goal; the other, again, the hindrance. Yet this revived Oedipal struggle is not and must not be interpreted as exclusively or even primarily a sexual one. It is a turn toward the earliest origins, an attempt to resolve a diffusion of early introjects and to rebuild shaky childhood identifications—in other words, a wish to be born again, to learn once more the very first steps toward reality and mutuality and to be given renewed permission to develop again the functions of contact, activity, and competition.

A young patient who had found himself blocked in college nearly read himself blind during the initial phase of his treatment, apparently in a destructive overidentification with father and therapist, both of whom were professors. Guided by a resourceful "painter in residence," he came upon the fact that he had an original talent to paint, an activity which was prevented only by his advancing treatment from becoming a self-destructive overactivity. As painting proved to be a valuable asset in the patient's gradual acquisition of a sense of identity of his own, one night he dreamed a different version of a dream which previously had always ended in frightened awakening. As always, he was fleeing from fire and persecution, but this time he fled into a stand of trees which he had sketched himself, and as he fled into it the charcoal drawing turned into a real forest with infinite perspectives.

THE CHOICE OF THE NEGATIVE IDENTITY

The loss of a sense of identity is often expressed in a scornful and snobbish hostility toward the roles offered as proper and desirable in one's family or immediate community. Any aspect of the required role, or all of it—be it masculinity or femininity, nationality or class membership—can become the main focus of the young person's acid disdain. Such excessive contempt for their backgrounds occurs among the oldest Anglo-Saxon and the newest Latin or Jewish families; it can become a general dislike for everything American and an irrational overestimation of everything foreign, or the reverse. Life and strength seem to exist only where one is not, while decay and danger threaten wherever one happens to be. This typical fragment from a case report illustrates the superego's triumph of depreciation over a young man's faltering identity: "A voice within him which was disparaging him began to increase at about this time. It went to the point of intruding into everything he did. He said, 'If I smoke a cigarette, if I tell a girl I like her, if I make a gesture, if I listen to music, if I try to read a book—this third voice is at me all the time—"You're doing this for effect; you're a phony." ' This disparaging voice became rather relentless. One day on the way from home to college, his train crossed through the New Jersey swamplands and some poorer sections of cities, and he felt overwhelmingly that he was more congenial with people who lived there than he was with people on the campus or at home. Life seemed to exist only in those places, and the campus, in contrast, was a sheltered, effeminate place."

In this example, it is important to recognize not only an overweening superego, overclearly perceived as a deprecating inner voice (but not integrated enough to lead the young man into an alternative career), but also the acute identity confusion as projected on segments of society. An analogous case is that of a French-American girl from a rather prosperous mining town who felt panicky to the point of paralysis when alone with a boy. It appeared that numerous superego injunctions and identity conflicts had, as it were, short-circuited in the obsessive idea that every boy had a right to expect from her a yielding to sexual practices popularly designated as "French."

Such estrangement from national and ethnic origins rarely

leads to a complete denial of *personal identity*, although the
angry insistence on being called by a particular given name or
nickname is not uncommon among young people who try to
find refuge in a new name label. Yet, confabulatory reconstruc-
tions of one's origin do occur. An especially inventive high
school girl from Middle-European stock secretly sought the
company of Scottish immigrants, carefully studying and easily
assimilating their dialect and their social habits. With the help of
history books and travel guides she reconstructed for herself a
childhood in a given milieu in an actual township in Scotland,
which was apparently quite convincing to some descendants of
that country throughout long evening talks. She spoke of her
American-born parents as "the people who brought me over
here," and when sent to me introduced herself as "Lorna" and
described her childhood "over there" in impressive detail. I
went along with the story, saying that it had more inner truth
than reality to it. And indeed the inner truth turned out to be a
memory, namely, the girl's erstwhile attachment to a woman
neighbor who had come from the British Isles and who had
given her more of the kind of love she wanted than her parents
did or could. The force behind the near-delusional power of the
invented "truth" was in turn a death wish against her parents,
which is latent in all severe identity crises. The semideliberate-
ness of the delusion came to the fore when I finally asked the girl
how she had managed to marshall all the details of life in Scotland. "Bless you, sir," she said, in a pleading Scottish brogue, "I
needed a past." Needless to say, with such gifts for language,
histrionics, and personal warmth, a "delusion" is very different
in nature and prognosis from a truly psychotic condition.

On the whole, however, our patients' conflicts find expression
in a more subtle way than the abrogation of personal identity.
They choose instead a *negative identity*, i.e., an identity perversely based on all those identifications and roles which, at critical stages of development, had been presented to them as most
undesirable or dangerous and yet also as most real. For example, a
mother whose first-born son died and who, because of compli-

cated guilt feelings, had never been able to attach to her later surviving children the same amount of religious devotion that she bestowed on the memory of her dead child, aroused in one of her sons the fateful conviction that to be sick or dead was a better assurance of being "recognized" than to be healthy and about. A mother who was filled with unconscious ambivalence toward a brother who had disintegrated into alcoholism again and again responded selectively only to those traits in her son which seemed to point to a repetition of her brother's fate, with the result that this "negative" identity sometimes seemed to have more reality for the son than all his natural attempts at being good. He worked hard at becoming a drunkard, and, lacking the necessary ingredients, ended up in a state of stubborn paralysis of choice.

In other cases the negative identity is dictated by the necessity of finding and defending a niche of one's own against the excessive ideals either demanded by morbidly ambitious parents or indeed actualized by superior ones. In both cases the parents' weaknesses and unexpressed wishes are recognized by the child with catastrophic clarity. The daughter of a man of brilliant showmanship ran away from college and was arrested as a prostitute in the Negro quarter of a southern city, while the daughter of an influential southern Negro preacher was found among narcotic addicts in Chicago. In such cases it is of utmost importance to recognize the mockery and vindictive pretense in such role playing, for the white girl had not really prostituted herself, and the colored girl had not really become an addict—yet. Needless to say, however, each of them had put herself into a marginal social area, leaving it to law enforcement officers and psychiatric agencies to decide what stamp to put on such behavior. A corresponding case is that of a boy presented to a psychiatric clinic as "the village homosexual" of a small town. On investigation, it appeared that the boy had succeeded in assuming this fame without any actual acts of homosexuality except one, much earlier in his life, when he had been raped by some older boys.

Such vindictive choices of a negative identity represent, of course, a desperate attempt at regaining some mastery in a situation in which the available positive identity elements cancel each other out. The history of such a choice reveals a set of conditions in which it is easier for the patient to derive a sense of identity out of a total identification with that which he is least supposed to be than to struggle for a feeling of reality in acceptable roles which are unattainable with his inner means. The statement of a young man that "I would rather be quite insecure than a little secure" and of a young woman that "at least in the gutter I'm a genius," circumscribe the relief following the total choice of a negative identity. Such relief is, of course, often sought collectively in cliques and gangs of young homosexuals, addicts, and social cynics.

Some forms of upper-class snobbism must be included here because they permit some people to deny their identity confusion through recourse to something they did not earn themselves, such as their parents' wealth, background, or fame, or to some things they did not create, such as styles and art forms. But there is a "lower lower" snobbism too, which is based on the pride of having achieved a semblance of nothingness. At any rate, many a sick or desperate late adolescent, if faced with continuing conflict, would rather be nobody or somebody totally bad or, indeed, dead—and this by free choice—than be not-quite-somebody. The word "total" is not accidental in this connection; we have endeavored to describe in Chapter II a human proclivity to a "totalistic" reorientation when, at critical stages of development, reintegration into a relative "wholeness" seems impossible. The totalistic solution of a psychotic break cannot be discussed here.[14]

SPECIFIC FACTORS IN FAMILY AND CHILDHOOD

In the discussion of patients who share a relevant pathogenic trend, we are apt to ask ourselves what their parents have in common. I think one may say that a significant number of the mothers in our case histories have in common several outstand-

ing traits, which are not necessarily dependent on their actual social status. First, a pronounced status awareness of the climbing
and pretentious or the "hold-on" variety. They would at almost
any time be willing to overrule matters of honest feeling and intelligent judgment for the sake of a façade of wealth or status,
propriety and "happiness"; in fact, they try to coerce their sensitive children into a pretense of a "natural" and "glad-to-be-
proper" sociability. Secondly, they have the special quality of
penetrating omnipresence; their ordinary voices as well as their
softest sobs are sharp, plaintive, or fretful and cannot be escaped
within a considerable radius. One patient all through childhood
had a repetitive dream of a pair of snipping scissors flying
around a room: the scissors proved to symbolize his mother's
voice, cutting and cutting off.[15] These mothers love, but they
love desperately and intrusively. They are themselves so hungry
for approval and recognition that they burden their young children with complicated complaints, especially about the fathers,
almost pleading with them to justify their mothers' existence by
their existence. They are highly jealous and highly sensitive to
the jealousy of others. In our context it is especially important
that the mother is intensely jealous of any sign that the child
may identify primarily with the father or, worse, base his very
identity on that of the father. It must be added that whatever
these mothers are, they are more so toward the patient. Behind
the mother's persistent complaints, then, that the father failed to
make a woman out of her is the complaint, deeply perceived by
both mother and child, that the patient failed to make a mother
of her. The conclusion is inescapable that these patients in turn
have, from the very beginning of their lives, deeply hurt their
mothers by shying away from them because of an utter intolerance of what at first looks like extreme temperamental differences. These differences, however, turn out to be only extreme
expressions of an essential affinity, by which I mean to imply
that the patient's excessive tendency to withdraw or to act ran-
domly, and the mother's desperate social intrusiveness have in
common a basic social vulnerability.

What I describe here is, in its milder forms, so usual a type that it cannot possibly be "blamed" for the child's illness, especially since not all children in the family seem to respond with equal malignancy. We must also bear in mind that we usually meet these mothers when they are already doubly on the defensive. But I think we can say with assurance that we have here again a *reciprocal negative reaction* of mother and child which is the malignant opposite of mutuality.

The fathers, although usually successful and often outstanding in their fields, do not stand up against their wives at home because of an excessive dependence on them, in consequence of which the fathers also are deeply jealous of their children. What initiative and integrity they have either surrenders to the wife's intrusiveness or tries guiltily to elude her, and as a result the mother becomes all the more needy, plaintive, and "sacrificial" in her demands upon all or some of her children.

Of the relationship of our patients to their brothers and sisters I can only say that it seems to be more symbiotic than most sibling relationships are. Because of an early identity hunger, our patients are apt to attach themselves to one brother or sister in a way resembling the behavior of twins [16] except that here we have one twin, as it were, trying to treat a non-twin as a twin. They seem apt to surrender to a total identification with at least one sibling in ways which go far beyond the "altruism by identification" described by Anna Freud.[17] It is as if our patients surrendered their own identity to that of a brother or sister in the hope of regaining a bigger and better one by some act of merging. For periods they succeed, but the letdown which must follow the breakup of the artificial twinship is only the more traumatic. Rage and paralysis follow the sudden insight—also possible in one of a pair of twins—that there is enough identity only for one, and that the other seems to have made off with it.

The early childhood histories of our patients are, on the whole, remarkably bland. Some infantile autism is often observed but it is usually rationalized by the parents. Yet one has the general impression that the degree of malignancy of the acute identity confusion in late adolescence depends on the extent of this early autism, and that it will determine the depth of regression and the extent of the return to old introjects. As to particular traumata in childhood or youth, one item seems frequent, namely, a severe physical trauma either in the Oedipal period or in early puberty, usually in connection with a separation from home. This trauma may consist of an operation or a belatedly diagnosed physical defect or it may be an accident or a severe sexual traumatization.

Otherwise, the early pathology conforms with that which we have come to regard as typical for the dominant psychiatric diagnosis given. Obviously, identity confusion is not a clinical diagnosis. But there remains always the decisive question whether, for example, an identity confusion of the paranoic type is to be taken as a case of paranoia that happens to occur in youth or as a disposition for paranoia aggravated by acute identity confusion, which is relatively reversible if the confusion can be made to subside. This "technical" question cannot be dealt with here. But another critical problem is obvious from our whole discussion. It is the danger, discussed in sociological terms by Kai T. Erikson,[18] that the patient of this age group will choose the very role of patient as the most meaningful basis for an identity formation.

4. SOCIETAL: FROM INDIVIDUAL CONFUSION TO SOCIAL ORDER

I.

Having offered a picture of the whole condition of acute identity confusion, I would like now to take up each of the part-symptoms described and relate it to two phenomena seemingly remote from one another: the individual's childhood and cultural history. Since we take it for granted that the conflicts we meet in our case histories in vastly aggravated form are, in principle, common to all individuals, so that the picture presented is only a distorted reflection of the normal adolescent state, we may now inquire, first, how this state can be shown to revive old childhood conflicts and, second, what are the various avenues which cultures offer to "normal" youths so that they may overcome the forces that pull them back into infantile regressions and find ways of mobilizing their inner strength for future-oriented pursuits.

First, then, the pull back into childhood, the regressive aspects of adolescent conflict. I hope I will not complicate this matter unbearably by reintroducing the chart in order to "locate" regressive trends in our scheme of psychosocial development. I know that some readers will have wondered what to do with the as yet unassigned parts of the chart. Others would probably prefer to read on and leave the diagram to those interested in such charting. I will, therefore, insert here a paragraph intended only for chart fanciers, explaining to them the way in which, throughout this section, the numbers after certain items refer to the chart. Other readers may ignore this next paragraph as well as all subsequent numbers in parentheses. To them, I hope, the text will speak for itself.

Only the *diagonal* of the epigenetic chart (p. 94) has been fully discussed in Chapter III. It depicts, we said, the ontogenetic unfolding of the main components of psychosocial vitality (I.1–VIII.8). We have also filled in some aspects of the vertical leading from infancy to identity, from I.5 to V.5. These are the specific contributions which previous stages make directly to the development of identity, namely, the primitive *trust* in mutual recognition; the rudiments of a *will* to be oneself; the *anticipation* of what one might become; and the capacity to *learn* how to be, with skill, what one is in the process of becoming. But this also means that each of these stages contributes a particular estrangement to identity confusion: the earliest would come about with an "autistic" inability to establish mutuality. The most radical forms of identity confusion, we have just seen, can be traced back to such early disturbances. Here, a basic confusion of contradictory introjects undermines, as it were, all future identifications and thus also their integration in adolescence. Taking our cues, then, from the clinical picture just described, and experimenting with the chart, we will now distribute the various *part-symptoms* of confusion on horizontal V of the chart, and indicate how we would trace them downward along the "regressive" verticals 1, 2, 3, and 4 to their antecedents in childhood. The reader need only let his eye wander along these verticals to find the location of the numbers which appear after the major items.

Let us begin with the first item of pathology just described, the mistrust of time itself and the dominance of *time confusion* (V.1). A loss of the ego's function of maintaining perspective and expectancy is a clear regression to a time in early infancy when time did not exist. The experience of time arises only from the infant's adaptation to initial cycles of need tension, delay of satisfaction, and satiation. In the infant, as tension increases, future fulfillment is anticipated in a "hallucinatory" way; as fulfillment is delayed, moments of impotent rage occur in which trust seems obliterated; any signs of an approaching satisfaction gives time again a quality of intense hope, while further delay causes redoubled rage. Our patients, as we saw, do not trust time and are not convinced that sufficient satisfaction is sufficiently predictable to make wanting and "working" worth while.

Our most malignantly regressed young people are in fact clearly possessed by general attitudes which represent something of a mistrust of time as such: every delay appears to be a deceit, every wait an experience of impotence, every hope a danger, every plan a catastrophe, every possible provider a potential traitor. Therefore, time must be made to stand still, if necessary by the magic means of catatonic immobility. These are the extremes which are manifest in few but latent in many cases of identity confusion, and every adolescent, I would believe, knows at least fleeting moments of being thus at odds with time itself. In its normal and transitory form, this new kind of mistrust quickly or gradually yields to outlooks permitting and demanding an intense and even fanatic investment in a future, or a rapid succession in a number of possible futures. These, to the elders, often seem quite inconsistent with each other and at any rate quite "utopian," that is, based on expectations which would call for a change in the laws of historical change. But then, again, youth can attach itself to seemingly utopian world images which somehow prove to be realizable in part, given the right leader— and historical luck. Time confusion, then, is more or less typical for all adolescents at one stage or another, although it becomes pathologically marked only in some.

What does the social process do about this, from culture to culture, and from one era to another? I can only offer some suggestive examples. Thus, there was the romantic period, when youth (and artists and writers) were preoccupied with the ruins left by a dead past which seemed more "eternal" than the present. To be emphasized here, however, is not the mere turning to a distant past, but a concomitant change in the whole quality of temporal experience. This, under different cultural or historical conditions, can be acquired in settings as different (to choose from examples already mentioned in this book) as a vision-quest in the blinding prairie sun or dancing to drumbeat throughout the night; in utterly passive drug-induced floating in "absolute" time or in goose stepping to blaring trumpets in preparation for the Thousand Year Reich. There is, in fact, an indispensable temporal aspect to all ideology, including the ideological significance which the goals and values of different civilizations have for youth, be they bent on salvation or reform, adventure or conquest, reason or progress, in accordance with newly developing identity potentials. For among the essentials which they provide for youth is a sensually convincing *time perspective* compatible with a coherent world image. It makes supreme sense that today, when the standardization of anticipated futures is at its height, thousands of young people would choose to behave as if the moratorium were a way of life and a separate culture. As they choose to forget about their future, society forgets that theirs is only a modern—that is, more populous and more publicized—form of an old phenomenon, as is clearly revealed by the quality of revival in some of our young people's display.

We also diagnosed *identity-consciousness* among the ingredients of identity confusion, and we meant by it a special form of painful self-consciousness which dwells on discrepancies between one's self-esteem, the aggrandized self-image as an autonomous person, and one's appearance in the eyes of others. In our patients an occasional total obliteration of self-esteem contrasts sharply with a narcissistic and snobbish disdain of the judgment of others. But again, we see corresponding, if less extreme, phenomena in that sensitivity of adolescents which alternates with defiant shamelessness in the face of criticism. Again, these are primitive defenses, upholding a shaky self-certainty against the sense of *doubt* and *shame* (II.2) which we discussed in the last chapter. While this is normally a transitory matter, it persists in some character formations and remains characteristic of many creative people who experience, according to their own testimony, repeated adolescences and with them the full cycle of sensitive withdrawal and forceful self-exhibition.

Self-consciousness (V.2) is a new edition of that original doubt which concerned the trustworthiness of the parents and of the child himself—only in adolescence, such self-conscious doubt concerns the reliability of the whole span of childhood which is now to be left behind and the trustworthiness of the whole social universe now envisaged. The obligation now to commit oneself with a sense of free will to one's autonomous identity can arouse a painful over-all ashamedness somehow comparable to the original shame and rage over being visible all around to all-knowing adults—only such shame now adheres to one's having a public personality exposed to age mates and to be judged by leaders. All of this, in the normal course of events, is outbalanced by that *self-certainty* (V.2) now characterized by a definite sense of independence from the family as the matrix of self-images, and a sureness of anticipation.

Among the societal phenomena corresponding to this second conflict there is a universal trend toward some form of uniformity either in special uniforms or in distinctive clothing through which incomplete self-certainty, for a time, can hide in a group certainty. Such certainty has always been provided by the age-old badges as well as the sacrifices of investitures, confirmations, and initiations, but it can also be temporarily and arbitrarily created by those who care to differ, radically, and yet must evolve a certain uniformity of differing (zoot-suiters, beatniks). These and less obvious uniformities are enforced by comprehensive shaming among peers, a judgmental give-and-take and a cruel banding together which leaves outsiders "holding the bag" in painful, if sometimes creative, isolation.

The display of a total commitment to a *role fixation* (V.3) as against a free *experimentation* with available roles has an obvious connection with earlier conflicts between free initiative and Oedipal guilt in infantile reality, fantasy, and play. Where our patients regress below the Oedipal crisis to a total crisis of trust, the choice of a self-defeating role often remains the only acceptable form of initiative on the way back and up, and this in the form of a complete denial of ambition as the only possible way of totally avoiding guilt. The normal expression of relatively guilt-free and in fact more or less "delinquent" initiative in youth, however, is an experimentation with roles which follows the unwritten codes of adolescent subsocieties and thus is not lacking a discipline of its own.

Of the social institutions which undertake to channel as they encourage such initiative and to provide atonement as they appease guilt, we may point here, again, to initiations and confirmations: they strive within an atomosphere of mythical timelessness to combine some badge of sacrifice or submission with an energetic push toward sanctioned ways of action—a combination which, where it works, assures the development in the novice of an optimum of compliance with a maximum sense of free choice and solidarity. This special proclivity of youth—namely, the achievement of a sense of free choice as the very result of ritual regimentation—is, of course, universally utilized in army life.

Extreme *work paralysis* (V.4) is the logical sequence of a deep sense of the inadequacy of one's general equipment. Such a sense of inadequacy, of course, does not usually reflect a true lack of potential; it may, rather, convey the unrealistic demands made by an ego ideal willing to settle only for omnipotence or omniscience; it may express the fact that the immediate social environment does not have a niche for the individual's true gifts; or it may reflect the paradoxical fact than an individual in early school life was seduced into a specialized precocity which outdistanced his identity development. For all these reasons, then, the individual may be excluded from that experimental competition in play and work through which he learns to find and insist on his own kind of achievement and his work identity. This can become especially relevant in an early turn to delinquency— delinquents being, in many ways, the "positive" counterparts of our patients because at least they act out in company what the isolate suppresses. Some mockery of work and yet a competition with it is obvious in such delinquent phrases as "doing a job" (that is, a burglary) or "making a good job of it" in the sense of completing a destruction. From here it is only one step to another obvious consideration, namely, that young people must have learned to enjoy a sense of *apprenticeship* (IV.4) in order not to need the thrill of destruction. Schizoids and delinquents have in common a mistrust of themselves, a disbelief in the possibility that they could ever complete anything of value. This, of course, is especially marked in those who, for some reason or other, do not feel that they are partaking of the technological identity of their time. The reason may be that their own gifts have not found contact with the productive aims of the machine age or that they themselves belong to a social class (here "upper-upper" is remarkably equal to "lower-lower") that does not partake of the stream of progress.

Social institutions support the strength and distinctiveness of the budding work identity by offering those who are still learning and experimenting a certain status of *apprenticeship*, a moratorium characterized by defined duties and sanctioned competitions as well as by special license.

These, then, are the regressive trends in the identity crisis which are particularly clearly elaborated in the symptoms of identity confusion and some of the social processes which counteract them in daily life. But there are also aspects of identity formation which anticipate future development. The first of these is what we may call a *polarization of sexual differences* (V.6), i.e., the elaboration of a particular ratio of masculinity and femininity in line with identity development. Some of our patients suffer more lastingly and malignantly from a state not uncommon in a milder and transient form in all adolescence: the young person does not feel himself clearly to be a member of one sex or the other, which may make him the easy victim of the pressure emanating, for example, from homosexual cliques, for to some persons it is more bearable to be typed as something, anything, than to endure drawn-out bisexual confusion. Some, of course, decide on an ascetic turning away from sexuality which may result in dramatic breakthroughs of bewildering impulses. For *bisexual confusion* (V.6) in adolescence joins *identity-consciousness* in the establishment of an excessive preoccupation with the question of what kind of man or woman, or what kind of intermediate or deviate, one might become. In his totalistic frame of mind, an adolescent may feel that to be a little less of one sex means to be much more, if not all, of the other. If at such a time something happens that marks him socially as a deviant, he may develop a deep fixation, reinforced by the transvaluation of a negative identity, and true intimacy will then seem dangerous. Here the sexual mores of cultures and classes make for immense differences in the psychosocial differentiation of masculine and feminine and in the age, kind, and ubiquity of genital activity. These differences can obscure the common fact discussed above, namely, that the development of psychosocial intimacy is not possible without a firm sense of identity. Induced by special mores, young people in confusion may foreclose their identity development by concentrating on early genital activity without intimacy; or, on the contrary, they may concentrate on social, artistic, or intellectual aims which underplay the genital element to an extent that there is a permanent weakness of genital polarization with the other sex.

Social institutions here offer ideological rationales for widely different patterns of partial sexual moratoria such as complete sexual abstinence for a specified period, promiscuous genital activity without personal commitment, or sexual play without genital engagement. What a group's or an individual's "libido economy" will stand depends both on the kind of childhood left behind and on the identity gain which accrues from such preferred sexual behavior.

But youth also makes an important step toward parenthood and adult responsibility in learning to take *leadership* as well as to assume *followership* (V.7) among peers and to develop what often amounts to an astonishing foresight in the functions thus assumed. Such foresight can be, as it were, ahead of the individual's over-all maturity precisely because the prevailing ideology provides a framework for an orientation in leadership. By the same token, the common "cause" permits others to follow and to obey (and the leader himself to obey higher leaders) and thus to replace the parent images set up in the infantile superego with the hierarchy of leader-images inhabiting the available gallery of ideals—a process as typical for delinquent gangs as for any highly motivated group. Where a youth can neither obey nor give orders he must make do with an isolation which can lead to malignant withdrawal but which also, if he is lucky and gifted, will help him respond to guiding voices who speak to him (as if they knew him) over the centuries, through books, pictures, and music.

We now come to that system of ideals which societies present to the young in the explicit or implicit form of an ideology. From what has been said so far we can ascribe to ideology the function of offering youth (1) a simplified perspective of the future which encompasses all foreseeable time and thus counteracts individual "time confusion"; (2) some strongly felt correspondence between the inner world of ideals and evils and the social world with its goals and dangers; (3) an opportunity for exhibiting some uniformity of appearance and behavior counteracting individual identity-consciousness; (4) inducement to a collective experimentation with roles and techniques which help overcome a sense of inhibition and personal guilt; (5) introduction into the ethos of the prevailing technology and thus into sanctioned and regulated competiton; (6) a geographic-historical world image as a framework for the young individual's budding identity; (7) a rationale for a sexual way of life compatible with a convincing system of principles; and (8) submission to leaders who as super-human figures or "big brothers" are above the ambivalence of the parent-child relation. Without some such *ideological commitment*, however implicit in a "way of life," youth suffers a *confusion of values* (V.8) which can be specifically dangerous to some but which on a large scale is surely dangerous to the fabric of society.

In the conclusion of a pathographic sketch, then, I have also sketched in some phenomena which are the domain of social science. I can justify this only in the belief that clinical work, in trying to arrive at some workable generalities in regard to individual pathology, may well come upon aspects of the social process which the social sciences have by necessity neglected. A psychosocial study of the case history or the life history cannot afford to neglect them. So we return, once more, to Shaw's formulation, and let it lead us to a few concluding thoughts.

II.

Shaw was a studiedly spectacular man who knowingly worked as hard on the public identity of G.B.S. as he worked on any of his stage characters. But to extend the Shavianism quoted earlier: a clown is often not only the best but also the most sincere part of the Great Show. It is, therefore, worth while at this point to review the words chosen by Shaw to characterize the story of his "conversion" as a young man:

I was *drawn into* the Socialist *revival* of the early eighties, among Englishmen *intensely serious* and *burning with indignation* at very *real* and very *fundamental evils* that affected *all the world*.

The words here italicized convey to me the following connotations. "Drawn into": an ideology has a compelling power. "Revival": consists of a traditional force in the state of rejuvenation. "Intensely serious": permits even the cynical to make an investment of sincerity. "Burning with indignation": gives to the need for repudiation the sanction of righteousness. "Real": projects a vague inner evil on a circumscribed horror in social reality. "Fundamental": promises participation in an effort at basic reconstruction of society. "All the world": gives structure to a totally defined world image. Here, then, are the elements of a group identity which harnesses the young individual's aggressive and discriminative energies in the service of an ideology and helps to stamp, as it completes, the individual's identity. Thus, identity and ideology are two aspects of the same process. Both provide the necessary condition for further individual maturation and, with it, for the next higher form of identification, namely, the solidarity linking common identities in joint living, acting, and creating.

The immediate need to combine in one ideational system both the irrational self-hate of one's negative identity and the irrational repudiation of inimical otherness makes young people, on occasion, mortally compulsive and intrinsically conservative just where and when they seem most anarchic and radical. The same need makes them highly argumentative in their search for a world image held together by what Shaw called "a clear comprehension of life in the light of an intelligible theory," although what seems intelligible often is only the logic of the past as absorbed in childhood but expressed in shockingly new terms.

As far as Fabian socialists are concerned, Shaw seems fully justified in using terms characterizing an ideology of marked intellectual brilliance. More generally, however, an ideological system is a coherent body of shared images, ideas, and ideals which, whether based on a formulated dogma, an implicit *Weltanschauung*, a highly structured world image, a political creed, or, indeed, a scientific creed (especially if applied to man), or a "way of life," provides for the participants a coherent, if systematically symplified, over-all orientation in space and time, in means and ends.

The word "ideology," of course, has a somewhat bad name. By their very nature explicit and propagandistic ideologies contradict other ideologies as "inconsistent" and hypocritical, and an over-all critique of ideology characterizes its most persuasive simplifications as a systematic form of collective pseudologia. We have no reason, however, to abandon this word to the contemporary political connotation which limits its significantly wider meaning. What could be called hypocrisy, it is true, is the other side of the coin. There could be no ideological simplification without a factual pretense which runs counter to the level of intellectual sophistication otherwise achieved. It is also true that the average adult and, in fact, the average community, if not acutely engaged in some ideological polarization, are apt to consign ideology—as soon as the shooting and the shouting are over—to a well-circumscribed compartment in their lives, where it remains handy for periodical rituals and rationalizations but will do no undue harm to other business at hand. Yet the fact that ideologies are simplified conceptions of what is to come, and thus later can serve as rationalizations for what has come about, does not preclude the possibility that at certain stages of individual development and at certain periods in history, ideological polarization leading to militant conflict and to radically new commitment corresponds to an inescapable inner need. Youth needs to base its rejections and acceptances "normally" on ideological alternatives vitally related to the existing range of alternatives for identity formation, and in periods of radical change, this essentially adolescent propensity comes to dominate the collective mind.

Ideologies, then, seem to provide meaningful combinations of the oldest and the newest in a group's ideals. They thus channel the forceful earnestness, the sincere asceticism, and the eager indignation of youth toward that social frontier where the struggle between conservatism and radicalism is most alive. On that frontier, fanatic ideologists do their busy work and psychopathic leaders their dirty work; but there, also, true leaders create significant solidarities. But ideologies must ask, as the prize for the promised possession of a future, for uncompromising commitment to some absolute hierarchy of values and some rigid principle of conduct, be that principle total obedience to tradition, if the future is the earthly kingdom of the ancestors; total resignation, if the future is to be of another world altogether; total martial discipline, if the future is reserved for some brand of armed superman; total inner reform, if the future is perceived as an advance facsimile of heaven on earth; or finally (to mention only one of the ideological ingredients of our time) complete pragmatic abandon to human teamwork and to the processes of production if unceasing production seems to hold present and future together. It is by this very totalism of ideologies that the infantile superego is apt to regain its territory from adolescent identity: for when established identities become outworn and while new ones remain vulnerable, special crises compel men to wage holy wars, by the cruelest means, against those who seem to question or threaten their as yet unsafe ideological bases.

In conclusion, we may ponder once more the over-all fact that the technological and economic developments of our day encroach upon all traditional group identities and solidarities which may have developed in agrarian, feudal, patrician, or mercantile eras. As has been shown by many writers, such over-all development seems to result in a loss of a sense of cosmic wholeness, of providential planfulness, and of heavenly sanction for the means of production—and destruction. In large parts of the world this apparently leads to a ready fascination with totalistic world views, views predicting milleniums and cataclysms and advocating self-appointed mortal gods. Technological centralization today can give small groups of such fanatic ideologists the concrete power of totalitarian state machines, and of small and secret or large and open machineries of extermination.

THIS MAY BE the place for another biographic item, namely,

the moratorium of a man whom I could not have listed with Bernard Shaw because he probably never laughed from his heart and never made anyone else laugh heartily in his life—Adolf Hitler. A man who was Hitler's one and only boyhood friend recounts how during his youth Hitler disappeared completely for two years, after which he emerged with a fanatic ideological direction.[19]

This totally anonymous moratorium, spent in extreme isolation, followed a severe disappointment in his late adolescence. As a youth, Hitler had wanted desperately to be a city planner; he walked around for days (and as if in a daze) rebuilding his hometown of Linz. To rebuild, of course, he had to imagine all the large buildings destroyed, but no doubt he tried to be "constructive" on a vast, if almost delusional, scale. It was when he finally sent his plans for a new opera house in Linz to a prize committee which paid no attention to them that he really broke with society and disappeared, to reappear only as an avenger. But in his very last days, after having destroyed much of Europe and having finally been cornered in his bunker, he carefully planned his self-liquidation, but not without putting the last touches on his plans for the opera house in Linz, which he had almost come to build. To such an eerie extent does a late-adolescent commitment persist even in a person of excessive destructive needs.

I am not suggesting here that a personality like Hitler's could have been "cured," although there are claims that he sought analytic treatment for isolated symptoms. Nor do I wish to imply that even a man like Hitler could have imposed his particular mixture of abysmal destructiveness and contructive make-believe on the world without a fateful coincidence of his evil genius with a historical catastrophe. As we saw in Chapter II, Germany's defeat and the Treaty of Versailles resulted in a widespread traumatic identity loss, especially in German youth, and thus in a historical identity confusion conducive to a state of national delinquency under the leadership of a gang of overgrown adolescents of criminal make-up. But as we ponder such national catastrophes, we should not let our abhorrence blind us to the constructive potentialities which, in a given nation, can be perverted largely by the default of other nations.

I HAVE POINTED in Chapter II to the role which technological developments have played in making this and other totalitarian undertakings so shockingly successful. But I should admit again that we know as yet little about the question of how man changes in his depth as he wields his new technological powers.

III.

Finally, a word about a new nation. I once had an opportunity in a seminar in Jerusalem to discuss with Israeli scholars and clinicians the question of what the identity of an "Israeli" is, and thus to envisage one extreme of contemporary ideological orientation.[20] Israel fascinates both her friends and her enemies. A great number of ideological fragments from European history have found their way into the consciousness of this small state, and many of the identity problems which have occupied a century and a half of American history are being faced in Israeli within a few decades. Out of oppressed minorities from many lands a new nation is established on a "frontier" which does not seem to "belong" to anybody, and a new national identity is created out of imported ideals which are libertarian, puritanic, and messianic. Any discussion of Israel's manifold and most immediate problems sooner or later leads to the extraordinary accomplishments and the extraordinary ideological problems posed by the pioneer Zionist settlers who made up what is known as the kibbutz movement. These European ideologists, given as it were a geographic-historical moratorium created by the peculiar international and national status of Palestine first in the Ottoman Empire and then in the British mandate, were able to establish and fortify a significant utopian bridgehead for Zionist ideology. In his "homeland," and tilling his very home soil, the "ingathered" Jew was to overcome such evil identities as result from eternal wandering, merchandising, and intellectual-

izing and was to become whole again in body and mind as well
as in nationality. That the kibbutz movement has created a
hardy, responsible, and inspired type of individual, nobody can
deny, although certain details of its educational system (such as
the raising of children from birth in Children's Houses and the
rooming together of boys and girls through the high school
years) are under critical scrutiny, both in Israel and abroad.
But it is senseless to apply metropolitan standards of a utopian
mental hygiene to conditions on a frontier exposed all around,
a historical fact which alone provides the framework for judging
the rationale and the rationalizations of the style of life which
ensued. For no doubt these pioneers provided a new nation,
sprung up overnight, with a historical ideal. A legitimate question, however, and one not so foreign to this country's historians, concerns the relationship of a revolutionary elite to those
who subsequently crowd into and thrive on the lands occupied
and on the gains made.[21] In Israel, the now somewhat exclusive elite of kibbutzniks—who have played in their country's
tradition a role comparable to our pioneers—faces that incom-
parably larger part of the population which represents an all but
indigestible mixture ideologically: the masses of African and
Oriental immigrants, powerful organized labor, the big-city
dwellers, the religious orthodoxy, the new state bureaucracy—
and then, of course, the "good old" mercantile class of middle-
men. Furthermore, the more uncompromising part of the kibbutz movement has not failed to place itself between the two
worlds with which Zionism maintains strong historical bonds:
American and British Jewry (which bought much of the kibbutz
land from Arab absentee landlords) and Soviet communism, to
which the communalistic Kibbutz movement[22] felt ideologically close—only to be repudiated by Moscow as another form
of deviationism.

The kibbutz movement thus is one example of a modern
ideological actuality which on the basis of what looked like
utopian ideals freed unknown energies in youths who considered
themselves as of one "people" and created a group ideal of per-

vading significance, if of quite unpredictable historical fate in an industrial world. However, Israel is, undoubtedly, one of the most ideology-conscious countries that ever existed. No "peasants" or workmen ever argued more about the logic-and-meaning of daily decisions. I think one learns most about the importance of ideology for identity formation by comparing such highly verbal and strongly institutionalized ideologies with those often unformulated and more transitory symptoms of conversion and aversion which exist as the most meaningful part of a young person's or a young group's life, without the understanding or, indeed, curiosity of the adults around them. At any rate, many of the extreme tastes, opinions, and slogans which occupy the arguments of youths anywhere, and many of the sudden impulses to join in destructive behavior, are a joint expression of historical identity fragments waiting to be tied together by some ideology.

In the pathographic section of this book I pointed to the total choice of a negative identity in individuals who could achieve such escape on the basis of autistic and regressive proclivities. The escape of many gifted if unstable young individuals into a private utopia might not be necessary were it not for a general development to which they feel unable to submit, namely, the increasing demand for conformity, uniformity, and standardization which characterizes the present stage of this, our "individualistic" civilization. In this country the demand for large-scale conformity has not developed into explicit totalitarian ideologies; so far it shuns political ideology and associates itself instead with the puritan dogmas of churches and with the stereotypes of businesslike behavior. As we study it we appreciate the capacity of our youth to manage the identity confusion of an industrial democracy with simple trustfulness, playful dissonance, technical virtuosity, "other-minded" solidarity—and a distaste for ideological explicitness. What exactly the implicit ideology of American youth, this most technological youth in the world, is—that is a fateful question, not to be rightly approached in a book of this kind. Nor would one dare to assess in passing the changes which may be taking place in this implicit ideology as a result of a world struggle which makes a military identity a part of young adulthood in peacetime.

As yet it is easier to delineate that malignant turn toward a negative group identity which prevails in some of the youth, especially in our large cities, where conditions of economic, ethnic, and religious marginality provide poor bases for positive identities. There negative group identities are sought in spontaneous clique formations ranging all the way from neighborhood gangs to dope rings, homosexual circles, and criminal gangs. Clinical experience can be expected to make significant contributions to this problem. Yet we may well warn ourselves against an uncritical transfer of clinical terms, attitudes, and methods to such public problems. Rather, we may come back to a point made earlier. Teachers, judges, and psychiatrists who deal with youth come to be significant representatives of that strategic act of "recognition," the act through which society "identifies" and "confirms" its young members and thus contributes to their developing identity, which was described at the beginning of this book. If, for simplicity's sake or in order to accommodate ingrown habits of law or psychiatry, they diagnose and treat as a criminal, as a constitutional misfit, as a derelict doomed by his upbringing, or indeed as a deranged patient a young person who, for reasons of personal or social marginality, is close to choosing a negative identity, that young person may well put his energy into becoming exactly what the careless and fearful community expects him to be—and make a total job of it.

It is hoped that the theory of identity, in the long run, can contribute more to this problem than a warning. Nor do I propose to leave the matter in this condition: studies taking into account the specific dynamic nature of selected media—case history, life history, history, dream life—must follow.[23]

5. BIOGRAPHIC II: THE CONFUSION RETURNS— PSYCHOPATHOLOGY OF EVERY NIGHT

At the beginning of this book I quoted two men, Sigmund Freud and William James, who seem to me to have formulated forcefully and poetically what a vital sense of identity feels (or should I say, felt) like. They can now help us to look again "beyond identity." For it so happens that both of these men have recorded and reported dreams which illustrate the return of a sense of identity confusion and the restoration of the late-adolescent identity in dream life. Dreams, of course, are the most sensitive indicators of an individual's continuing struggles with earlier crises, and in all those individuals who have successfully mastered other regressions, the identity crisis remains to be re-lived in succeeding crises of later life, but "subliminally" and in symbolical acts which at the most may belong to the psycho-pathology of every day—or every night. Such reliving pre-supposes, of course, that the identity crisis was once lived through and that its basic formulae have survived sufficiently to be restored by normal means. Freud's dream illustrates an iden-tity problem in the stage of generativity, James's in that of old-age despair.[24]

I. FREUD'S DREAM OF IRMA

After having quoted Freud's declaration of the "positive" identity which bound him to Judaism—i.e., the identity of one who, gifted with an uninhibited intelligence, works in self-chosen isolation from "the compact majority"—I indicated that we may recognize in another singular confession, namely, Freud's analysis of his dream of his patient Irma,[25] the traces of the corresponding *negative identity* which, by definition, fol-lows the positive one like a shadow. Now Freud had the Irma dream when he was about to enter the fifth decade of his life, to which we would ascribe the generativity crisis—and indeed, as I have pointed out elsewhere,[26] the Irma dream is concerned with a middle-aged man's cares, with the question of how much of what he has started he can also take care of, and whether or not he is not at times too careless to be able to sustain his ambi-tions. I will excerpt from the earlier paper only such items as will serve to indicate the reliving of an identity crisis in the terms of this later crisis.

It is, first of all, important to relate the dream to the moment in Freud's life when it was dreamed—the moment when creative thought gave birth to the interpretation of dreams. For the dream of Irma owes its significance not only to the fact that it was the first dream reported elaborately in *The Interpretation of Dreams*. In a letter sent to his friend Fliess, Freud indulges in a fancy of a possible tablet which (he wonders) may some day adorn his summer home. Its inscription would tell the world that "In this house, on July 24, 1895, the Mystery of the Dream unveiled itself to Dr. Sigm. Freud."[27] The date is that of the Irma dream.

Here, then, was a thirty-nine-year-old doctor, a specialist in neurology in the city of Vienna. He was a Jewish citizen of a Catholic monarchy which was once the Holy Roman Empire of German nationality and now swayed both by liberalism and increasing anti-Semitism. His family had grown rapidly; in fact, his wife at the time was again pregnant. The dreamer just then wished to fortify his position and, in fact, his income by gaining academic status. The wish had become problematic, not only because he was a Jew but also because in a recent joint publication with an older colleague, Dr. Breuer, he had committed himself to theories so unpopular and universally disturbing that the senior co-author himself had disengaged himself from the junior one. The book in question, *Studies in Hysteria*, had emphasized the role of sexuality in the etiology of the "defense neuropsychoses," i.e., nervous disorders caused by the necessity of defending consciousness against repugnant and repressed ideas primarily of a sexual nature. The junior worker felt increasingly committed to these ideas; he had begun to feel, with a pride often overshadowed by despair, that he was destined to make a revolutionary discovery by "undreamed-of" means.

It had occurred to Freud by then that the dream was, in fact, a normal equivalent of a hysterical attack, "a little defense neuropsychosis." In the history of psychiatry, the comparison of normal phenomena with abnormal ones was not new: the Greeks had called orgasm "a little epilepsy." But if hysterical symptoms, if even dreams, were based on inner conflict, on an involuntary defense against unconscious thoughts, what justification was there for blaming patients for the fact that they could not easily accept, long remember, or consistently utilize the interpretations which the psychiatrist offered them? It was soon to dawn on Freud that in order to give shape to these tools, a basic shift from physiologic concepts to purely psychological ones, and from authoritative medical techniques to emphatic and intuitive observation, even to self-observation, was necessary.

This, then, is the situation: within an academic milieu which seemed to restrict his opportunities because he was a Jew; at an age when he seemed to notice with alarm the first signs of aging, and, in fact, of disease; burdened with the responsibility for a fast-growing family—a medical scientist is faced with the decision of whether to employ his brilliance, as he had shown he could, in the service of conventional practice and research or to accept the task of substantiating in himself and of communicating to the world a new insight, namely, that man is demonstrably unconscious of the best and of the worst in himself. Soon after the Irma dream, Freud was to write to his friend Fliess with undisguised horror that in trying to explain psychological defense he had found himself explaining something "out of the core of nature." At the time of this dream, then, he knew that he would have to bear a great discovery—and "bear" here has a "pregnant" double meaning. The question, then, was whether he should live up to the core of his identity—that very core later formulated as the fate of the lone investigator discarding the support of the "compact majority." But, of course, his future work was already *in statu nascendi*, and, at any rate, he could not seriously doubt his commitment—except in his dreams.

The evening before the dream was dreamed, Freud had an experience which had painfully spotlighted his inner doubts. He had met a colleague, "Otto," who had just returned from a summer resort. There he had seen a mutual friend, a young woman, who was Freud's patient: "Irma." This patient, by Freud's effort, had been cured of hysterical anxiety but not of certain somatic symptoms, such as intense retching. Before going on vacation Freud had offered her an interpretation as the solution of her problems, but she had been unable to accept it. Now Freud apparently had heard some reproach in Otto's voice regarding the condition of the patient who appeared "better, but not well"; and behind the reproach he thought he detected the stern authority of "Dr. M.," a man who was "the leading personality in our circle." On his return home, and under the impression of the encounter, Freud had written a lengthy case report for "Dr. M." explaining his views on Irma's illness.

He had apparently gone to bed with a feeling that this report would settle matters so far as his own peace of mind was concerned. Yet that very night the personages concerned in this incident, namely, Irma, Dr. M., Dr. Otto, and another doctor, Dr. Leopold, constituted themselves the population of a dream.

A great hall—a number of guests, whom we are receiving—among them Irma, whom I immediately take aside, as though to answer her letter, and to reproach her for not yet accepting the "solution" [his interpretation]. . . . She answers: "If you only knew what pains I have."

The concerned dreamer now takes the patient in a corner, looks into her throat, and, indeed, finds somatic symptoms which puzzle him.

I quickly call Dr. M., who repeats the examination and confirms it. . . . Now, my friend, Otto, too, is standing beside her, and my friend Leopold percusses her covered chest and says: "She has a dullness below, on the left," and also calls attention to an infiltrated portion of skin on the left shoulder (which I can feel [the dreamer means: on his own body] in spite of the dress). M. says, "There's no doubt that it's an infection, but it doesn't matter; dysentery will follow and the poison will be eliminated." . . . We know, too, precisely (unmittelbar) how the infection originated. My friend, Otto, not long ago, gave her, when she was feeling unwell, an injection of a preparation of propyl . . . propyls . . . propionic acid . . . trimethylamin (the formula of which I see before me, printed in heavy type). . . . One doesn't give such injections so rashly. . . . Probably, too, the syringe was not clean.

A doctor's dream, then, and one about a medical circle. Freud at the time used this dream in order to explain the fact that dreams fulfill wishes.

... For the result of the dream is that it is not I who am to blame for the pain which Irma is still suffering, but that Otto is to blame for it. ... The whole plea—for this dream is nothing else—recalls vividly the defense offered by a man who was accused by his neighbor of having returned a kettle in a damaged condition. In the first place, he said, he had returned the kettle undamaged; in the second place, it already had holes in it when he borrowed it; and in the third place, he had never borrowed it at all.

The implication seen in Dr. Otto's remark on the preceding evening, namely, that the dreamer may be a careless doctor, had apparently awakened infantile feelings of unworthiness. But as we can now see, they had also put in question the tenets of his identity, namely, his sanction to work and think independently. For Irma is not "just a patient," she was a test case. And Freud's interpretation of hysteria was not just another diagnostic category, it was to be the breakthrough to an altered image of man. For higher sanction, however, man looks to compact ritual, and I submit (radically excerpting for this purpose) that in the Irma dream (as in equally significant "creative" dreams such as Descartes's dream trilogy) we can recognize the outlines of a ritual joining, a dream-rite, which brings to the troubled dreamer the sanction for sinfully original ideas, here from the same colleagues who, on another level of the dream, are ridiculed and, in life, resisted. I will paraphrase the dream once more, and add in parentheses what I suggest is the outline of a ritual.

The *festive occasion* (ceremonial gathering), the *pronounced We-ness* (congregation), and the dreamer's dominant position (we receive) give to the beginning of the dream a ceremonial setting which, however, is soon lost in the concern over the patient (isolation, self-blame). A mood of urgency takes over. The dreamer *quickly calls* Dr. M. (appeal to higher authority). This call for help is answered not only by Dr. M., but also by Dr. Leopold and Dr. Otto (ordained circle). As the examination of the patient proceeds, the dreamer suddenly feels, and feels on *his own body*, one of the patient's symptoms. The doctor and man thus fuses with the *patient* and *woman*, that is, he becomes the *sufferer* and the *examined* (prostration, submission). By implication, it is now he that is open for *inspection* (trial, confession). Dr. M. recites with great assurance something senseless (ritual formula, Latin, Hebrew) which seems to be *magically effective* in that it awakes in the dreamer and the dream population the *immediate conviction* (revelation) that the *causality* in the case is now understood (magic, divine will). This common conviction restores in the dream an intellectual (spiritual) *"We-ness"* (communion, congregation) which had been lost when the dreamer's wife and the festive guests had disappeared. At the same time it restores to the dreamer a *belongingness* (brotherhood) to a hierarchic group *dominated by an authority* (priest) in whom *he believes implicitly* (faith). He immediately benefits from his newly won state of grace: he sees a *formula* before him (revelatory apparition) *printed in heavy type* (truth), and he now has sanction for turning all blame on Dr. O. (the infidel). With the *righteous indignation* which is the believer's reward and weapon, he can now mark his erstwhile accuser as a careless doctor (an unclean one).

The presence of these ritual parallels in Freud's dream suggests questions which I will not try to answer here. Freud, of course, had grown up as a member of a Jewish community in a predominantly Catholic culture: could the over-all milieu of the Catholic environment have impressed itself on this child of a minority? Much speaks for this. Freud informs Fliess that during a most critical period in his childhood—namely, when he, the "first-born son of a young mother," had to accept the arrivals of a brother and a sister—an old and superstitiously religious Czech woman used to take him around to various churches in his home town.[28] He obviously was so impressed with such events that when he came home he (in the words of his mother) preached to his family and showed them how God carries on (*"wie Gott macht"*); this apparently referred to the priest, whom he took to be God. And yet the described configuration is representative of a basic ritual which has found collective expression in other religions, Jewish, Catholic or otherwise. At any rate, the dreamer of the Irma dream can be shown both to belittle and yet also temporarily seek membership in a "compact" majority, in this case, the medical world which doubted him. The dream at the same time defends him against their reproaches, permits him to join them in a mock ritual, and reaffirms his daytime preoccupation, namely, the strong urge to investigate, unveil, and recognize—the cornerstone of the dreamer's identity.

For it was in Freud's youth (as he recounts, on hearing Goethe's "Ode to Nature") that the "naturalist" ideology replaced all the religiosity in him which may have been temporarily awakened by Judaism or (in his earliest childhood) by all-engulfing Catholicism. And if we seem to recognize in this dream of an aging man something of a puberty rite, we probably touch on a matter mentioned more than once in Freud's letters, that is, the "repeated adolescence" of creative minds. The creative mind seems to face more than once what most men, once and for all, settle in late adolescence or young adulthood. The "normal" individual combines the various prohibitions and challenges of the ego ideal in a sober, modest, and workable unit more or less well consolidated in a set of techniques and in the roles which go with them. The restless individual and, above all, the original one must, for better or for worse, alleviate a persistently revived Oedipal guilt by the reassertion of his unique identity. Yet where the *positive identity* may be allied with highest ideals leading, as in Freud's case, to a new form of dogmatic and ritual association (the psychoanalytic technique, the "psychoanalytic movement," and psychoanalytic institutes), the *negative identity* has its roots in the types despised in childhood. A careful reading of Freud's dreams makes it clear that the negative identity he had to live down (or dream down) is something akin to the Jewish *Schlemiel* or the German *Dummkopf*. At any rate, one of the most pervasive and influential events of his early life (according to the *Interpretation of Dreams*) was his father's declaration—under especially embarrassing circumstances, namely, the boy's urinating in an inappropriate place—that "that boy is never going to amount to anything." In the Irma dream, then, the grown man who was just about to amount to quite something had to struggle with this "curse," and this primarily, one suspects, because amounting to something after all was a defeat of his father's prediction—a defeat, of course, fervently hoped for by many fathers who challenge their little boys by shaming them.

II. WILLIAM JAMES'S TERMINAL DREAM

To return to the second of our great initial witnesses we will quote [29] what is probably the most incisive report of an identity confusion in dreams—incisive no doubt just because the dreamer could reassert his positive identity, that of a researcher, and remember and record the dream the next day. The date of *his* dream is important, too, for it was probably the last dream recorded and certainly the last publicly reported in James's life; he died half a year later at the age of sixty-four. No wonder, then, that in this dream identity confusion is part of an inner storm denoting a loss of hold on the world—the kind of storm which Shakespeare in *King Lear*, according to dramatic laws of representation, projects on nature and yet clearly marks as an inner storm. James had this dream in a period when he was seeking to break out from the bonds of "natural" psychology and to understand certain mystical states in which man transcends his own boundaries. He complains, however, that this dream was the "exact opposite of mystical illumination" and thus permits us to claim it as a product of the conflict between man's lasting hopes for a higher Integrity and his terminal despair.

In fact, James illustrates much of what we have been saying here in descriptive terms so close to our generalizations that it seems necessary to say that this dream came to my attention only recently. No doubt, however—and this is why I had reason to refer to him in the introduction to the Harvard doctors' book on emotional problems among students [30]—James knew from personal experience what we have described as "borderline" psychotic states in these pages. However, apparently, he never came as close to a truly psychotic experience as in this dream—a fact which I ascribe to the depth of "ultimate concerns" at this stage of his life.

I despair of giving the reader any just idea of the bewildering confusion of mind into which I was thrown by this, the most intensely peculiar experience of my whole life. I wrote a full memorandum of it a couple of days after it happened and appended some reflections. Even though it should cast no light on the conditions of mysticism, it seems as if this record might be worthy of publication, simply as a contribution to the descriptive literature of pathological mental states. I let it follow, therefore, as originally written, with only a few words altered to make the account more clear.

Since I would not wish to interrupt this account with astonished comments, I will ask the reader to take note of the clarity with which the characteristics of an acute identity confusion appear in this dream: the discontinuity of time and space; the twilight between waking and sleeping; the loss of ego boundaries and, with it, the experience of being dreamed by the dream rather than actively "having" it; and many other criteria which will occur to the reader:

San Francisco, Feb. 14th 1906.—The night before last, in my bed at Stanford University, I woke at about 7:30 A.M., from a quiet dream of some sort, and whilst "gathering my waking wits," seemed suddenly to get mixed up with reminiscences of a dream of an entirely different sort, which seemed to telescope, as it were, into the first one, a dream very elaborate, of lions, and tragic. I concluded this to have been a previous dream of the same sleep; but the apparent mingling of two dreams was something very queer, which I had never before experienced.

On the following night (Feb. 12–13) I awoke suddenly from my first sleep, which appeared to have been very heavy, in the middle of a dream, in thinking of which I became suddenly confused by the contents of two other dreams that shuffled themselves abruptly in between the parts of the first dream, and of which I couldn't grasp the origin. Whence come *these dreams?* I asked. They were close to *me,* and fresh, as if I had just dreamed them; and yet they were far away *from the first dream.* The contents of the three had absolutely no connection. One had a cockney atmosphere, it had happened to someone in London. The other two were American. One involved the trying on of a coat (was this the dream I seemed to wake from?) the other was a sort of nightmare and had to do with soldiers. Each had a wholly distinct emotional atmosphere that made its individuality discontinuous with that of the others. And yet, in a moment, as these three dreams alternately telescoped into and out of each other, and I seemed to myself to have been their common dreamer, they seemed quite as distinctly *not* to have been dreamed in succession, in that one sleep. *When*, then? Not on a previous night, either. *When*, then, and *which* was the one out of which I had just awakened? I *could no longer tell:* one was as close to me as the others, and yet they entirely repelled each other, and I seemed thus to belong to three different dream-systems at once, no one of which would connect itself either with the others or with my waking life. I began to feel curiously confused and *scared*, and tried to wake myself up wider, but I seemed already wide-awake. Presently cold shivers of dread ran over me: *am I getting into other people's dreams?* Is this a "telepathic" experience? Or an invasion of double (or treble) personality? Or is it a thrombus in a cortical artery? and the beginning of a general mental "confusion" and disorientation which is going on to develop who knows how far?

Decidedly I was losing hold of my "self," and making acquaintance with a quality of mental distress that I had never known before, its nearest analogue being the sinking, giddying anxiety that one may have when, in the woods, one discovers that one is really "lost." Most human troubles look towards a terminus. Most fears point in a direction and concentrate towards a climax. Most assaults of the evil one may be met by bracing oneself against something, one's principles, one's courage, one's will, one's pride. But in this experience all was diffusion from a centre, and foothold swept away, the brace itself disintegrating all the faster as one needed its support more direly. Meanwhile vivid perception (or remembrance) of the various dreams kept coming over me in alternation. Whose? *whose?* WHOSE? Unless I can *attach* them, I am swept out to sea with no horizon and no bond, getting *lost*. The idea aroused the "creeps" again, and with it the fear of again falling alseep and renewing the process. It had begun the previous night, but then the confusion had only gone one step, and had seemed simply curious. *This* was the second step—where might I be after a third step had been taken?

And now to that aspect of the account which, I feel, reinstates (as did Freud's dream) the dreamer's *activity* in the terms of his professional identity. Having come close to being a "patient" and feeling close to life's "terminus," he now assumes the psychologist's prerogative of "objective" empathy and systematic compassion, and this, at first, in words with which we would have been more than glad to conclude our own description of identity confusion:

At the same time I found myself filled with a new pity towards persons passing into dementia with *Verwirrtheit*, or into invasions of secondary personality. *We* regard them as simply *curious;* but what *they* want in

the awful drift of their being out of its customary self, is any principle of
steadiness to hold on to. We ought to assure them and reassure them that
we will stand by them, and recognize the true self in them, to the end.
We ought to let them know that we are with *them* and not (as too often
we must seem to them) a part of the world that but confirms and pub-
lishes their deliquescence.

Evidently I was in full possession of my reflective wits; and whenever I
thus objectively thought of the situation in which I was, my anxieties
ceased. But there was a tendency to relapse into the dreams and reminiscences, and to relapse vividly; and then the confusion recommenced,
along with the emotion of dread lest it should develop farther.

Then I looked at my watch. Half-past twelve! Midnight, therefore.
And this gave me another reflective idea. Habitually, on going to bed, I
fall into a very deep slumber from which I never naturally awaken until
after two. I never awaken, therefore, from a midnight dream, as I did to-
night, so of midnight dreams my ordinary consciousness retains no recol-
lection. My sleep seemed terribly heavy as I woke to-night. Dream states
carry dream memories—why may not the two succedaneous dreams
(whichever two of the three *were* succedaneous) be memories of *twelve
o'clock dreams of previous nights*, swept in, along with the just-fading
dream, into the just-waking system of memory? Why, in short, may I
not be tapping in a way precluded by my ordinary habit of life, *the midnight stratum* of my past?

This idea gave great relief—I felt now as if I were in full possession of
my *anima rationalis* . . . it seems, therefore, merely as if the threshold
between the rational and the morbid state had, in my case, been temporarily lowered, and as if similar confusions might be very near the line of
possibility in all of us.

And even as one often feels (and especially in the case of the
Irma dream) that Freud's dreams were dreamed to reveal the
nature of dreams, so James ends by reporting that this dream,
which was "the exact opposite of mystical illumination," was
permeated with "the sense that reality was being uncovered"—a
sense which he found in itself to be"mystical in the highest
degree." And, in his eagerness for and closeness to transcendence, he ended by feeling that his dream had been dreamed "in
reality"—by another "I," by a mysterious stranger.

CHAPTER
V

Theoretical Interlude

I MUST NOW ASK a few theoretical questions—questions which it took a decade to formulate—of my colleagues and of those students of human behavior who are sympathetically close to our clinical and theoretical concerns. This is, by now, an unfathomably large group; but not every reader may find all of this chapter congenial to his experience and interest.

1. EGO AND ENVIRONMENT

So far I have tried out the term identity almost deliberately—I like to think—in many different connotations. At one time it seemed to refer to a conscious sense of individual uniqueness, at another to an unconscious striving for a continuity of experience, and at a third, as a solidarity with a group's ideals. In some respects the term appeared to be colloquial and naïve, a mere manner of speaking, while in others it was related to existing concepts in psychoanalysis and sociology. And on more than one occasion the word slipped in more like a habit that seems to make things appear familiar than as a clarification. I must now come back once more to the concept of ego because when I first reported on the subject (in "A Clinician's Notebook" in Chapter II) I called what I was exploring Ego-Identity.

Identity in its vaguest sense suggests, of course, much of what has been called the self by a variety of workers, be it in the form of a self-concept,[1] a self-system,[2] or in that of fluctuating self-experience described by Schilder,[3] Federn,[4] and others. Within psychoanalytic ego psychology, Hartmann, above all, has circumscribed this general area more clearly when, in discussing the so-called libidinal cathexis of the ego in narcissism, he comes to the conclusion that it is rather a self which is thus being cathected. He advocates the term "self-representation," as differentiated from "object representation." [5] This self-representation was, less systematically, anticipated by Freud in his occasional references to the ego's "attitudes toward the self" and to fluctuating cathexes bestowed upon this self in labile states of "self-esteem." [6]

Here we are at first concerned with the genetic continuity of such a self-representation, a continuity which must certainly be ascribed to the work of the ego. No other inner agency could accomplish the selective accentuation of significant identifications throughout childhood and the gradual integration of self-images which culminates in a sense of identity. It is for this reason that I at first called identity "ego identity." In choosing a name analogous to "ego ideal," however, I have raised the question of the relationship of ego ideal and ego identity.

Freud assigned the internalization of environmental influences to the functions of the "superego or ego ideal" which was to represent the commands and the prohibitions emanating from the environment and its traditions. Let us compare two statements of Freud's which are relevant here.

The super-ego of the child is not really built up on the model of the parents, but on that of the parents' super-ego; it takes over the same content, it becomes the vehicle of tradition and of all the age-long values which have been handed down in this way from generation to generation. You may easily guess what great help is afforded by the recognition of the super-ego in understanding the social behavior of man, in grasping the problem of delinquency, for example, and perhaps, too, in providing us with some practical hints upon education. . . . Mankind never lives completely in the present. The ideologies of the super-ego perpetuate the past, the traditions of the race and the people, which yield but slowly to the influence of the present and to new developments, and, as long as they work through the super-ego, play an important part in man's life.[7]

Freud, it is to be noted here, speaks of the "ideologies of the super-ego," thus giving the superego ideational content; yet he also refers to it as a "vehicle," i.e., as a part of the psychic system through which such traditional ideals work. It would seem that by ideologies of the superego Freud means to define something prerational, in line with the superego's affinities to the archaic, and that at the same time he ascribes a magic inner coerciveness to them. But he obviously also uses the term "ideology" differently from its exclusively political usage, as I, in turn, have attempted to approach the ideological as a psychological fact and need related to, but not explained by, political phenomena.

In a second statement Freud also acknowledges the social side of the ego ideal.

The ego-ideal is of great importance for the understanding of group psychology. Besides its individual side, this ideal has a social side; it is also the common ideal of a family, a class, or a nation.[8]

It would seem that here the terms superego and ego ideal have come to be distinguished by their different relation to the onto-genetic and the phylogenetic history of the race. The superego is conceived as a more archaic, more thoroughly internalized and more unconscious representative of man's inborn proclivity toward the development of a primitive, categorical conscience. Allied with early introjects, the superego thus remains a rigidly vindictive and punitive inner agency of "blind" morality. The ego ideal, however, seems to be more flexibly and consciously bound to the ideals of the particular historical era as absorbed in childhood. It is closer to the ego function of reality testing: ideals can change.

What I once called ego identity would in comparison be even closer to changing social reality in that it would test, select, and integrate the self-images derived from the psychosocial crises of childhood in the light of the ideological climate of youth. While the imagery of the ego ideal could be said to represent a set of to-be-striven-for but forever not-quite-attainable ideal goals for the Self, ego identity could be said to be characterized by the actually attained but forever to-be-revised sense of the reality of the Self within social reality.

However, in using the word self in the sense of Hartmann's self-representation, one opens this terminology to a radical consideration. The ego, if understood as a central and partially unconscious organizing agency, must at any given stage of life deal with a changing Self which demands to be synthesized with abandoned and anticipated selves. This suggestion would be applicable to the body ego, which could be said to be that part of the Self provided by the experience of one's body and, therefore, might more appropriately be called the *body self*. It concerns the ego ideal as the representative of the ideas, images, and configurations which serve the persistent comparison with an *ideal self*. It, finally, would apply to part of what I have called ego identity, namely, that part which consists of role images. What could consequently be called the *self-identity* emerges from experiences in which temporarily confused selves are successfully reintegrated in an ensemble of roles which also secure social recognition. Identity formation, thus, can be said to have a self-aspect and an ego aspect.

Ego-Identity, then, is the result of the synthesizing function on one of the ego's frontiers, namely, that "environment" which is social reality as transmitted to the child during successive childhood crises. Identity, in this connection, has a claim to recognition as the adolescent ego's most important accomplishment in that it helps simultaneously in the containing of the postpubertal id and in the balancing of the then newly invoked superego as well as the appeasing of the often rather lofty ego ideal—all in the light of a foreseeable future structured by an ideological world image. One can then speak of ego identity when one discusses the ego's synthesizing power in the light of its central psychosocial function, and of self-identity when the integration of the individual's self- and role-images are under discussion.

This may be the place to discuss briefly my replacement of the term identity diffusion with that of identity confusion. The wrong connotations of the first term have been repeatedly pointed out to me, and this especially by anthropologist friends. To them the commonest meaning of the term diffusion is a strictly spatial one: a centripetal distribution of elements from a center of origin. In culture diffusion, for example, a technological object, an art form, or a linguistic item may have been transferred by way of migration or steplike transmission from one culture to another far away. In this use of the term, nothing disorderly or confused is implied. In identity diffusion, however, a split of self-images is suggested, a loss of center and a dispersion. This last word might have been a better choice, although dispersion would again suggest that an identity may be transmitted from one to many rather than falling apart within itself, while confusion is perhaps too radical a word; a young individual may be in a state of mild identity diffusion without feeling thoroughly confused.

But since confusion is obviously the better word for both the subjective and the objective aspects of the state to be described, it will be best to emphasize "mild" confusion on one end of the continuum and "aggravated" and "malignant" confusion at the other.

2. CONFUSION, TRANSFERENCE, AND RESISTANCE

This would seem to be the place to approach the whole matter from the traditional focus of clinical observation.

On facing therapy, some patients undergo a phase of particular malignancy. While the depth of regression and the danger of acting out must, of course, guide our diagnostic decisions, it is important to recognize, from the start, a mechanism present in such turns for the worse: I would call it the "rock-bottom attitude." This consists of the patient's quasideliberate surrender to the pull of regression, a radical search for the rock-bottom—i.e., both the ultimate limit of regression and the only firm foundation for a renewed progression. The assumption of such a deliberate search for the "base line" seems to carry Ernst Kris's "regression in the service of the ego" to a dangerous extreme. But the fact that the recovery of our patients sometimes coincides with the discovery of previously hidden artistic gifts suggests further study of this very point.

The element of deliberateness added here to "true" regression is often expressed in pervasive mockery which characterizes the initial therapeutic contact with these patients and by that strange air of sadomasochistic satisfaction which often makes it hard to see and harder to believe that their self-depreciation and their willingness to "let the ego die" harbor a devastating sincerity. As one patient said: "That people do not know how to succeed is bad enough. But the worst is that they do not know how to fail. I have decided to fail well." This almost "deadly" sincerity is to be found in the patient's very determination to trust nothing but mistrust, and yet to watch from a dark corner of the mind (and, indeed, often from the corner of an eye) for new experiences simple and forthright enough to permit a renewal of the most basic experiments in trustful mutuality. The therapist, manifestly faced with a mocking and defiant young adult, actually must take over the task (but not the "posture") of a mother who introduces a baby to life's trustworthiness. In the center of the treatment is the patient's need to redelineate himself and thus rebuild the foundation of his identity. At the beginning these delineations shift abruptly, even as violent shifts in the patient's experience of his ego boundary take place before our eyes. The patient's mobility may suddenly undergo a "catatonic" slow-down; his attentiveness may turn into overwhelming sleepiness; his vasomotor system may overreact to the point of producing sensations of fainting; his sense of reality may yield to feelings of depersonalization; or the remnants of his self-assurance may disappear in a miasmic loss of a sense of physical presence. Cautious but firm inquiry will reveal the probability that a number of contradictory impulses preceded the "attack." There is first a sudden intense impulse to destroy the therapist completely, accompanied, it seems, by an underlying "cannibalistic" wish to devour his essence and his identity. At the same time, or in alternation, there may be a fear and a wish to be devoured, thus to gain an identity by being absorbed in the therapist's essence. Both tendencies, of course, are often dissimilated or somatized for long periods, during which they find covert expression only after the therapeutic hour. This manifestation may be an impulsive flight into sexual promiscuity acted out without sexual satisfaction or any sense of participation; enormously absorbing rituals of masturbation or food intake; excessive drinking or wild driving; or self-destructive marathons of reading or listening to music without thought of food or sleep.

We see here the most extreme form of what may be called identity resistance which, as such, far from being restricted to the patients described here, is a universal form of resistance regularly experienced but often unrecognized in the course of some analyses. Identity resistance is, in its milder and more usual forms, the patient's fear that the analyst, because of his particular personality, background, or philosophy, may carelessly or deliberately destroy the weak core of the patient's identity and impose instead his own. I would not hesitate to say that some of the much-discussed unsolved transference neuroses in patients, as well as in candidates in training, is the direct result of the fact that the identity resistance often is, at best, analyzed only quite unsystematically. In such cases the analysand may resist throughout the analysis any possible inroad on his identity of the analyst's values while surrendering on all other points; or the patient may absorb more of the analyst's identity than is manageable within his own means; or he may leave the analysis with a lifelong sense of not having been provided with something essential owed him by the analyst.

In cases of acute identity confusion, this identity resistance becomes the core problem of the therapeutic encounter. Variations of psychoanalytic technique have this one problem in common: the dominant resistance must be accepted as the main guide to technique, and interpretation must be fitted to the patient's ability to utilize it. In these cases the patient sabotages communication until he has settled some basic—if contradictory—issues. The patient insists that the therapist accept his negative identity as real and necessary—which it is, or rather was—without concluding that this negative identity is "all there is to him." If the therapist is able to fulfill both these demands, he must prove patiently through many severe crises that he can maintain understanding and affection for the patient without either devouring him or offering himself for a totem meal. Only then can better-known forms of transference, if ever so reluctantly, emerge.

These are nothing more than a few hints regarding the phenomenology of identity confusion as reflected in the most outstanding and immediate transferences and resistances. Individual treatment, however, is only one facet of therapy in the cases under discussion. The transferences of these patients remain diffused, while their acting out remains a constant danger. Some, therefore, need to undergo treatment in a hospital environment in which their stepping out of the therapeutic relationship can be observed and limited and in which first steps beyond the newly won bipolar relationship to the therapist meet with the immediate support of sympathetic but firm nurses, co-operative fellow patients, and competent instructors in a sufficiently wide choice of activities.

In a hospital setting, the patient's progress can be charted from a determined "oneliness" (as the young woman patient put it), through his attempts to exploit and provoke the hospital environment and his growing ability to utilize it, and finally to his growing capacity to leave this kind of institutionalized moratorium and return to his old or new place in society. The hospital community makes it possible for the clinical researcher to be a participant observer not only in the individual patient's personal treatment, but also in the "therapeutic design" which is to meet the legitimate demands of patients who share a life problem—in this case, identity confusion. It stands to reason that such a common problem receives elucidation as the hospital community adapts to the difficulties specifically aggravated by it. In this case the hospital becomes a planfully institutionalized world-between-worlds; it offers the young individual support in the rebuilding of those most vital ego functions which —as far as he ever built them—he has relinquished. The relationship to the individual therapist is the cornerstone for the establishment of a new and honest mutuality of function which must set the patient's face toward an ever so dimly perceived and ever so strenuously refuted future. Yet it is the hospital community in which the patient's first steps of renewed social experimentation take place. For this reason a program of activities—not "occupational therapy"—is of primary importance, a program which permits each patient to develop talents under the guidance of professional instructors who themselves pursue their craft with full commitment but who do not force the patient into any premature occupational decisions. It is especially urgent that the patient submit as soon as possible to the privileges and obligations of a communal design which will strive to meet his fellow patients' needs as well—and, incidentally, also those of the staff. For it stands to reason that a communal setting such as a hospital is characterized not only by the identity needs of those who happen to be the patients, but also of those who choose to become their brothers' and sisters' keepers. There is much discussion of the ways in which the professional hierarchy distributes the functions, rewards, and status of such keepership and opens the door to a variety of countertransferences and "cross-transferences" which, indeed, make the hospital a facsimile of a home. From the present point of view, such studies also reveal the danger of the patient's choosing the very role of a patient as the basis of his crystallizing identity, for this role may well prove more meaningful than any potential identity experienced before.

3. I, MY SELF, AND MY EGO

In order to clarify and even quantify man's attitudes toward himself, philosophers and psychologists have created such nouns as the "I" or the "Self," making imaginary entities out of a manner of speaking. Habits of syntax, it seems to me, say much about this obscure subject.

No one who has worked with autistic children will ever forget the horror of observing how desperately they struggle to grasp the meaning of saying "I" and "You" and how impossible it is for them, for language presupposes the experience of a coherent "I." By the same token, work with deeply disturbed young people confronts the worker with the awful awareness of the patients' incapacity to *feel* the "I" and the "You" which are cognitively present and of the fear that life may run out before such feeling has been experienced—in love. No other affliction makes it equally clear that ego psychology alone cannot encompass certain central human problems which so far have been left to poetry or metaphysics.

What the "I" reflects on when it sees or contemplates the body, the personality, and the roles to which it is attached for life—not knowing where it was before or will be after—are the various selves which make up our composite Self. There are constant and often shocklike transitions between these selves: consider the nude body self in the dark or suddenly exposed in the light; consider the clothed self among friends or in the company of higher-ups or lower-downs; consider the just awakened drowsy self or the one stepping refreshed out of the surf or the one overcome by retching and fainting; the body self in sexual excitement or in a rage; the competent self and the impotent one; the one on horseback, the one in the dentist's chair, and the one chained and tortured—by men who also say "I." It takes, indeed, a healthy personality for the "I" to be able to speak out of all of these conditions in such a way that at any given moment it can testify to a reasonably coherent Self.

The counterplayers of the "selves" are the "others," with which the "I" compares the selves continually—for better and for worse. It is for this reason also that I would follow Heinz Hartmann's suggestion that psychoanalysts discontinue the use of the word "ego" when they mean the self as the object of the "I," and, for example, speak of an ideal self rather than an ego-ideal as the image of what we would like our self to be like, and of self-identity rather than ego identity insofar as the "I" perceives its selves as continuous in time and uniform in substance. For if the "I" admires the image of its body self (as Narcissus did), it is not in love with its ego (for otherwise Narcissus might have kept his balance) but with one of its selves, the mirrored body self as perceived by autoerotized eyes.

Only after we have separated the "I" and the selves from the ego can we consign to the ego that domain which it has had ever since it came from neurology into psychiatry and psychology in Freud's earliest days: the domain of an inner "agency" safeguarding our coherent existence by screening and synthesizing, in any series of moments, all the impressions, emotions, memories, and impulses which try to enter our thought and demand our action, and which would tear us apart if unsorted and unmanaged by a slowly grown and reliably watchful screening system.

One should really be decisive and say that the "I" is all-conscious, and that we are truly conscious only insofar as we can say I and mean it. (A drunken person says "I" but his eyes belie it, and later he will not remember what he said with drugged conviction.) The selves are mostly preconscious, which means they can become conscious when the "I" makes them so *and* insofar as the ego agrees to it. The ego, however, is unconscious. We become aware of its work, but never of it. To sacrifice in any respect the concept of an unconscious ego, which manages to do for us, as the heart and the brain do, what we could never "figure out" or plan consciously, would mean to abandon psychoanalysis as an instrument, as well as the beauty (to speak thomistically) which it alone can make us see. On the other hand, to ignore the conscious "I" in its relation to its existence (as psychoanalytic theory has done) means to delete the core of human self-awareness, the capacity which, after all, makes self-analysis possible.

But who or what is the counterplayer of the ego? First, of course, the id and the superego, and then, so theory says, the "environment." The first two are awkward terms in English, which does not cultivate the academic-mythical grandeur of German, where "*das Es*" or "*das Ueber-Ich*" are never thinglike entities, but demonic and primal givens. The ego's over-all task is, in the simplest terms, to turn passive into active, that is, to screen the impositions of its counterplayers in such a way that they become volitions. This is true on the inner frontier where what is experienced as "id" must become familiar, even tame, and yet maximally enjoyable; where what feels like a crushing burden of conscience must become a bearable, even a "good" conscience. That much has been clearly demonstrated under conditions of psychoanalysis in which a paralyzed ego could be seen to have become passive or, as I would say, inactivated in its defensive and adaptive functions. Yet, id and superego can truly be the ego's allies, as can be seen in sexual abandon and in rightful action.

It is, then, again the "environment" which, as indicated in these pages, lacks specificity as the ego's counterplayer. As also pointed out, this is a consequence of a really outmoded naturalist habituation to speak of "the" organism and "its" environment. Ecology and ethology have decisively gone beyond this simplification. Members of the same species and of other species are always part of each other's *Umwelt*. By the same token, then, and accepting the fact that the human environment is social, the *outerworld of the ego* is made up of the *egos of others* significant to it. They are significant because on many levels of crude or subtle communication my whole being perceives in them a hospitality for the way in which my inner world is ordered and includes them, which makes me, in turn, hospitable to the way they order their world and include me—a mutual affirmation, then, which can be depended upon to activate my being as I can be depended upon to activate theirs. To this, at any rate, I would restrict the term *mutuality*, which is the secret of love. I would call *reciprocal negation*, on the other hand, the denial on the part of others to take their place in my order and to let me take mine in theirs. Nothing in nature, in all probability, resembles the hate which this arouses, and nothing the ambivalence which makes us uncertain where in these respects we stand in relation to one another, although the mixture of rage, discomfort, and fear displayed by some animals in ambiguous situations and the enormous investment of affect in greeting ceremonials—their and ours—give us a good idea of the phylogenetic precursors of "ambivalence." At any rate, foremost among the complexities of human life is communication on the ego level, where each ego tests all the information received sensorily and sensually, linguistically and subliminally for the confirmation or negation of its identity. The persistent effort, then, of jointly ordering these processes into a psychosocial "territory" of trusted mutualities and defined reciprocal negations is what we mean by a "group ego"; and I have indicated the further complication that the boundary of this territory runs right through each constituent ego, dividing it into a positive and a negative identity. Here again, conflict within (as ambivalence without) arouses a specifically human anxiety, and only when, in our linked orders, we confirm or negate ourselves and each other clearly, is there identity—psychosocial identity.

But "I" is nothing less than the verbal assurance according to which I feel that I am the center of awareness in a universe of experience in which I have a coherent identity, and that I am in possession of my wits and able to say what I see and think. No quantifiable aspect of this experience can do justice to its subjective halo, for it means nothing less than that I am alive, that I *am* life. The counterplayer of the "I" therefore can be, strictly speaking, only the deity who has lent this halo to a mortal and is Himself endowed with an eternal numinousness certified by all "I"s who acknowledge this gift. That is why God, when Moses asked Him who should he say had called him, answered: "I AM THAT I AM." He then ordered Moses to tell the multitude: "I AM has sent me unto you." And, indeed, only a multitude held together by a common faith shares to that extent a common "I," wherefore "brothers and sisters in God" can appoint each other true "You"s in mutual compassion and joint veneration. The Hindu greeting of looking into another's eyes—hands raised close to the face with palms joined—and saying "I recognize the God in you" expresses the heart of the matter. But then, so does a lover by his mere glance recognize the numinosity in the face of the beloved, while feeling, in turn, that his very life depends on being so recognized. Those few, however, who turn their faces totally toward that of the deity, must avoid all love except that of brotherhood: "unless you are willing to forsake . . ."

4. A COMMUNALITY OF EGOS

The so-called basic biological orientation of psychoanalysis has, it seems, gradually become (out of mere habituation) a kind of pseudobiology, and this especially in the conceptualization of man's "environment." In psychoanalytic writings the terms "outer world" or "environment" are often used to designate an uncharted area which is said to be outside merely because it fails to be inside—inside the individual's somatic skin, or inside his psychic systems, or inside his self in the widest sense. Such a vague and yet omnipresent "outerness" by necessity assumes a number of ideological and certainly unbiological connotations, such as an antagonism between organism and environment. Sometimes "the outer world" is conceived of as "reality's" conspiracy against the infantile organism's instinctual wish world and sometimes as the indifferent or annoying fact of the existence of other people. But even in the recent admission of the at least partially benevolent presence of maternal care, a stubborn tendency persists to treat the "mother-child relationship" as a "biological" entity more or less isolated from its cultural surroundings which then, again, become an "environment" of vague supports or of blind pressures and mere "conventions." Thus, step by step, we are encumbered by the remnants of juxtapositions which were once necessary and fruitful enough, for it was important to establish the fact that moralistic and hypocritical social demands are apt to crush the adult's and exploit the child's instinctuality. It was important to conceptualize certain intrinsic antagonisms between the individual's and society's interests. However, the implicit conclusion that an individual ego could exist against or without a specifically human "environment," and that means social organization, is senseless; and as a pseudobiological orientation, such an implicit assumption threatens to isolate psychoanalytic theory from the rich ecological insights of modern biology.

It is, again, Hartmann who opens the way to new considerations.[9] His statement that the human infant is born preadapted to an "average expectable environment" implies a more truly biological as well as an inescapably societal formulation. For not even the very best of mother-child relationships could, by themselves, account for that subtle and complex "milieu" which permits a human baby not only to survive but also to develop his potentialities for growth and uniqueness. Man's ecology demands constant natural, historical, and technological readjustment, which makes it at once obvious that only a perpetual, if ever so imperceptible, restructuring of tradition can safeguard for each new generation of infants anything approaching an "average expectability" of environment. Today, when rapid technological changes have taken the lead the world over, the matter of establishing and preserving in flexible forms an "average expectable" continuity for child rearing and education everywhere has, in fact, become a matter of human survival.

The specific kind of preadaptedness of the human infant—namely, the readiness to grow by epigenetic steps through psychosocial crises—calls not only for one basic environment, but for a whole sequence of "expectable" environments, for as the child adapts in spurts and stages he has a claim, at any given stage reached, to the next "average expectable environment." In other words, the human environment as a whole must permit and safeguard a series of more or less discontinuous and yet culturally and psychologically consistent developments, each extending further along the radius of expanding life tasks. All of this makes man's so-called biological adaptation a matter of life cycles developing within their community's changing history. Consequently, a psychoanalytic sociology faces the task of conceptualizing man's environment as the persistent endeavor of the generations to join in the organizational effort of providing an integrated series of "average expectable environments."

In a paper which reviews efforts at approaching the relation of culture and personality, Hartmann, Kris, and Loewenstein state: "Cultural conditions could and should be viewed also with the question in mind which and what kind of opportunities for ego functions in a sphere free from conflict they invite or inhibit." [10] In regard to the possibility of studying the reflection of such "cultural conditions" in the psychoanalysis of individuals, the writers seem less encouraging. They state:

Analysts too are aware of differences of behavior caused by cultural conditions; they are not devoid of that common sense which has always stressed these differences, but their impact on the analytic observer tends to decrease as work progresses and as available data move from the periphery to the center, that is from manifest behavior to data, part of which is accessible only to an analytic investigation.

I venture to suggest, and I hope that even the mere fragments of case material presented in this book have helped to indicate, that rather central problems of ego development—which are, indeed, "accessible only to an analytic investigation"—demand that the psychoanalyst's awareness of cultural differences go well beyond that "common sense" which the three authors seem to find sufficient in this particular area of observation, while they would assuredly urge a more "analyzed" common sense in other areas. For, as we have suggested, the relationship between the organized values and institutional efforts of societies, on the one hand, and the nature of ego synthesis, on the other, is more systematic, and that, from a psychosocial point of view at any rate, basic social and cultural processes can *only* be viewed as the joint endeavor of adult egos to develop and maintain, through joint organization, a maximum of conflict-free energy in a mutually supportive psychosocial equilibrium. Only such organization is likely to give consistent support to the egos of growing and grown beings at every step of their development. For, as was indicated in Chapter III, the older generation needs the younger one as much as the younger one depends on the older for the strength of their respective egos; and it would seem that it is in the sphere of this mutuality of drives and ego interests through-out the development of the older as well as the younger genera-tions that certain basic and universal values, in all of their com-pensatory power and defensive strength, become and remain important joint achievements of individual ego development and of the "group ego." In fact, so our clinical histories begin to reveal, these values provide indispensable support for the ego development of the growing generations, in that they give some specific superindividual consistency to parental conduct, al-though different kinds of consistency—including consistent kinds of being inconsistent—vary with value systems and per-sonality types.

Only societal processes representing a multiple mutuality, then, will re-create the "average expectability" of the environ-ments either through ceremonial rededication or systematic re-formulation. In both cases, elected or self-selected leaders and elites feel, ever again, called upon to demonstrate a convincing, "charismatic" kind of generalized generativity, i.e., a super-personal interest in the maintenance and the rejuvenation of in-stitutions. In recorded history some such leaders are registered as "great"; they, it seems, are able, out of the deepest personal con-flicts to derive the energy which meets their period's specific need for a resynthesis of the prevalent world image. At any rate, only through constant rededication will institutions gain the active and inspired investment of new energy from their young members. More theoretically stated: only by maintaining a meaningful correspondence between its values and the main cri-ses of ego development does a society manage to have at the dis-posal of its particular group identity a maximum of the conflict-free energy accrued from the childhood crises of a majority of its young members.

One can only conclude that the functioning ego, while guard-ing individuality, is far from isolated, for a kind of communality links egos in a mutual activation. Something in the ego process, then, and something in the social process is—well, identical.[11]

5. THEORY AND IDEOLOGY

In studying the ego's relation to changing historical reality, psychoanalysis approaches a new phalanx of unconscious resistances. It is implicit in the nature of psychoanalytic investigation that such resistances be located and appraised in the observers, and in their *habits of conceptualization*, before their presence in the observed can be understood and treated. When investigating man's instinctuality the psychoanalyst knows that his drive to investigate is partially instinctual in nature. He knows that he responds with a partial countertransference to the patient's transference, i.e., that for special reasons of his own he may indulge the patient's ambiguous wish to satisfy infantile strivings in the very therapeutic situation which is to cure them. The analyst acknowledges all this, yet works methodically toward that margin of freedom where the clear delineation of the inevitable makes consuming resistances unnecessary and frees energy for creative work.

It is, then, a commonplace that the psychoanalyst must be aware of the historical determinants of what made him what he is before he can hope to perfect that human gift: the ability to understand that which is different from him.

A new kind of common sense enlightened by a new trend of self-analysis has been the mark of advance wherever a new conceptual trend became part of psychoanalytic practice. If I seriously suggest that a psychosocial point of view may become part of psychoanalytic concerns I will also have to take into consideration the possibility that specific resistances may formerly have been in the way of such insight, and only the nature of the insight resisted can point to the nature of the resistance. In this case it would be the relationship of the professional identity of a generation of observers to the ideological trends of their time.

The question of the "admission" of social considerations into "official" psychoanalysis has had a stormy history ever since the publication of the work of Alfred Adler, and one cannot escape the impression that this has continued to be an ideological as well as a methodological issue. What was at stake, it seems, was, on the one hand, Freud's treasured assumption that psychoanalysis could be a science like any other without a world view (a "*Weltanschauung*") other than that of natural science; and, on the other hand, the persistent conviction among many of the most gifted younger psychoanalysts that psychoanalysis as a critique of society should join the revolutionary orientation which in Europe had earned the solidarity of many of the most original minds. Behind this is a rather gigantic Marx-Freud polarization which was the result of an intrinsic antagonism between these views, as though they were really two reciprocally exclusive ideologies—which, up to a point, they, indeed, were at first, the evidence being the total exclusion of each by the other to the point of a dogmatic neglect of rather obvious common interests and insights.

It would seem, then, that in the long run some of the most heated and stubborn answers to the questions of what the nature of psychoanalysis is or is not originate in another question of great immediacy, namely, what psychoanalysis must be, or must remain or become, to a particular worker because a particular world image has become a necessity for his identity as a man, a professional, and a citizen.

Now, psychoanalysis has offered rich opportunities for a variety of professional identities. It gave new function and scope to such divergent endeavors as natural philosophy and Talmudic argument, medical tradition and missionary teaching, literary demonstration and the building of theory, social reform and the making of money. Psychoanalysis as a movement has harbored a variety of world images and utopias which originated in the various stages of its history in a variety of countries. This, I think, is a result of an inescapable necessity, for man, in order to be able to interact efficiently with other human beings and especially so if he wishes to cure and to teach, must at intervals make a total orientation out of a given stage of partial knowledge. Individual students of Freud thus found their identity best verified in isolated theses of his which promised a particular psychoanalytic ideology and, with it, the possibility of a stable professional orientation. Similarly, overstated anti-theses to some of Freud's tentative and transient theses have served as dogmatic bases for the professional and scientific orientation of other workers in the field. Thus, new "schools" become irreversible systematizations which put themselves beyond argument—or self-analysis.

As I look back on my early days as an immigrant psychoanalyst in this country, I become belatedly aware of another ideological factor in the history of the diaspora of psychoanalysis. I was granted by my patients a kind of moratorium during which I could gloss over my abysmal ignorance of the English language, not to mention all those colloquial nuances which alone convey a patient's milieu, and could cling tenaciously to what the books said was common to everyone everywhere and the more unconscious the better. In this, I now understand, the patients (and the candidates) conspired with me, because I represented an integrated belief system which promised to replace the brittle remnants of their parents' and grandparents' fundamentalisms, whether religious or political. If I was able to join some of my American friends (Margaret Mead, John Dollard, Scudder Mekeel) in their persuasive cultural relativism, and could learn to see the cultural differences described in my Notebook, it was no doubt due to special motivations rooted in my own life history which had made me marginal in regard to family, nation, religion, and profession and had prepared me for feeling at home in an immigrant ideology.

This seems to be a rather personalistic way of concluding some theoretical remarks. However, I am not trying to "relativize" these matters, but rather to introduce into them the necessary social and historical relativity. Least of all do I wish to neglect the original ideological power and source of inspiration which has emanated from the theoretical and technical tenets of Freud's psychoanalysis. Just because some of the psychoanalytic "revisionists" have, to my mind, taken unnecessary chances with that foundation (discussing ponderously as scientific differences what were ideological ones), I have not been able to give much thought to the question as to how my methodological and term-inological suggestions may or may not fit theirs. It has been more important to me to advance my teaching in psychoanalytic institutes by small steps without abandoning our unique ideo-logical foundations. For the best work is often initiated in cata-combs, and many of us are nostalgic for the days when we sat and learned in social and academic isolation. Such isolation was once the almost spiritual setting for a truly creative idea, the *therapeutic* idea which invited the patient to join an enormously demanding psychotherapeutic process by which he and the analyst observed the phenomena and the laws of the internalized world, thus simultaneously strengthening (as I like to think we still do at our best) inner freedom and outer realism. At our best: that is, when the patient happens to be the kind of person who has it in him to join the kind of person we therapists are in benefiting from the kind of clarification which our method affords. And by "kind of person" I really mean "identity," for psychoanalytic treatment presupposes in therapist and patient not only a communality of observation, but also a strength and direction of a therapeutic ideology which makes such commu-nality fruitful to both. This has generated, in generations of workers, an undreamed-of intellectual energy, but it also sup-poses that the process be kept alive, and that analyst and patient (and training analyst and candidate) do not become dependent on the common dogmatic conspiracy of calling only that real which happens to fit into a past ideological state of the theory and into a particular local or regional trend in the political or-ganization of psychoanalysis itself.

There is another job to be done in a field which can only develop further by becoming conscious of its own history. Every psychological term concerning a central human issue is originally adopted with ideological connotations which range from what Freud called the "age-old ideologies of the Super-Ego" to the influence of contemporary ideologies. Both, of course, are soon superseded if and when the term becomes habitual and ritualized, especially in different languages. Take the superego itself: the German *"Ueber"* can have a very different meaning (*"Ueber allen Wipfeln . . ."*) from the English "super" ("super-jet"). A relatively small group of workers can, of course, agree on what the term means, especially when delineated against other items such as the id and the ego. But as the field spreads, individual workers and groups of workers ascribe new meanings to each term in accordance with their own past and present. As I have indicated repeatedly, the most fundamental of our terms, *"Trieb,"* and its adjective, *"triebhaft,"* had in their original usage a nature-philosophic quality of an ennobling as well as elemental force (*"die suessen Triebe"*—"sweet drives," the German poet could say, and, as pointed out, stern physiologists could speak of "forces of dignity"); wherefore, in addition to reasons of parsimony, Freud had to be eminently restrained before appointing a new "basic" element to the Olympus of Triebe. Other (American) psychologists could think of long lists of drives with a small "d," the aim of which was verification, not mythological conviction.

Similarly, *"die Realitaet"* by the very fact that it could be used with an article was an almost personalized power comparable to Anangke or Fate, and called for much more than reasonable adjustments to factual reality. Reality itself is one of the most corruptible terms in use, since it can mean a world image substantiated as real by all who jointly and self-denyingly use reason to establish what can be consensually agreed on and lived by, while to many it means the sum of all that one can get away with without feeling too sinful or coming into avoidable conflict with rules and regulations insofar as they happen to be enforced. Probably the term most vulnerable to changing connotations, however, is that of the ego, for to some it will never quite lose the odium of egotism, to others that of self-centeredness, while to many it retains the quality of a closed system in the process of inner transformations. Finally, there is the term "mechanism." If Anna Freud says that

All through childhood a maturation process is at work which, in the service of an increasing knowledge and adaptation to reality, aims at perfecting (ego) functions, at rendering them more and more objective and independent of the emotions until they become as accurate and reliable as a mechanical apparatus.[12]

she describes a tendency which the ego has in common, in more than one sense, with the nervous system and the brain (wherefore man can create machines) but she certainly does not intend to advocate mechanical adaptation as the goal of human life. In fact, her "mechanisms of defence," while a highly necessary *part* of mental life, render the person *dominated* by them impoverished and stereotyped. And yet, where man overidentifies with his machines he may want to become (and make others become) more manageable by finding smooth methods of mechanical adjustment. In summary, I am not denying that one can agree on what a term means logically, nor am I advocating (God forbid) that richly suggestive terms be avoided in social science; but I am pointing out that an awareness of the changing connotations of its most important terms is one of the requirements of a "self-analytic" psychosocial orientation.

In speaking of scientific proof and scientific progress, then, in a field which deals directly with the immediate needs of men, it is necessary to account not only for methodological, practical, and ethical factors, but also for the necessity of a professional ideology. For this reason psychoanalytic training will have to encompass the varieties of professional identity formation while theoretical teaching must throw light also on the ideological background of principal differences in what is felt to be most practical, most true, and most right at various stages of a developing field. If here another universal resistance, namely, identity resistance, seems to call for analysis in analogy to "id" and "superego" resistances, I should repeat, in conclusion, that anything concerning identity is closer to the historical day than are the other counterplayers of the ego. This kind of resistance, then, can be countered not only by an additional stress in individual analysis but, above all, by a joint effort to reapply applied psychoanalysis to psychoanalysis.[13]

I may add that I am only too aware of the fact that in steering in a new direction one is apt to hold to a one-sided course, temporarily ignoring well-traveled courses and alternate directions suggested in the pioneer work of others. But the important theoretical question is: will a new direction lead to new observations?

CHAPTER
VI

Toward Contemporary Issues:
Youth

1.

THE DESCRIPTION AND ANALYSIS of what is most sick and most depraved in individuals and conditions has developed into a style of social critique, both in textbooks and in fiction, which often feeds on itself. For as the young see themselves, as it were, negatively glorified in the mass media, their sense of identity can only make the most of the power they seem to wield at least as living symptoms. But I have found it necessary for other than reasons of "public relations" to ask myself what may be the balance to the psychopathology which we have learned to recognize, and what may be the positive goals built into each stage of development. "Positive" in many circles often suggests a delusional turning away from ugly reality; but is it not part of any over-all clinical attitude to study the "natura" which, with our therapeutic help, is to do the "curat"? I have already indicated in Chapter III that I would assign to each stage its own vital strength, and to all stages an epigenetic system of such strengths which make for human (and here that means generational) vitality. If, in a militant mood, I called these strengths basic virtues, I did so in order to indicate that without them all other values and goodnesses lack vitality. My justification for the use of the word was that it once had the connotation of an inherent strength and of an active quality in something to be described: a medicine or a drink, for example, was said to be "without virtue" when it had lost its spirit. In this sense, I think, one may use the term "vital virtues" to connote certain qualities which begin to animate man pervasively during successive stages of his life, Hope being the first and the most basic.[1]

The use of such a term, however, for the conceptualization of a quality emerging from the interplay of individual growth and social structure recalls to the mind of many readers the "naturalist fallacy," that is, the naïve attempt to ascribe to evolution the intention of developing certain types of ornamentative goodness in man. Yet, newer concepts of environment (such as the *Umwelt* of the ethologists) imply an optimum relation of inborn potentialities to the structure of the environment. And even if man is the creature who adjusts to a great variety of environments or, rather, is apt to readjust himself and his environments according to his own inventions, he nevertheless remains a creature who has evolved with a specific life cycle fitting his kind of modified environment—and this can only mean the potential of an ever-renewed vital adaptation. If it is part of this evolved arrangement that man can make himself sick and survive in a fashion that no other creature would call living, he also has the capacity for diagnosis and cure, critique and change. These in turn rely on a revitalization of strength, a revival of values, a restoration of productive forces. It is in this sense, then, that I claim for the life cycle a generational principle which would tend to perpetuate a series of vital virtues from *hope* in infancy to *wisdom* in old age. As to youth and the question of what is in the center of its most passionate and most erratic striving, I have concluded that *fidelity* is the vital strength which it needs to have an opportunity to develop, to employ, to evoke—and to die for. Having made such a "basic" claim, I can only repeat some of the variations on the theme of youth presented so far, to see whether fidelity, indeed, is recognizable as pervasive.

Although I will not review here the other stages of life and the specific strengths and weaknesses contributed by each to man's precarious adaptation, we will take one more look at the stage of life which immediately precedes youth, the school age, and then turn to youth itself.

The school age, which intervenes between childhood and youth, finds the child, previously dominated by play, ready, willing, and able to apply himself to those rudimentary skills which form the necessary preparation for his culture's tools and weapons, symbols and concepts. Also, it finds him eager to realize actual roles (previously play-acted) which promise him eventual recognition within the specializations of his culture's technology. I would say, then, that *competence* is the specific strength emerging in man's school age. However, the stage-by-stage acquisition during human childhood of each of man's evolutionary gains leaves the mark of infantile experience on his proudest achievements. As the play age bequeaths to all methodical pursuits a quality of grandiose delusion, the school age leaves man with a naïve acceptance of "what works."

As the school child makes methods his own, he also permits accepted methods to make him their own. To consider as good only what works, and to feel accepted only if things work, to manage and to be managed can become his dominant delight and value. And since technological specialization is an intrinsic part of the human horde's or tribe's or culture's system and world image, man's pride in the tools that work with materials and animals extends to the weapons which work against other humans as well as against other species. That this can awaken a cold cunning as well as an unmeasured ferocity rare in the animal world is, of course, due to a combination of developments. Among these we will be most concerned (because it comes to the fore during youth) with man's need to combine technological pride with a sense of identity: a double sense of personal selfsameness slowly accrued from infantile experiences and of shared sameness experienced in encounters with an ever-widening community.

This need, too, is an evolutionary necessity as yet to be understood and influenced by planning, for men—not being a natural species any more, and not a mankind as yet—need to feel that they are of some special kind (tribe or nation, class or caste, family, occupation, or type) whose insignia they will wear with vanity and conviction, and defend (along with the economic claims they have staked out for their kind) against the foreign, the inimical, the not-so-human kinds. Thus it comes about that they can use all their proud skills and methods most systematically against other men, even in the most advanced state of rationality and civilization, with the conviction that they could not morally afford not to do so.

It is not our purpose, however, to dwell on the easy perversion and corruptibility of man's morality, but to determine what those core virtues are which—at this stage of psychosocial evolution—need our concerted attention and ethical support, for antimoralists as well as moralists easily overlook the bases in human nature for a strong ethics. As we have indicated, fidelity is that virtue and quality of adolescent ego strength which belongs to man's evolutionary heritage, but which—like all the basic virtues—can arise only in the interplay of a life stage with the individuals and the social forces of a true community.

The evidence in young lives of the search for something and somebody to be true to can be seen in a variety of pursuits more or less sanctioned by society. It is often hidden in a bewildering combination of shifting devotion and sudden perversity, sometimes more devotedly perverse, sometimes more perversely devoted. Yet in all youth's seeming shiftiness, a seeking after some durability in change can be detected, whether in the accuracy of scientific and technical method or in the sincerity of obedience; in the veracity of historical and fictional accounts or the fairness of the rules of the game; in the authenticity of artistic production, and the high fidelity of reproduction, or in the genuineness of convictions and the reliability of commitments. This search is easily misunderstood, and often it is only dimly perceived by the individual himself, because youth, always set to grasp both diversity in principle and principle in diversity, must often test extremes before settling on a considered course. These extremes, particularly in times of ideological confusion and widespread marginality of identity, may include not only rebellious but also deviant, delinquent, and self-destructive tendencies. However, all this can be in the nature of a moratorium, a period of delay in which to test the rock-bottom of some truth before committing the powers of body and mind to a segment of the existing (or a coming) order. "Loyal" and "legal" have the same root, linquistically and psychologically, for legal commitment is an unsafe burden unless shouldered with a sense of sovereign choice and experienced as loyalty. To develop that sense is a joint task of the consistency of individual life history and the ethical potency of the historical process.

2.

Let a great tragic play tell us something of the elemental nature of the crisis man encounters here. If it is a prince's crisis, let us not forget that the "leading families" of heaven and history at one time personified man's pride and tragic failure. Prince Hamlet is in his twenties, some say early, some late. We will say he is in the middle of his third decade, a youth no longer young, about to forfeit his moratorium. We find him in a tragic conflict in which he cannot follow the one principle of action demanded simultanesouly by his age and his sex, his position, and his historical responsibility, namely, royal revenge.

To make Shakespeare's insight into one of "the ages of man" explicit will seem a reprehensible endeavor to the students of drama, especially if undertaken by a trained psychologist. Everybody else (how could he do otherwise?) interprets Shakespeare in the light of some prevailing if usually naïve psychology. I will not try, however, to solve the riddle of Hamlet's inscrutable nature, if for no other reason than that I believe his inscrutability to be his nature. I feel sufficiently warned by Shakespeare himself, who lets Polonius speak like the caricature of a psychiatrist:

> And I do think—or else this brain of mine
> Hunts not the trail of policy so sure

> As it has us'd to do—that I have found
> The very cause of Hamlet's lunacy.

Hamlet's decision to play insane is a secret which the audience shares with him from the start, without their ever getting rid of the feeling that he is on the verge of slipping into the state he pretends. "His madness," says T. S. Eliot, "is less than madness, and more than feigned."

If Hamlet's madness is more than feigned, it appears to be aggravated at least fivefold by habitual melancholy, an introverted personality, Danishness, an acute state of mourning, and love. All this makes a regression to the Oedipus complex, postulated by Ernest Jones as the main theme of this as of other great tragedies, entirely plausible.[2] This would mean that Hamlet cannot forgive his mother's recent illegitimate betrayal because he had not been able as a child to forgive her for having betrayed him quite legitimately with his father; but, at the same time, he is unable to avenge his father's recent murder, because as a child he had himself betrayed him in fantasy and wished him out of the way. Thus he forever postpones—until he ruins the innocent with the guilty—his uncle's execution, which alone would free the ghost of his beloved father from the fate of being

> Doomed for a certain term to walk the night,
> And for the day confined to fast in fires.

No audience, however, can escape the feeling that he is a man of superior conscience, and advanced, in fact, beyond the legal concepts of his time which would have permitted him to take revenge without scruples.

One further suggestion is inescapable, namely, that Hamlet displays some of the playwright's and the actor's personality, for where others lead men and change the course of history, he reflectively moves characters about on the stage (the play within the play); in brief, where others act, he play-acts. And indeed, Hamlet, historically speaking, may well stand for an abortive leader, a stillborn rebel. Instead, he is the morbid young intellectual of his time, for did he not recently return from studies at

Wittenburg, the hotbed of humanist corruption, his time's counterpart to Sophist Athens and to today's centers of learning infested by existentialism, psychoanalysis—or worse?

There are five young men in the play, all Hamlet's age mates and all sure (or even overdefined) in their identities as dutiful sons, courtiers, and future leaders. But they are all drawn into the moral swamp of infidelity, which seeps into the fiber of all those who owe allegiance to "rotten" Denmark, drawn by the multiple intrigue which Hamlet hopes to defeat with his own intrigue: the play within the play.

Hamlet's world, then, is one of diffuse realities and fidelities. Only through the play within the play and through the madness within the insanity does Hamlet, the actor within the play-actor, reveal the noble identity within the pretended identities—and the superior fidelity in the fatal pretense.

His estrangement is one of identity confusion. Estrangement from existence itself is the theme of the famous soliloquy. He is estranged from being human and from being a man: "Man delights me not; no, nor woman either," and estranged from love and procreation: "I say we will have no more marriage." He is estranged from the ways of his country, "though I am native here and to the manner born," and, much like our "alienated" youth, he is estranged from and describes as "alienated" the overstandardized man of his day, who "only got the tune of time and outward habit of encounter."

Yet Hamlet's single-minded and tragically doomed search for fidelity breaks through all this. Here is the essence of the historical Hamlet, that ancient model who was a hero on the folk stage for centuries before Shakespeare modernized and eternalized him: [3]

He was loth to be thought prone to lying about any matter, and wished to be held a stranger to any falsehood; and accordingly he mingled craft and candor in such a wise that, though his words did not lack truth, yet there was nothing to betoken the truth and to betray how far his keenness went.

It accords with the general diffusion of truth in *Hamlet* that this central theme is announced in the old fool's message to his son:

Polonius: This above all: to thine own self be true,
And it must follow, as the night the day,
Thou canst not then be false to any man.

Yet it is also the central theme of Hamlet's most passionate pronouncements, which make his madness but an adjunct to his nobility. He abhors conventional sham and advocates genuineness of feeling:

Seems, madam! Nay, it is; I know not "seems."
'Tis not alone my inky cloak, good mother,
Nor customary suits of solemn black,
Nor windy suspiration of forc'd breath,
No, nor the fruitful river in the eye,
Nor the dejected havior of the visage,
Together with all forms, moods, shapes of grief
That can denote me truly. These indeed seem,
For they are actions that a man might play:
But I have that within which passes show;
These but the trappings and the suits of woe.

He searches for what only an elite will really understand— "honest method":

I heard thee speak me a speech once but it was never acted; or, if it was, not above once; for the play, I remember, pleased not the million . . . ! It was (as I received it, and others, whose judgements . . . cried in the top of mine) an excellent play, well digested in the scenes, set down with as much modesty and cunning. I remember one said there were no sallets in the lines to make the matter savoury, nor no matter in the phrase that might indict the author of affection; but called it an honest method.

He fanatically insists on purity of form and fidelity of reproduction:

. . . let your own discretion be your tutor. Suit the action to the word, the word to the action, with this special observance, that you o'erstep not the modesty of nature; for anything so overdone is from the purpose of playing whose end, both at the first and now, was and is to hold, as 'twere, the mirror up to nature, to show virtue her own feature, scorn her own image and the very age and body of the time his form and pressure.

And finally, the eager (and overeager) acknowledgment of genuine character in his friend:

> Since my dear soul was mistress of her choice
> And could of men distinguish, her election
> Hath sealed thee for herself; for thou hast been
> As one in suffering all, that suffers nothing,
> A man that fortune buffets and rewards
> Hast ta'en with equal thanks; and bless'd are those
> Whose blood and judgement are so co-mingled
> That they are not a pipe for fortune's finger
> To sound what stop she please. Give me that man
> That is not passion's slave, and I will wear him
> In my heart's core, ay in my heart of heart,
> As I do thee. Something too much of this.

This, then, is the Hamlet within Hamlet. It fits the combined play-actor, the intellectual, the youth, and the neurotic that his words are his better deeds, that he can say clearly what he cannot live, and that his fidelity must bring doom to those he loves, for what he accomplishes at the end is what he tried to avoid at first. He succeeds in actualizing only what we would call his negative identity and in becoming exactly what his own ethical sense could not tolerate: a mad revenger. Thus do inner reality and historical actuality conspire to deny tragic man the positive identity for which he seems exquisitely chosen. Of course, the audience all along has sensed in Hamlet's very sincerity an element of deadliness. At the end he gives his "dying voice" to his counterplayer on the historical stage, victorious young Fortinbras, who in turn insists on having him

> . . . born like a soldier to the stage
> For he was likely, had he been put on,
> To have prov'd most royal.

The ceremonial fanfares, blaring and hollow, announce the end of this singular youth. He is confirmed by his chosen peers, with the royal insignia of his birth. But the audience feels that a special person is being buried, certified as royal and yet beyond insignia.

3.

To be a special kind, we have said, is an important element in the human need for personal and collective identities—all, in a sense, pseudospecies. "Pseudo" suggests falsehood, and might suggest that I am trying to emphasize the deviation from fact in all mythologizing. Now, it should be clear that man is the lying animal just because he tries to be the only truthful one: both distortion and correction are part of his verbal and ideational equipment. To have steady values at all, he must absolutize them; to have style, he must believe himself to be the crown of the universe. To the extent, then, that each tribe or nation, culture or religion will invent a historical and moral rationale for its exclusively God-ordained uniqueness, to that extent are they pseudospecies, no matter what else they are and accomplish. On the other hand, man has also found a transitory fulfillment in his greatest moments of cultural identity and civilized perfection, and each such tradition of identity and perfection has highlighted what man could be, could he be all these at one time. The utopia of our own era predicts that man will be one species in one world, with a universal technological identity to replace the illusory pseudo-identities which have divided him and with an international ethics replacing all moral systems of superstition, repression, and suppression. In the meantime, ideological systems vie for the distinction of being able to offer not only the most practical, but also the most universally convincing political and private morals to that future world; and universally convincing means, above all, credible in the eyes of youth.

In youth, ego strength emerges from the mutual confirmation of individual and community, in the sense that society recognizes the young individual as a bearer of fresh energy and that the individual so confirmed recognizes society as a living process which inspires loyalty as it receives it, maintains allegiance as it attracts it, honors confidence as it demands it. Let us go back, then, to the origins of that combination of drivenness and disciplined energy, of irrationality and courageous capability which belong to the best discussed and the most puzzling phenomena of the life cycle. The puzzle, we must grant throughout, is in the essence of the phenomenon. For the unity of the personality must be unique to be united, and the functioning of each new generation unpredictable to fulfill its function.

Of the three sources of new energy, physical growth is the most easily measured and systematically exercised, although its contribution to the aggressive drives is little understood—except that it seems certain that any hindrance in applying physical energies in truly meaningful activities results in a subdued rage which can become destructive or self-destructive. The youthful powers of comprehension and cognition can be experimentally studied and, with planning, applied to apprenticeship and study, but their relation to ideological imagination is less well known. Finally, the long-delayed genital maturation is a source of untold energy, but also of a drivenness accompanied by intrinsic frustration.

When maturing in his physical capacity for procreation, the human youth is as yet unable either to love in that binding manner which only two persons with reasonably formed identities can offer each other, or to care consistently enough to sustain parenthood. The two sexes, of course, differ greatly in these respects, and so do individuals, while societies provide different opportunities and sanctions within which individuals must fend for their potentials—and for their potency. A psychosocial moratorium, then, seems to be built into the schedule of human development. Like all "latencies" in man's developmental schedules, the delay of adulthood can be prolonged and intensified to a forceful and fateful degree; thus it accounts for very special human achievements and also for the very special weaknesses in such achievements. For whatever the partial satisfactions and partial abstinences that characterize premarital sex life in various cultures—whether the pleasure and pride of forceful genital activity without commitment, or erotic states without genital consummation, or disciplined and devoted delay—ego development uses the psychosexual powers of adolescence for enhancing a sense of style and identity. Here, too, man is never an animal: even where a society furthers the genital closeness of the sexes, it does so in a stylized manner. On the other hand, the sex act, biologically speaking, is the procreative act, and there is an element of psychobiological dissatisfaction in any sexual situation not favorable in the long run to procreative consummation and care—a dissatisfaction which can be tolerated by otherwise healthy people, as all partial abstinences can be borne, for a certain period and under conditions otherwise favorable to the aims of identity formation. In the woman, no doubt, this dissatisfaction plays a much greater role, owing to her deeper engagement, physiologically and emotionally, in the sex act as the first step in a procreative commitment of which her monthly cycle is a regular bodily and emotive reminder; this will be discussed more fully in the next chapter.

The various hindrances to a full consummation of adolescent genital maturation have many deep consequences for man which pose an important problem for future planning. Best known is the regressive revival of that earlier stage of psychosexuality which preceded the emotionally quiet first school years, that is, the infantile genital and locomotor stage with its tendency toward autoerotic manipulation, grandiose fantasy, and vigorous play.[4] But in youth, autoerotism, grandiosity, and playfulness are all immensely amplified by genital potency and locomotor maturation and are vastly complicated by what we will presently describe as the youthful mind's new historical perspective.

The most widespread expression of the discontented search of youth as well as of its native exuberance is the craving for locomotion, whether expressed in a general "being on the go," "tearing after something," or "running around" or in locomotion proper, as in vigorous work, absorbing sports, rapt dancing, shiftless *Wanderschaft*, and the employment and misuse of speedy animals and machines. But it also finds expression through participation in the movements of the day (whether the riots of a local commotion or the parades and campaigns of major ideological forces), if they only appeal to the need for feeling "moved" and for feeling essential in moving something along toward an open future. It is clear that societies offer any number of ritual combinations of ideological perspective and vigorous movement (dance, sports, parades, demonstrations, riots) to harness youth in the service of their historical aims, and that where societies fail to do so these patterns will seek their own combinations in small groups occupied with serious games, good-natured foolishness, cruel prankishness, and delinquent warfare. In no other stage of the life cycle, then, are the promise of finding oneself and the threat of losing oneself so closely allied.

In connection with locomotion, we must mention two great industrial developments: the motor engine and the motion picture. The motor engine, of course, is the very heart and symbol of our technology, and its mastery the aim and aspiration of much of modern youth. In connection with immature youth, however, it must be understood that both motor car and motion pictures offer to those so inclined passive locomotion with an intoxicating delusion of being intensely active. The prevalence of car thefts and motor accidents among juveniles is much decried (although it is taking the public a long time to understand that a theft is an appropriation for the sake of gainful possession, while automobiles more often than not are stolen by the young in search of a kind of automotive intoxication, which may literally run away with car and youngster). Yet, while vastly inflating a sense of motor omnipotence, the need for active locomotion often remains unfulfilled.

Motion pictures expecially offer the onlooker, who sits, as it were, with the engine of his emotions racing, fast and furious motion in an artificially widened visual field interspersed with close-ups of violence and sexual possession—all without making the slightest demand on intelligence, imagination, or effort. I am pointing here to a widespread imbalance in adolescent experience because I think it explains new kinds of abolescent outbursts and points to new necessities of mastery. Such mastery is suggested in the newest dance styles which combine a machinelike pulsation with a semblance of rhythmic abandon and ritualistic sincerity. Each dancer's isolation, underscored by fleeting melodies, which permits him to join his partner sporadically, seems to reflect the needs of adolescence more truly than did the spurious intimacy of partners glued together and yet staring vacantly past each other.

The danger of feeling overwhelmed simultaneously by inner impulse and the ceaseless pulse of motorization is partly balanced in that part of youth which can take active charge of technical development and manages to learn and to identify with the ingeniousness of invention, the improvement of production, and the care of machinery, thus being in command of a new and unlimited application of youthful capacities. Where youth is underprivileged in such technical experience, it must explode in riotous motion; where it is ungifted, it will feel estranged from the modern world, until technology and nontechnical intelligence have come to a certain convergence.

The cognitive gifts developing during the first half of the second decade add a powerful tool to the tasks of youth. Piaget calls the gains in cognition made toward the middle teens the achievement of "formal operations." [5] This means that the youth can now operate on hypothetical propositions and can think of possible variables and potential relations—and think of them in thought alone, independent of certain concrete checks previously necessary. As Jerome S. Bruner puts it, the child now can "conjure up systematically the full range of alternative possibilities that could exist at any given time." [6] Such cognitive orientation forms not a contrast but a complement to the need of the young person to develop a sense of identity, for, from among all possible and imaginable relations, he must make a series of ever-narrowing selections of personal, occupational, sexual, and ideological commitments.

Here again diversity and fidelity are polarized: they make each other significant and keep each other alive. Fidelity without a sense of diversity can become an obsession and a bore; diversity without a sense of fidelity, an empty relativism.

4.

The sense of identity, then, becomes more necessary (and more problematical) wherever a wide range of possible identities is envisaged. In the preceding chapter I have indicated how very

complicated the real article is; here we add the overriding meaning of a sense of sameness, a unity of personality which is
acceptable and, if possible, proudly so, as an irreversible historical fact.

We have described the prime danger of this age, therefore, as
identity confusion, which can express itself in excessively prolonged moratoria (Hamlet offered an exalted example), or in
repeated impulsive attempts to end the moratorium with sudden
choices—that is, to play with historical possibilities—and then
deny that some irreversible commitment has already taken place,
or sometimes also in severe regressive pathology, as illustrated in
the preceding chapter. The dominant issue of this as of any
other stage, therefore, is the assurance that the active, the selective, ego is in charge and enabled to be in charge by a social structure which grants a given age group the place it needs—and in
which it is needed.

In a letter to Oliver Wendell Holmes, William James speaks
of wanting to "rebaptize himself" in their friendship, and this
one word says much of what is involved in the radical direction
of the social awareness and the social needs of youth. From the
middle of the second decade, the capacity to think and the
power to imagine reach beyond the persons and personalities in
which youth can immerse itself so deeply. Youth loves and hates
in people what they "stand for" and chooses them for a significant encounter involving issues that often, indeed, are bigger than
you and I. We have heard Hamlet's declaration of love to his
friend Horatio, a declaration quickly broken off as "something
too much here." It is a new reality, then, for which the individual wishes to be reborn, with and by those whom he chooses
as his new ancestors and his genuine contemporaries.

This mutual selection, while frequently associated with, and
therefore interpreted as, a rebellion against or withdrawal from
the parental environment, is an expression of a truly new perspective which I have already called "historical"—in one of
those loose uses of an ancient and overspecialized word which
sometimes become necessary in making new meanings specific.

By "historical perspective" I mean something which the human being comes to develop only during adolescence. It is a sense of the irreversibility of significant events and an often urgent need to understand fully and quickly what kind of happenings in reality and in thought determine others, and why. As we have seen, psychologists such as Piaget recognize in youth the capacity to appreciate that any process can be understood when it is retraced in its steps and thus reversed in thought. Yet it is no contradiction to say that he who comes to understand such a reversal also realizes that in reality, among all the events that can be thought of, a few will determine and narrow one another with historical fatality, whether (in the human instance) deservedly or undeservedly, intentionally or unintentionally.

Youth, therefore, is sensitive to any suggestion that it may be hopelessly determined by what went before in life histories or in history. Psychosocially speaking, this would mean that irreversible childhood identifications would deprive an individual of an identity of his own; historically, that vested powers would prevent a group from realizing its composite historical identity. For these reasons, youth often rejects parents and authorities and wishes to belittle them as inconsequential, for it is in search of individuals and movements who claim, or seem to claim, that they can predict what is irreversible, thus getting ahead of the future—which means reversing it. This in turn accounts for the acceptance by youth of mythologies and ideologies predicting the course of the universe or the historical trend; for even intelligent and practical youth can be glad to have the larger framework settled so that it can devote itself to the details which it can manage, once it knows (or is convincingly told) what they stand for and where it stands. Thus, "true" ideologies are verified by history—for a time; for if they can inspire youth, youth will make the predicted history come more than true.

By pointing to what, in the mind of youth, people "stand for," I do not mean to overemphasize the ideological explicitness in the meaning to youth of admired individuals. The selection of meaningful individuals can take place in the framework of pointed practicalities such as schooling or job selection as well as in religious and ideological fellowship, while the methods of selecting heroes can range from banal amenity and enmity to dangerous play with the borderlines of sanity and legality. But the occasions have in common a mutual sizing up and a mutual plea for recognition as individuals who can be more than they seem to be and whose potentials are needed by the order that is, or will be. The representatives of the adult world thus involved may be advocates and practitioners of technical accuracy, of a method of scientific inquiry, of a convincing rendition of truth, of a code of fairness, of a standard of artistic veracity, or of a way of personal genuineness. They become representatives of an elite in the eyes of the young quite independently of whether or not they are thus viewed in the eyes of the family, the public, or the police. The choice can be dangerous, but to some youths the danger is a necessary ingredient of the experiment. Elemental things are dangerous, and if youth could not overcommit itself to danger it could not commit itself to the survival of genuine values—one of the primary steering mechanisms of psychosocial evolution. The elemental fact is that only when fidelity has found its field of manifestation is the human as ready as, say, the nestling in nature when it can rely on its own wings and take its adult place in the ecological order.

If in human adolescence this field of manifestation is alternately one of devoted conformism or extreme deviancy, of re-dedication or rebellion, we must remember the necessity for man to react (and to react most intensively in his youth) to the diversity of conditions. In the setting of psychosocial evolution, we can ascribe a long-range meaning to the idiosyncratic individualist and to the rebel as well as to the conformist, albeit under different historical conditions. For healthy individualism and devoted deviancy contain an indignation in the service of a wholeness that is to be restored, without which psychosocial evolution would be doomed. Thus human adaptation has its loyal deviants, its rebels, who refuse to adjust to what so often is called, with an apologetic and fatalistic misuse of a once good phrase, "the human condition."

Loyal deviancy and identity formation in extraordinary individuals are often associated with neurotic and psychotic symptoms, or at least with a prolonged moratorium of relative isolation in which all the estrangements of adolescence are suffered. In *Young Man Luther* I attempted to put the suffering of a great young man into the context of his greatness and his historic position.[7] Unfortunately, however, such work leaves unanswered what to many youths remains the most urgent question, namely, the exact relation of special giftedness to neurosis. One can only say that there is often an intrinsic relation between the originality of an individual's gift and the depth of his personal conflicts. But biographies detailing the emergence of both in the life of a man already certified as original or great are of little help and may be confusing to those who have deep conflicts and original gifts today. For better or for worse, we do have psychiatric enlightenment today and, in fact, a psychiatric form of self-consciousness which joins all the other factors making for identity confusion. It makes little sense to ask, then, (as the Chancellor of St. Paul's Cathedral half facetiously did in a review of my book) whether young Luther's genius would have survived the administrations of psychiatry. Nor does it help young contemporaries very much to compare their doubts with the kind of scruples that were experienced before our "therapeutic" age. It may seem heartless to say so, but originality and creativity today will have to take their sovereign chances with *our* dominant values—and that may include taking chances with accepting therapy or refusing it. In the meantime, a simple test can be found in asking oneself whether one seems *to have* some kind of a neurosis along with other manageable complexities, or whether one seems to *be had* by it, in which case it should not be too demeaning or dangerous to accept help in changing the second, the passive, predicament back into the first, the active one. Originality takes care of itself, and, at any rate, it should be suspect as the pillar of one's identity if it depends on a denial of the need for help.

5.

To return, once more, to the history of psychiatry: in the classical case of a youthful neurosis, Freud's first published encounter with an eighteen-year-old girl suffering from "*petite hystérie* with the commonest of all . . . symptoms," it is interesting to recall that at the end of treatment Freud was puzzled as to "what kind of help" the girl wanted from him. He had communicated to her his interpretation of the structure of her neurotic disorder, an interpretation which became the central theme of his classical publication on the psychosexual factors in the development of hysteria.[8] Freud's clinical reports, however, remain astonishingly fresh over the decades, and today his case history clearly reveals the psychosocial centering of the girl's story in matters of fidelity. In fact, one might say, without seriously overdoing it, that three words characterize her social history: sexual *infidelity* on the part of some of the most important adults in her life; the *perfidy* of her father's denial of his friend's attempts to seduce her which had, in fact, been the precipitating cause of the girl's illness; and a strange tendency on the part of all the adults around the girl to make her a *confidante* in any number of matters, without having enough confidence in her to acknowledge the truths relevant to her illness.

Freud, of course, focused on other matters, opening up, with the concentration of a psychosurgeon, the symbolic meaning of her symptoms and their history; but, as always, he reported relevant data on the periphery of his interests. Thus, among the matters which somewhat puzzled him, he reports that the patient was "almost beside herself at the idea of its being supposed that she had merely fancied" (and thus invented) the conditions which had made her sick, and that she kept "anxiously trying to make sure whether I was being quite straightforward with her" —or perfidious like her father. When at the end she left analyst and analysis "in order to confront the adults around her with the secrets she knew," Freud considered such aggressive truthfulness an act of revenge on them, and on him; and within the trend of his interpretations this partial interpretation, too, stands. Nevertheless, as we can now see, there was more to this insistence on the historical truth than the denial of an inner truth, especially in an adolescent. For the question as to what confirms them irreversibly as a truthful or a cheating, a sick or a rebellious type is paramount in the minds of adolescents; and the further question—whether or not they were right in the abhorrence of the conditions which made them sick—is as important to them as any insight into the "deeper" meaning of their sickness can ever be. In other words, they insist that the fact of their sickness find recognition within a reformulation of a historical truth which points beyond itself to the possibility of new and altered conditions and not according to the corrupt terms of the environment which wishes them to adjust or (as Dora's father had put it when he brought her to Freud) to be "brought to reason."

No doubt Dora by then *was* a hysteric, and the unconscious symbolic meaning of her symptons *was* psychosexual; but the sexual nature of her disturbance and of the precipitating events in this case should not blind us to the fact that infidelity was the common theme in all the suggested sexual situations, and that other infidelities (in the form of other perfidies, familial and communal) also cause adolescents to fall sick in a variety of ways in other ages and places.

Only when adolescence is reached, in fact, does the capacity for a systematic symptom formation occur: only when the historical function of the mind is consolidated can significant omissions and repressions become marked enough to cause consistent symptom formation and identifiable deformation of character. The depth of regression determines the severity of the pathology and, with it, the therapy to be employed. However, the pathographic picture sketched in Chapter IV as common to all sick youth is clearly discernible in Dora's total state, although hysteria, as the "highest" of all neurotic afflictions, renders the various components less malignant and even somewhat histrionic. This picture, so we said, is characterized by refusal to acknowledge the flux of time while all parental premises are re-tested; and Dora suffered from a "*taedium vitae* which was probably not entirely genuine." But such slowing up makes the moratorium of illness an end in itself. At this time death and suicide can become, so we said, a spurious preoccupation—"not entirely genuine" and yet sometimes leading unpredictably to suicide; and Dora's parents found "a letter in which she took leave of them because she could no longer endure life. Her father . . . guessed that the girl had no serious suicidal intentions." Such a finite decision would cut off life itself before it could lead to adult commitment. There is also a social isolation which excludes any sense of solidarity and can lead to a snobbish isolation: Dora "tried to avoid social intercourse" and was "distant" and "unfriendly." The flare-up of violent repudiation which can accompany the first steps of an identity formation is in neurotics turned against the self—"Dora was satisfied neither with herself nor with her family."

A repudiated self in turn cannot offer loyalty and, of course, fears the fusion of love or of sexual encounters. The work inhibition often connected with this picture (Dora suffered from "fatigue and lack of concentration") is really a career inhibition, in the sense that every exertion of skill or method is suspected of binding the individual to the role and status suggested by the activity; thus, again, any genuine moratorium is impossible. Where fragmentary identities are formed, they are highly self-conscious and are immediately put to a test: Dora obviously defeated her own wish to be a woman intellectual and to compete with her successful brother. This self-consciousness is a strange mixture of snobbish superiority—a conviction that one is really too good for his community, his period of history, or, indeed, this life— and an equally deep sense of being nobody.

6.

We have sketched the most obvious social symptoms of adolescent psychopathology, in part to indicate that the unconscious meaning and complex structure of neurotic symptoms is accompanied by a behavioral picture so open that one sometimes wonders whether the patient lies by telling so simple a truth or tells the truth even when evading it most obviously. The answer is that one must listen to what they *are* saying, and not only to the symbolism implicit in their message.

The sketch presented, however, also serves as a comparison of the isolated adolescent sufferer with those youths who try to solve their doubt in their elders by joining deviant cliques and gangs. Freud found that "psychoneuroses are, so to speak, the negative of perversions," [9] which means that neurotics suffer under the repression of tendencies which perverts try to "live out." This formula can be applied to the fact that isolated sufferers try to solve by withdrawal what the joiners of deviant cliques and gangs attempt to solve by conspiracy.

If we now turn to this form of adolescent pathology, the denial of the irreversibility of historical time appears to be expressed in a clique's or a gang's self-appointment as a "people" or a "class" with a tradition and an ethics all its own. The pseudohistorical character of such groups is expressed in such names as "The Navahos," "The Saints," or "The Edwardians," while their provocaton is countered by society (remember the Pachucos of the war years) with a mixture of impotent rage whenever murderous excess does occasionally occur, and with a phobic overconcern followed by vicious suppression whenever these "secret societies" are really no more than fads lacking any organized purpose. But they display an unassailable inner sense of callous rightness which is a psychological necessity for each member and the rationale for their solidarity, as can best be understood by briefly comparing the torment of the isolated youngster with the temporary gains derived by the joiner from the mere fact that he has been taken into a pseudosociety. The time diffusion attending the isolate's inability to envisage a career is "cured" by the joiner's attention to "jobs"—theft, destruction, fights, murder, or acts of perversion or addiction, conceived on the spur of the moment and executed forthwith. This "job" orientation also takes care of the work inhibition, because the members of a clique or gang are always "busy," even if they

just "hang around." Their lack of any readiness to wince under
any shaming accusation is often considered the mark of a total
personal perdition, while in fact it is a trademark, the very insignia of the "species" to which the youngster (mostly marginal
in economic and ethnic respects) would belong unto death
rather than take his chances with a society so eager to confirm
him as a criminal and then to "rehabilitate" him as an ex-
criminal.

As to the isolate's tortured feelings of bisexuality or an immature need for love, the young joiner in social pathology, by
the very act of joining, has made a clear decision: the boy is male
with a vengeance; the girl a female without sentimentality. In
either case, they can deny both love and procreation as functions
of genitality and can make a semiperverse pseudoculture of what
is left. By the same token, they will acknowledge authority only
in the assertive form chosen in the act of joining, repudiating the
authorities of the official world; the isolate, on the other hand,
repudiates existence as such and, with it, himself.

The justification for repeating these comparisons lies in the
common denominator of fidelity: the impotent craving of the
isolated sufferer to be true to himself, and the energetic attempt
of the joiner to be true to a group and to its insignia and codes.
By this I do not mean to deny that the isolate is sick (as his physical and mental symptoms attest), or that the joiner can be on
the way to becoming a criminal, as his more and more irreversible acts and choices attest. Both theory and therapy, however,
lack the proper leverage, if the need for (receiving and giving)
fidelity is not understood, and especially if the young deviant is
confronted instead with radical diagnoses confirming him by
every act of the correctional or therapeutic authorities as a future criminal or a lifelong patient.

Young people driven into the extreme of their condition may,
in the end, find a greater sense of identity in being withdrawn or
in being delinquent than in anything society has to offer them.
Yet we underestimate the hidden sensitivity of these young
people to the judgment of society at large. As Faulkner puts it:

"Sometimes I think it ain't none of us pure crazy and ain't none of us pure sane until the balance of us talks him that-a-way." If the "balance of us" diagnose these young people as psychotic or criminal so as to dispose of them efficiently, it may be the final step in the formation of a negative identity. To a high proportion of young people, society is offering only this one convincing "confirmation." Gangs, naturally, become the subsocieties for those thus confirmed.

In Dora's case, I have tried to indicate the phenomenology of the need for fidelity. As to young delinquents, I can only quote again one of those rare newspaper reports which convey enough of a story to show the elements involved. Kai T. Erikson and I have used this example as an introduction to our article "The Confirmation of the Delinquent." [10]

Judge Imposes Road Gang Term for Back Talk

Wilmington, N.D. (UP)—A "smart alecky" youth who wore pegged trousers and flattop haircut began six months on the road gang today for talking back to the wrong judge.

Michael A. Jones, 20, of Wilmington, was fined $25 and costs in Judge Edwin Jay Roberts Jr.'s Superior Court for reckless operation of an automobile. But he just didn't leave well enough alone.

"I understand how it was, with your pegged trousers and flattop haircut," Roberts said in assessing the fine.

"You go on like this and I predict in five years you'll be in prison."

When Jones walked over to pay his fine, he overheard Probation Officer Gideon Smith tell the judge how much trouble the "smart alecky" young offender had been.

"I just want you to know I'm not a thief," interrupted Jones to the judge.

The judge's voice boomed to the court clerk: "Change that judgment to six months on the roads."

I quote the story here to add the interpretation that the judge in this case (neither judge nor case differs from a host of others) took as an affront to the dignity of authority what may also have been a desperate "historical" denial, an attempt to claim that a truly antisocial identity had not yet been formed, and that there was enough discrimination and potential fidelity left to be made something of by somebody who cared to do so.[11] But, instead, what the young man and the judge made of it was likely, of course, to seal the irreversibility and confirm the doom. I say "was likely to" because I do not know what happened in this case; we do know, however, the high recidivity of criminality in the young who, during the years of identity formation, are forced by society into an exclusive identification with hardened criminals.

7.

The psychopathology of youth, then, suggests a consideration of the same issues which we found operative in the evolutionary and developmental aspects of this stage of life. And if we now turn back to history it cannot be overlooked that at times political undergrounds of all kinds can and do make use not only of the "sure" need for fidelity to be found in any new generation looking for new causes but also of the store of wrath accumulated in those totally deprived in their need to develop any faith. Here social rejuvenation can make use of and redeem social pathology, even as in individuals special giftedness can be related to and redeem neurosis. However, adolescence being an intermediary state, all the devotion, courage, and resourcefulness of youth can also be exploited by demagogues, while all ideological idealism retains a juvenile element which can become mere pretense when historical actuality changes.

As THE strength of disciplined devotion, then, fidelity can be gained in the involvement of youth in many kinds of experiences if they only reveal the essence of some aspect of the era youth is to join—as the beneficiaries and guardians of tradition, as the practitioners of and inventors in technology, as renewers and innovators of ethical strength, as rebels bent on the destruction of the outlived, and as deviants with fanatical commitments. This, at least, seems to be the potential of youth in psychosocial evolution; and if this may sound like a rationalization endorsing any high-sounding self-delusion in youth, any self-indulgence masquerading as devotion, or any righteous excuse for blind destruction, it makes at least intelligible the tremendous waste attending this as of any other mechanism of human adaptation. As pointed out, our understanding of these wasteful processes is only partially furthered by the "clinical" reduction of adolescent phenomena to their infantile antecedents and to an underlying dichotomy of drive and conscience. We must also understand the function of adolescence in society and history, for adolescent development comprises a new set of identification processes, both with significant persons and with ideological forces, which thereby take over both the strength and (as we must now specify) the weaknesses of the juvenile mind.

In youth, the life history intersects with history; here individuals are confirmed in their identities and societies regenerated in their life style. But this process also implies a fateful survival of adolescent modes of thinking and of juvenile enthusiasm in man's historical and ideological perspectives, and a split between adult reason and idealistic conviction which is only too obvious in oratory, both political and clerical.

As pointed out in Chapter II, historical processes have already entered the individual's core in childhood. Past history survives in the ideal and evil prototypes which guide the parental imagery and which color fairy tale and family lore, superstition and gossip, and the simple lessons of early verbal training. Historians on the whole make little of this; they account only for the contest of autonomous historical ideas and are unconcerned with the fact that these ideas reach down into the lives of generations and re-emerge through the daily awakening and training of historical consciousness in young individuals: via the mythmakers of religion and politics, of the arts and the sciences, of drama, cinema and fiction—all contributing more or less consciously, more or less responsibly to the historical logic absorbed by youth. And today we must add to these, at least in the United States, psychiatry and the social sciences, and all over the world, the press, which force all significant behavior into the open and add immediate reportorial distortion and editorial response.

To enter history, we said, each generation of youth must find an identity consonant with its own childhood and consonant with an ideological promise in the perceptible historical process. But in youth the tables of childhood dependence begin slowly to turn: no longer is it merely for the old to teach the young the meaning of life. It is the young who, by their responses and actions, tell the old whether life as represented to them has some vital promise, and it is the young who carry in them the power to confirm those who confirm them, to renew and regenerate, to disavow what is rotten, to reform and rebel.

And then there are the "youth leaders" who, one way or another, are "identified with youth." I have spoken of Hamlet as an abortive ideological leader. His drama combines all the elements of which successful ideological leaders are made: they are often the postadolescents who make out of the very contradictions of their protracted adolescence the polarities of their charisma. Individuals with an uncommon depth of conflict, they also often have uncanny gifts and uncanny luck with which they offer to the crisis of a whole generation the solution of their own personal crisis—always, as Woodrow Wilson put it, being "in love with activity on a large scale," always feeling that their one life must be made to count in the lives of all, always convinced that what shook them as youths was a curse, a fall, an earthquake, a thunderbolt—in short, a revelation to be shared with their generation and with many to come. Their humble claim to being chosen against their will does not preclude a wish for universal power. "Fifty years from now," wrote Kierkegaard in the journal of his spiritual soliloquy, "the whole world will read my diary." He sensed, maybe, and not necessarily with a sense of triumph, that the impending deadlock of mass ideologies would cause a vacuum ready for the ideology of parallel isolation, existentialism. We must study the question (I have approached it in my study of young Luther) of what ideological leaders do to history—whether they first aspire to power and then face spiritual qualms, or first face spiritual perdition and then seek universal influence. Their answers often manage to subsume under the heading of a more embracing identity all that ails man, especially young man, at critical times: danger from new inventions and weapons, anxiety from the childhood traumata typical for the time, and existential dread of the ego's limitations, magnified in times of disintegrating superidentities.

And, come to think of it, does it not take a special, strange sense of calling to dare and to care to give such inclusive answers? Is it not probable and, in fact, demonstrable that among the most passionate ideologists there are unreconstructed adolescents transmitting to their ideas the proud moment of their transient ego recovery, of their temporary victory over the forces of existence and history, but also the pathology of their deepest isolation, the defensiveness of their forever adolescing egos—and their fear of the calm of adulthood? "To live beyond forty," says Dostoevsky's undergound diarist, "is bad taste." It warrants study, both historical and psychological, to see how some of the most influential leaders have turned away from parenthood only to despair in middle age of the issue of their leadership as well.

It is clear that today the ideological needs of all but intellectual youth of the humanist tradition are beginning to be taken care of by a subordination of ideology to the technological superidentity in which even the American dream and the Marxist revolution come to meet. If their competition can be halted before it leads to mutual annihilation, it is just possible that a new mankind, seeing that it can now both build and destroy on a gigantic scale, will focus its intelligence (feminine as well as masculine) on the ethical question concerning the workings of human generations—beyond products, powers, and ideas. Ideologies in the past have also contained an ethical corrective, but a new ethics must eventually transcend the alliance of ideology and technology, for the great question will be how man, on ethical and generational grounds, will *limit* the use of technological expansion even where it might, for a while, enhance prestige and profit.

Moralities sooner or later outlive themselves, ethics never: this is what the need for identity and for fidelity, reborn with each generation, seems to point to. Morality in the moralistic sense can be shown to be predicated on superstitions and irrational inner mechanisms which, in fact, ever again undermine the ethical fiber of generations; but old morality is expendable only where new and more universal ethics prevail. This is the wisdom that the words of many religions have tried to convey to man. He has tenaciously clung to the ritualized words even though he has understood them only vaguely and in his actions has disregarded or perverted them completely. But there is much in ancient wisdom which now, perhaps, can become knowledge.

As in the near future peoples of different tribal and national pasts join what must eventually become the identity of one mankind, they can find an initial common language only in the workings of science and technology. This in turn may well help them to make transparent the superstitions of their traditional moralities and may even permit them to advance rapidly through a historical period during which they must put a vain superidentity of neonationalism in the place of their much-exploited historical identity weakness. But they must also look beyond the major ideologies of the now "established" world, offered them as ceremonial masks to frighten and attract them. The overriding issue is the creation not of a new ideology but of a universal ethics growing out of a universal technological civilization. This can be advanced only by men and women who are neither ideological youths nor moralistic old men, but who know that from generation to generation the test of what you produce is the *care* it inspires. If there is any chance at all, it is in a world more challenging, more workable, and more venerable than all myths, retrospective or prospective: it is in historical reality, at last ethically cared for.

VII

Womanhood
and the Inner Space

1.

THERE ARE A GREAT NUMBER OF economic and practical reasons for an intensified awareness of woman's position in the modern world. But there are also more elusive and darker reasons. The ubiquity of nuclear threat, the breakthrough into outer space, and increasing global communication are all bringing about a total change in the sense of geographic space and historical time, and thus they necessitate nothing less than a redefinition of the identity of the sexes within a new image of man. I cannot here go into the alliances and oppositions of the two sexes in previous styles of war and peace. This is a history as yet to be written and, indeed, discovered. But it is clear that the danger of man-made poison dropping invisibly from outer space into the marrow of the unborn in the wombs of women has suddenly brought one major male preoccupation, namely, the "solution" of conflict by periodical and bigger and better wars, to its own limits. The question arises whether such a potential for annihilation as now exists in the world should continue to exist without the representation of the mothers of the species in the councils of image-making and decision.

The special dangers of the nuclear age clearly have brought

male leadership close to the limit of its adaptive imagination. The dominant male identity is based on a fondness for "what works" and for what man can make, whether it helps to build or to destroy. For this very reason the all too obvious necessity to sacrifice some of the possible climaxes of technological triumph and of political hegemony for the sake of the mere preservation of mankind is not itself an endeavor enhancing the male sense of identity. True, an American president felt impelled to say, and said with deep feeling: "A child is not a statistic"; yet the almost desperate urgency of his pleas made clear enough the need for a new kind of political and technological ethics. Maybe if women would only gain the determination to represent publicly what they have always stood for privately in evolution and in history (realism of householding, responsibility of upbringing, resourcefulness in peacekeeping, and devotion to healing), they might well add an ethically restraining, because truly supranational, power to politics in the widest sense.

This, I think, many men and women hope openly and many more, secretly. But their hope collides with dominant trends in our technological civilization and with deep inner resistances as well. Self-made man, in "granting" a relative emancipation to women, could offer only his self-made image as a model to be equaled, and much of the freedom thus won by women now seems to have been spent in gaining access to limited career competition, standardized consumership, and strenuous one-family homemaking. Thus woman, in many ways, has kept her place within the typologies and cosmologies which men have had the exclusive opportunity to cultivate and to idolize. In other words, even where equality is closer to realization it has not led to equivalence, and equal rights have by no means secured equal representation in the sense that the deepest concerns of women find expression in their public influence or, indeed, their actual role in the game of power. In view of the gigantic one-sidedness which is threatening to make man the slave of his triumphant technology, the now fashionable discussion, by women and by men, as to whether woman could and how she might become "fully human" is really a cosmic parody, and, for once, one is nostalgic for gods with a sense of humor. The very question as to what it is to be "fully human" and who has the right to grant it to whom indicates that a discussion of the male and female elements in the potentialities of human nature must include rather fundamental issues.

In approaching them, therefore, one cannot avoid exploring certain emotional reactions or resistances which hinder concerted discussion. We all have observed the fact that it seems almost impossible to discuss woman's nature or nurture without awaking the slogans for and against the all-too-recent emancipation. Moralistic fervor outlives changed conditions and feminist suspicion watches over any man's attempt to help define the uniqueness of womanhood, as though by uniqueness he could be expected to mean inborn inequality. Yet it still seems to be amazingly hard for many women to say clearly what they feel most deeply, and to find the right words for what to them is most acute and actual, without saying too much or too little and without saying it with defiance or apology. Some women who observe and think vividly and deeply do not seem to have the courage of their native intelligence, as if they were somehow afraid on some final confrontation to be found to have no "real" intelligence. Even successful academic competition has, in many, failed to correct this. Thus women are still tempted quickly to go back to "their place" whenever they feel out of place. A major problem also seems to exist in the relationship of leading women to each other and to their women followers. As far as I can judge, "leading" women are all too often inclined to lead in too volatile, moralistic, or sharp a manner (as if they agreed to the proposition that only exceptional and hard women can think) rather than to inform themselves of and give voice to what the mass of undecided women are groping to say and are willing to stand by, and thus what use they may wish to make of an equal voice in world affairs.

On the other hand, the hesitance of many men to respond responsibly to the new "feminist" alarm, and the agitated response of others, suggests explanations on many levels. No doubt there exists among men an honest sense of wishing to save, at whatever cost, a sexual polarity, a vital tension, and an essential difference which they fear may be lost in too much sameness, equality, and equivalence, or at any rate in too much self-conscious talk. Beyond this, the defensiveness of men (and here we must include the best educated) has many facets. Where men desire, they want to awake desire, not empathize or ask for empathy. Where they do not desire, they find it hard to empathize, especially where empathy makes it necessary to see the other in oneself and oneself in the other, and where therefore the horror of diffused delineations is apt to kill both joy in otherness and sympathy for sameness. It also stands to reason that where dominant identities depend on being dominant it is hard to grant real equality to the dominated. And, finally, where one feels exposed, threatened, or cornered, it is difficult to be judicious.

For all of this there are age-old psychological reasons. There appear to be themes of such strangeness that rational men will ignore them, preferring to take off on some tangent. Among these themes, the physiological changes and the emotional challenges of that everyday miracle, pregnancy and childbirth, have disquieted every man through childhood, youth, and beyond. In his accounts of cultures and historical periods, man acknowledges this merely as a probably necessary side show. He habitually ascribes man's survival to the proud coherence of the schemes of men, not remembering the fact that while each scheme was tested and many exploded, women met the challenge of keeping some essentials together, of rebuilding, and of bringing up rebuilders. A new balance of Male and Female, of Paternal and Maternal is obviously presaged not only in contemporary changes in the relation of the sexes to each other, but also in the wider awareness which spreads wherever science, technology, and genuine self-scrutiny advance. Yet discussion in the present climate still calls for an acknowledgement from the onset that ambivalences and ambiguities of ancient standing are apt to be temporarily aggravated rather than alleviated by attempts to share partial insight in these matters.

2.

There is another general consideration which must precede the discussion of a subject which is so incompletely formulated and which always retains an intense actuality. Every worker will and must begin where he stands, that is, where he feels his own field and his own work have succeeded in clarifying, failed to do justice to, the issue as he has come to see it. But whenever he begins he is apt to be confronted with the remark which a Vermont farmer made to a driver who asked him for directions: "Well, now, if I wanted to go where you want to go, I wouldn't start from here."

Here is where I am, and where I must start from. In my preface to the book which grew out of the Youth issue of *Daedalus*,[1] I pointed out that that extraordinary symposium failed to develop fully—although Bruno Bettelheim made a determined start—the problem of the identity of female youth. This I felt was a severe theoretical handicap. For the student of development and practitioner of psychoanalysis knows that the stage of life crucial for the emergence of an integrated female identity is the step from youth to maturity, the state when the young woman, whatever her work career, relinquishes the care received from the parental family in order to commit herself to the love of a stranger and to the care to be given to his and her offspring.

I have suggested that the mental and emotional ability to receive and give fidelity marks the conclusion of adolescence, while adulthood begins with the ability to receive and give love and care. For the strength of the generations (and by this I mean a basic disposition underlying all varieties of human value systems) depends on the process by which the youths of the two sexes find their individual identities, fuse them in intimacy, love, and marriage, revitalize their respective traditions, and together create and "bring up" the next generation. Here whatever sexual differences and dispositions have developed in earlier life become polarized with finality because they must become part of the whole process of production and procreation which marks adulthood. But how does the identity formation of women differ by dint of the fact that their somatic design harbors an "inner space" destined to bear the offspring of chosen men and, with it, a biological, psychological, and ethical commitment to take care of human infancy? Is not the disposition for this commitment (whether it be combined with a career, and even whether or not it be realized in actual motherhood) the core problem of female fidelity?

The psychoanalytic psychology of women, however, does not "start here." In line with its originological orientation, i.e., the endeavor to infer the meaning of an issue from its origins, it begins with the earliest experiences of differentiation, largely reconstructed from women patients necessarily at odds with their womanhood and with the permanent inequality to which it seemed to doom them. However, since the psychoanalytic method could be developed only in work with acutely suffering individuals, whether adults or children, it was necessary to accept clinical observation as the original starting point for investigating what the little girl, when becoming aware of sex differences, can know as observable fact, can investigate by sight or touch, can feel as intense pleasure or unpleasant tension, or may infer or intuit with the cognitive and imaginative means at her disposal. I think it is fair to say that the psychoanalytic view of womanhood has been strongly influenced by the fact that the first and basic observations were made by clinicians whose task it was to understand suffering and to offer a remedy, and that by necessity they had to understand the female psyche with male means of empathy and to offer what the ethos of enlightenment dictated, namely, the "acceptance of reality." It is in line with this historical position that they saw, in the reconstructed lives of little girls, primarily an attempt to observe what could be seen and grasped (namely, what was there in boys and hardly there in girls) and to base on this observation "infantile sexual theories" of vast consequence.

From this point of view, the most obvious fact, namely, that children of both sexes sooner or later "know" the penis to be missing in one sex, leaving in its place a woundlike aperture, has led to generalizations concerning women's nature and nurture. From an adaptive point of view, however, it does not seem reasonable to assume that observation and empathy, except in moments of acute or transitory disturbance, would so exclusively focus on what is not there. The female child under all but extreme urban conditions is disposed to observe evidence in older girls and women and in female animals of the fact that an inner-bodily space—with productive as well as dangerous potentials —does exist. Here one thinks not only of pregnancy and childbirth, but also of lactation and all the richly convex parts of the female anatomy which suggest fullness, warmth, and generosity. One wonders, for example, whether girls are quite as upset by observed symptoms of pregnancy or menstruation as are (certain) boys, or whether they absorb such observation in the rudiments of a female identity—unless, of course, they are "protected" from the opportunity of comprehending the ubiquity and the meaning of these natural phenomena. Now no doubt at various stages of childhood observed data will be interpreted with the cognitive means then available, will be perceived in analogy with the organs then most intensely experienced, and will be endowed with the impulses then prevailing. Dreams, myths, and cults attest to the fact that the vagina has and retains (for both sexes) connotations of a devouring mouth and an eliminating sphincter, in addition to being a bleeding wound. However, the cumulative experience of being and becoming a man or a woman cannot, I believe, be entirely dependent upon fearful analogies and fantasies. Sensory reality and logical conclusion are given form by kinesthetic experience and by series of memories which "make sense," and in this total setting the existence of a productive inner-bodily space safely set in the center of female form and carriage has, I would think, greater actuality than has the missing external organ.

If I, then, take my start from here, it is because I believe that a future formulation of sex differences must at least include post-Freudian insights in order not to succumb to the repressions and denials of pre-Freudian days.

3.

Let me present here an observation which makes my point wordlessly, through the observation of children at play. The children were California boys and girls, aged ten, eleven, and twelve years, who twice a year came to be measured, interviewed, and tested in the "Guidance Study" of the University of California. It speaks for the feminine genius of the director of the study, Jean Walker Macfarlane, that for more than two decades the children (and their parents) not only came with regularity, but confided their thoughts with little reservation and, in fact, with much "zest"—to use Jean Macfarlane's favorite word. That means they were confident of being appreciated as growing individuals and eager to reveal and demonstrate what (they had been convincingly told) was useful to know and might be helpful to others. Since before joining the California study I had made it my business to interpret play behavior—a nonverbal approach which had helped me to understand what my very small patients were not able to communicate in words—it was decided that I would secure a number of play constructions from each child and then compare their form and context with other available data. Over a span of two years, I saw 150 boys and 150 girls three times and presented them, one at a time, with the task of constructing a "scene" with toys on a table. The toys were rather ordinary—a family, some uniformed figures (policemen, aviator, Indian, monk, etc.), wild and domestic animals, furniture, automobiles—but I also provided a large number of blocks. The children were asked to imagine that the table was a moving-picture studio; the toys, actors and props; and they themselves, moving-picture directors. They were to arrange on the table "an exciting scene from an imaginary moving picture," and then tell the plot. This was recorded, the scene photographed, and the child complimented. It may be necessary to add that no "inter-pretation" was given.[2]

The observer then compared the individual constructions with about ten years of biographic data to see whether it pro-vided some key to the major determinants of the child's inner development. On the whole this proved helpful, but that is not the point to be made here. The experiment also made possible a comparison of all play constructions with one another.

A few of the children went about the task with the somewhat contemptuous attitude of one doing something which was not exactly worth the effort of a young person already in his teens, but almost all of these bright and willing youngsters in somber jeans and gay dresses were drawn to the challenge by that eager-ness to serve and please which characterized the whole popula-tion of the study. And once they were involved, certain proper-ties of the task took over and guided them.

It soon became evident that among these properties the spatial one was dominant. Only half of the scenes were "exciting," and only a handful had anything to do with moving pictures. In fact, the stories told at the end were for the most part brief and in no way comparable to the thematic richness evidenced in verbal tests. But the care and (one is tempted to say) esthetic responsi-bility with which the children selected blocks and toys and then arranged them according to an apparently deeply held sense of spatial propriety was astounding. At the end, it seemed to be a sudden feeling of "now it's right" which made them come to a sense of completion and, as if awakening from a wordless experi-ence, turn to me and say, "I am ready now"—meaning, I am ready to tell you what this is all about.

I myself was most interested in observing not only imaginative themes but also spatial configurations in relation to stages of the life cycle in general and to the forms of neurotic tension in pre-puberty in particular. Sex differences thus were not the initial focus of my interest. I concentrated my attention on how the constructions-in-progress moved forward to the edge of the table or back to the wall behind it; how they rose to shaky heights or remained close to the table surface; how they were spread over the available space or constricted to a portion of that space. That all of this "says" something about the constructor is the open secret of all "projective techniques." This, too, cannot be discussed here. But soon I realized that in evaluating a child's play construction, I had to take into consideration the fact that girls and boys used space differently, and that certain configurations occurred strikingly often in the constructions of one sex and rarely in those of the other.

The differences themselves were so simple that at first they seemed a matter of course. History in the meantime has offered a slogan for it: the girls emphasized *inner* and the boys *outer* space.

This difference I was soon able to state in such simple configurational terms that other observers, when shown photographs of the constructions without knowing the sex of the constructor (nor, indeed, having any idea of my thoughts concerning the possible meaning of the differences), could sort the photographs according to the configurations most dominant in them, and this significantly in the statistical sense. These independent ratings showed that considerably more than two thirds of what I subsequently called the male configurations occurred in scenes constructed by boys, and more than two thirds of the "female" configurations in the constructions of girls. (I will here omit the finer points which still characterized the atypical scenes as clearly built by a boy or by a girl.) This, then, is typical: the girl's scene is a house *interior*, represented either as a configuration of furniture without any surrounding walls or by a simple *enclosure* built with blocks. In the girl's scene, people and animals are mostly *within* such an interior or enclosure, and they are primarily people or animals in a *static* (sitting or standing) position. Girls' enclosures consist of low walls, i.e., only one block high, except for an occasional *elaborate doorway*. These interiors of houses with or without walls were, for the most part, expressly *peaceful*. Often, a little girl was playing the piano. In a number of cases, however, the interior was *intruded*

by animals or dangerous men. Yet the idea of an intruding creature did not necessarily lead to the defensive erection of walls or
the closing of doors. Rather the majority of these intrusions
have an element of humor and pleasurable excitement.

Boys' scenes are either houses with elaborate walls or façades
with *protrusions* such as cones or cylinders representing orna-
ments or cannons. There are *high towers*, and there are entirely
exterior scenes. In boys' constructions more people and animals
are *outside* enclosures or buildings, and there are more *automotive* objects and animals *moving* along streets and intersections.
There are elaborate automotive *accidents*, but there is also traffic
channeled or arrested by the policeman. While *high structures*
are prevalent in the configurations of the boys, there is also
much play with the danger of *collapse* or downfall; *ruins* were
exclusively boys' constructions.

The male and female spaces, then, were dominated, respec-
tively, by height and downfall and by strong motion and its
channeling or arrest; and by static interiors which were open or
simply enclosed, and peaceful or intruded upon. It may come as
a surprise to some and seem a matter of course to others that
here sexual differences in the organization of a play space seem to
parallel the morphology of genital differentiation itself: in the
male, an external organ, erectable and intrusive in character, serving the channelization of mobile sperm cells; in the female, internal organs, with vestibular access, leading to statically expec-
tant ova. The question is: what is really surprising about this,
and what only too obvious, and in either case, what does it tell
us about the two sexes?

4.

Since I first presented these data a decade and a half ago to
workers in different fields, some standard interpretations have
not yielded an iota. There are, of course, derisive reactions
which take it for granted that a psychoanalyst would want to
read the bad old symbols into this kind of data. And indeed,
Freud did note more than half a century ago that "a house is the

only regularly occurring symbol of the (whole) human body in dreams." But there is quite a methodological step from the occurrence of a symbol in dreams and a configuration created in actual space. Nevertheless, the purely psychoanalytic or somatic explanation has been advanced that the scenes reflect the preadolescent's preoccupation with his own sexual organs.

The purely "social" interpretation, on the other hand, denies the necessity to see anything symbolic or, indeed, somatic in these configurations. It takes it for granted that boys love the outdoors and girls the indoors, or at any rate that they see their respective roles assigned to the indoors of houses and to the great outdoors of adventure, to tranquil feminine love for family and children and to high masculine aspiration.

One cannot help agreeing with both interpretations—up to a point. Of course, whatever social role is associated with one's physique will be expressed thematically in any playful or artistic representation. And, of course, under conditions of special tension or preoccupation with one part of the body, that part may be recognizable in play configurations: play therapy relies on that. The spokesmen for the anatomical and for the social interpretations are thus both right if they insist that neither possibility may be ignored. But this does not make either exclusively right.

A pure interpretation in terms of social role leaves many questions unanswered. If the boys thought primarily of their present or anticipated roles, why, for example, is the policeman their favorite toy, traffic stopped dead a frequent scene? If vigorous activity outdoors is a determinant of the boys' scenes, why did they not arrange any sports fields on the play table? (One tomboyish girl did.) Why did the girls' love for home life not result in an increase in high walls and closed doors as guarantors of intimacy and security? And could the role of playing the piano in the bosom of their families really be considered representative of what these girls (some of them passionate horseback riders and all future automobile drivers) wanted to do most or, indeed, thought they should pretend they wanted to do most?

Thus the boys' caution outdoors and the girls' goodness indoors in response to the explicit instruction to construct an exciting movie scene suggested dynamic dimensions and acute conflicts not explained by a theory of mere compliance with cultural and conscious roles.

I would suggest an altogether more inclusive interpretation, according to which a profound difference exists between the sexes in the experience of the ground plan of the human body. The emphasis here is on predisposition and predilection, rather than on exclusive ability, for both sexes (if otherwise matched in maturation and intelligence) learn readily to imitate the spatial mode of the other sex. Nothing in our interpretation, then, is meant to claim that either sex is doomed to one spatial mode or another; rather, it is suggested that in contexts which are not imitative or competitive these modes "come more naturally" for natural reasons which must claim our interest. The spatial phenomenon observed here would then express two principles of arranging space which correspond to the male and female principles in body construction. These may receive special emphasis in prepuberty, and maybe in some other stages of life as well, but they are relevant through life to the elaboration of sex roles in cultural space-times. Such an interpretation cannot be "proven," of course, by the one observation offered here. The question is whether it is in line with observations of spatial behavior in other media and at other ages; whether it can be made a plausible part of a developmental theory; and whether, indeed, it gives to other sex differences closely related to male and female structure and function a more convincing order. On the other hand, it would not be contradicted by the fact that other media of observation employed to test male and female performance might reveal few or no sexual differences in areas of the mind which have the function of securing verbal or cognitive agreement on matters dominated by the mathematical nature of the universe and the verbal agreement of cultural traditions. Such agreement, in fact, may have as its very function the correction of what differentiates the experience of the sexes, even as it also corrects the intuitive judgments separating other classes of men.

The play-constructing children in Berkeley, California, will lead us into a number of spatial considerations, especially concerning feminine development and outlook. Here I will say little about men; their accomplishments in the conquest of geographic space and of scientific fields and in the dissemination of ideas speak loudly for themselves and confirm traditional values of masculinity. Yet the play-constructing boys in Berkeley may give us pause: on the world scene, do we not see a supremely gifted yet somewhat boyish mankind playing excitedly with history and technology, following a male pattern as embarrassingly simple (if technologically complex) as the play constructions of the preadolescent? Do we not see the themes of the toy microcosm dominating an expanding human space: height, penetration, and speed; collision, explosion—and cosmic superpolice? In the meantime, women have found their identities in the care suggested in their bodies and in the needs of their issue, and seem to have taken it for granted that the outer world space belongs to the men.

5.

Before going on from here, I must retrace my steps to my earlier statement that the observations reported "while not expected seemed to confirm something long awaited." They served to clarify many doubts mentioned earlier regarding psychoanalytic theories of femininity. Many of the original conclusions of psychoanalysis concerning womanhood hinge on the so-called genital trauma, i.e., the little girl's sudden comprehension of the fact that she does not and never will have a penis. The assumed prevalence of envy in women; the assumption that the future baby is a substitute for the penis; the assumption that the the girl turns from the mother to the father because she finds that the mother not only cheated her out of a penis but has been cheated herself; and finally the woman's disposition to abandon (male) aggressiveness for the sake of a "passive-masochistic" orientation: all these depend on "the trauma," and all have been built into elaborate explanations of femininity. They all exist somewhere in all women and their existence has been shown over and over again in psychoanalyses. But it must always be suspected that a special method bares truths especially true under the circumstances created by the method, here the venting in free association of hidden resentments and repressed traumata. These same truths assume the character of very partial truths within a normative theory of feminine development in which they would appear to be subordinate to the early dominance of the productive interior. This would allow, then, for a shift of theoretical emphasis from the loss of an external organ to a sense of vital inner potential; from a hateful contempt for the mother to a solidarity with her and other women; from a "passive" renunciation of male activity to the purposeful and competent pursuit of activities consonant with the possession of ovaries, a uterus, and a vagina; and from a masochisic pleasure in pain to an ability to stand (and to understand) pain as a meaningful aspect of human experience in general and of the feminine role in particular. And so it is in the "fully feminine" woman, as such outstanding writers as Helene Deutsch have recognized, even though their nomenclature was tied to the psychopathological term "masochism"—a word significantly derived from the name of an Austrian man and novelist who described the perversion of being sexually aroused and satisfied by having pain inflicted on him (even as the tendency to inflict it has been named after the Marquis de Sade).

When this is seen, many now dispersed data fall into line. However, a clinician must ask himself in passing what kind of thinking may have permitted such a nomenclature and such a theory of development and their acceptance by outstanding women clinicians. This thinking is, I believe, to be traced not only to the psychiatric beginnings of psychoanalysis, but also to the original analytic-atomistic method employed by it. In science, our capacity to think atomistically corresponds to the nature of matter to a high degree and thus leads to the mastery over matter. But when we apply atomistic thinking to man, we break him down into isolated fragments rather than into constituent elements. In fact, when we look at man in the state of pathology, he is already fragmented, so that in psychiatry an atomizing mind may meet a phenomenon of fragmentation and mistake the fragments for atoms. In psychoanalysis we repeat for our own encouragement (and as an argument against others) that human nature can best be studied in a state of partial breakdown or, at any rate, of marked conflict because—so we say—a conflict delineates borderlines and clarifies the forces which collide on these borderlines. As Freud himself put it, we see a crystal's structure only when it cracks. But a crystal, on the one hand, and an organism or a personality, on the other, differ in the fact that one is inanimate and the other an organic whole which cannot be broken up without a withering of the parts. The ego, in the psychoanalytic sense of a guardian of inner continuity, insofar as it is in a pathological state is more or less inactivated; that is, it loses its capacity to organize personality and experience and to relate itself to other egos in mutual activation. To that extent its irrational defenses are "easier to study" in a state of conflict and isolation than is the ego of a person in vivid interaction with other persons. Yet I do not believe that we can entirely reconstruct the ego's normal functions from an understanding of its dysfunctions, nor that we can understand all vital conflict as neurotic conflict.

This, then, would characterize a post-Freudian position: the complexes and conflicts unearthed by psychoanalysis in its first breakthrough to human nature are recognized as existing; they do threaten to dominate the developmental and accidental crises of life. But the freshness and wholeness of experience and the opportunities arising with a resolved crisis can, in an ongoing life, transcend trauma and defense. To illustrate this, let me briefly remark on the often repeated statement that the little girl at a given stage "turns to" her father, whereas in all preceding stages she had been primarily attached to her mother. Actually, Freud insisted only that a theoretical "libido" was thus turning from one "object" to another, a theory which was, at one time, scientifically pleasing because it corresponded to a simple and (in principle) measurable transfer of energy. Developmentally seen, however, the girl turns to her father at a time when she is quite a different person from the one she was when primarily dependent on her mother. She has normally learned the nature of an "object relationship," once and for all, from her mother. The relationship to her father, then, is of a different kind, in that it becomes particularly significant when the girl has already learned to trust her mother and does not need to retest basic relationships. She now can develop a new form of love for a being who in turn is, or should be, ready to be responsive to the budding and teasing woman in her. The total process thus has many more aspects than can be condensed in the statement that the girl turns her libido from her mother to her father. Such transfer can, in fact, be reconstructed as an isolated "mechanism" only where the ego has been inactivated in some of its capacity to reorganize experience in line with emotional, physical, and cognitive maturation; and only then can it be said that the girl turns to her father because she is disappointed in her mother over what her mother has seemingly refused to give her, namely, a penis. Now, no doubt, some old disappointments and new expectations play an eminent role in all changes of attachment from an old to a new person or activity, but in any healthy change the fresh opportunities of the new relationship will outweigh the repetitious insistence on old disappointments. No doubt, also, new attachments prepare new disappointments, for the inner-productive role which we assume exists early in rudimentary form will cause in the small woman such fantasies as must succumb to repression and frustration—for example, in the insight that no daughter may give birth to her father's children. No doubt also the very existence of the inner productive space exposes women early to a specific sense of loneliness, to a fear of being left empty or deprived of treasures, of remaining unfulfilled and of drying up. This, no less than the strivings and disappointments of the little "Electra," has fateful consequences for the human in-

dividual and for the whole race. For this very reason it seems decisive not to misinterpret these feelings as totally due to a resent-
ment of not being a boy or of having been mutilated.

It will now be clear in what way the children's play constructions were unexpected and yet awaited. What was unexpected
was the domination of the whole space by the sex differences—a
"field" dominance going far beyond the power of any symbolic
representation of the sex organs. The data were "awaited,"
above all, as nonclinical and nonverbal support of pervasive
impressions concerning the importance of the "inner space"
throughout the feminine life cycle. The life histories of the girls
in the Guidance Study did not make sense without such an
assumption, but neither did the case histories of women patients
of all ages. For, as pointed out, clinical observation suggests that
in female experience an "inner space" is at the center of despair
even as it is the very center of potential fulfillment. Emptiness is
the female form of perdition—known at times to men of the
inner life (whom we will discuss later), but standard experience
for all women. To be left, for her, means to be left empty, to be
drained of the blood of the body, the warmth of the heart, the
sap of life. How a woman thus can be hurt in depth is a wonder
to many a man, and it can arouse both his empathic horror and
his refusal to understand. Such hurt can be re-experienced in each
menstruation; it is a crying to heaven in the mourning over a
child; and it becomes a permanent scar in the menopause. Clinically, this "void" is so obvious that generations of clinicians must
have had a special reason for not focusing on it. Maybe, even as
primitive men banned it with phobic avoidances and magic rituals of purification, the enlightened men of a civilization pervaded by technological pride could meet it only with the interpretation that suffering woman wanted above all what man had,
namely, exterior equipment and traditional access to "outer"
space. Again, such female envy exists in all women and is aggravated in some cultures; but the explanation of it in male terms
or the suggestion that it be borne with fatalism and compensated
for by a redoubled enjoyment of the feminine equipment (duly

certified and accepted as second rate) has not helped women to find their places in the modern world, for it has made of womanhood an ubiquitous compensation neurosis marked by a bitter insistence on being "restored."

I will generalize, then, in two directions. I submit that in psychoanalysis we have not ascribed due importance to the procreative patterns intrinsic to sexual morphology, and I will try to formulate the assumption that procreative patterns, in varying intensity, pervade every state of excitement and inspiration and, *if integrated*, lend power to all experience and to its communication.

In assigning a central place to generative modalities I, too, seem to repeat the often obsessive emphasis on sexual symbols in psychoanalytic theory and to ignore the fact that women as well as men have all-human organisms fit for, and most of the time enjoyed in, activities far removed from the sexual. But while both sexual repression and sexual monomania *isolate* sexuality from the total design of human actuality, we must be interested in how sex differences, once taken for granted, are *integrated* in that design. Sexual differences, however, besides offering a polarization of life styles and the maximization of mutual enjoyment (which now more than ever can be separated from procreation) nevertheless retain the morphology of procreation. It would even seem that such unashamed explorations of the inner space as those now medically conducted into human sexual response in St. Louis reveal a vigorous involvement of the procreative organs in the excitement of every kind of sexual act.

6.

If the "inner space" is so pervasive a configuration, it should be found to have its place in the evolutionary beginnings of social organization. Here, too, we can call on visual data.

Recent motion pictures taken in Africa by Washburn and deVore[3] demonstrate vividly the morphology of basic baboon organization. The whole wandering troop in search of food over a certain territory is so organized as to keep within a safe inner space the females who bear future offspring within their bodies or carry their growing young. They are protectively surrounded by powerful males who, in turn, keep their eyes on the horizon, guiding the troop toward available food and guarding it from potential danger. In peacetime the strong males also protect the "inner circle" of pregnant and nursing females against the encroachments of the relatively weaker and definitely more importunate males. Once danger is spotted, the whole wandering configuration stops and consolidates into an inner space of safety and an outer space of combat. In the center sit the pregnant females and mothers with their newborns. At the periphery are the males best equipped to fight or scare off predators.

I was impressed with these movies not only for their beauty and ingenuity, but because here I could see in the bush configurations analogous to those in the Berkeley play constructions. The baboon pictures, however, can lead us one step further. Whatever the morphological differences between the female and the male baboons' bony structures, postures, and behaviors, they are adapted to their respective tasks of harboring and defending the concentric circles, from the procreative womb to the limits of the defensible territory. Thus morphological trends "fit" given necessities and are therefore elaborated by basic social organization. And it deserves emphasis that even among the baboons the greatest warriors display a chivalry which permits the female baboons, for example, to have weaker shoulders and lesser fighting equipment. In both prehuman and human existence, then, the formula holds that whether, when, and in what respects a female anywhere can be said to be "weaker" is a matter to be decided not on the basis of comparative tests of isolated muscles, capacities, or traits but on that of the functional fitness of each item for an organism which, in turn, fits into an ecology of divided function.

Human society and technology has, of course, transcended evolutionary arrangement, making room for cultural triumphs of adaptation as well as for physical and mental maladaptation on a large scale. But when we speak of biologically given strengths and weaknesses in the human female, we may yet have to accept as one measure of all difference the biological rock-bottom of sexual differentiation. In this, the woman's productive inner space may well remain an inescapable criterion, whether conditions permit her to build her life partially or wholly around it or not. At any rate, many of the testable items on the long list of "inborn" differences between human males and females can be shown to have a meaningful function within an ecology which is built, as any mammalian ecology must be, around the fact that the human fetus must be carried inside the womb for a given number of months, and that the infant must be suckled or, at any rate, raised within a maternal world best staffed at first by the mother (and this for the sake of her own awakened motherliness, as well) with a gradual addition of other women. Here years of specialized womanhours of work are involved. It makes sense, then, that the little girl, the future bearer of ova and of maternal powers, tends to survive her birth more surely and turns out to be a tougher creature, to be plagued, to be sure, by many small ailments, but more resistant to some man-killing diseases (for example, of the heart) and with a longer life expectancy. It also makes sense that she is able earlier than boys to concentrate on details immediate in time and space, and has throughout a finer discrimination for things seen, touched, and heard. To these she reacts more vividly, more personally, and with greater compassion. More easily touched and touchable, however, she is said also to recover faster, ready to react again and elsewhere. That all of this is essential to the "biological" task of reacting to the differential needs of others, especially weaker ones, is not an unreasonable interpretation; nor should it, in this context, seem a deplorable inequality that in the employment of larger muscles woman shows less vigor, speed, and co-ordination. The little girl also learns to be more easily content within a limited circle of activities and shows less resistance to control and less impulsiveness of the kind that later leads boys and men to "delinquency." All of these and more certified "differences" could be shown to have corollaries in our play constructions.

Now it is clear that much of the basic schema suggested here as female also exists in some form in all men and decisively so in men of special giftedness—or weakness. The inner life which characterizes some artistic and creative men certainly also compensates for their being biologically men by helping them to specialize in that inwardness and sensitive indwelling (the German *Innigkeit*) usually ascribed to women. They are prone to cyclic swings of mood while they carry conceived ideas to fruition and toward the act of disciplined creation. The point is that in women the basic schema exists within an over-all optimum configuration such as cultures have every reason to nurture in the *majority of women*, for the sake of collective survival as well as individual fulfillment. It makes little sense, then, when discussing basic sex differences to quote the deviations and accomplishments (or both) of exceptional men or women without an inclusive account of their many-sided personalities, their special conflicts, and their complex life histories. On the other hand, one should also emphasize (and especially so in a post-Puritan civilization which continues to decree predestination by mercilessly typing individuals) that successive stages of life offer growing and maturing individuals ample leeway for free variation in essential sameness.

For example, woman's life too contains an adolescent stage which I have come to call a psychosocial moratorium, a sanctioned period of delay of adult functioning. The maturing girl and the young woman, in contrast to the little girl and the mature woman, can thus be relatively freer from the tyranny of the inner space. In fact, she may venture into "outer space" with a bearing and a curiosity which often appears hermaphroditic if not outright "masculine." A special ambulatory dimension is thus added to the inventory of her spatial behavior, which many societies counteract with special rules of virginal restraint. Where the mores permit, however, the young girl tries out a variety of possible identifications with the phallic-ambulatory male even as she experiments with the experience of being his counterpart and principal attraction—a seeming contradiction which will eventually be transformed into a polarity and a sexual and personal style. In all this, the inner space remains central to subjective experience but is overtly manifested only in persistent and selective attractiveness, for whether the young woman draws others to herself with magnetic inwardness, with challenging outwardness, or with a dramatic alternation of both, she selectively invites what seeks her.

Young women often ask whether they can "have an identity" before they know whom they will marry and for whom they will make a home. Granted that something in the young woman's identity must keep itself open for the peculiarities of the man to be joined and of the children to be brought up, I think that much of a young woman's identity is already defined in her kind of attractiveness and in the selective nature of her search for the man (or men) by whom she wishes to be sought. This, of course, is only the psychosexual aspect of her identity, and she may go far in postponing its closure while training herself as a worker and a citizen and while developing as a person within the role possibilities of her time. The singular loveliness and brilliance which young women display in an array of activities obviously removed from the future function of childbearing is one of those esthetic phenomena which almost seem to transcend all goals and purposes and therefore come to symbolize the self-containment of pure being—wherefore young women, in the arts of the ages, have served as the visible representation of ideals and ideas and as the creative man's muse, anima, and enigma. One is somewhat reluctant, therefore, to assign an ulterior meaning to what seems so meaningful in itself, and to suggest that the inner space is tacitly present in it all. A true moratorium must have a term and a conclusion: womanhood arrives when attractiveness and experience have succeeded in selecting what is to be admitted to the welcome of the inner space "for keeps."

Thus only a total configurational approach—somatic, historical, individual—can help us to see the differences of functioning and experiencing in context, rather than in isolated and senseless comparison. Woman, then, is not "more passive" than man simply because her central biological function forces her or permits her to be active in a manner tuned to inner-bodily processes, or because she may be gifted with a certain intimacy and contained intensity of feeling, or because she may choose to dwell in the protected inner circle within which maternal care can flourish. Nor is she "more masochistic" because she must accept inner periodicities in addition to the pain of childbirth, which is explained in the Bible as the eternal penalty for Eve's delinquent behavior and interpreted by writers as recent as de Beauvoir as "a hostile element within her own body." Taken together with the phenomena of sexual life and motherhood, it is obvious that woman's knowledge of pain makes her a "dolorosa" in a deeper sense than one who is addicted to small pains. She is, rather, one who "takes pains" to understand and alleviate suffering and can train others in the forebearance necessary to stand unavoidable pain. She is a "masochist," then, only when she exploits pain perversely or vindictively, which means that she steps out of, rather than deeper into, her female function. By the same token, a woman is pathologically passive only when she becomes too passive within a sphere of efficacy and personal integration which includes her disposition for female activity.

One argument, however, is hard to counter. Woman, through the ages (at any rate, the patriarchal ones), has lent herself to a variety of roles conducive to an exploitation of masochistic potentials: she has let herself be confined and immobilized, enslaved and infantilized, prostituted and exploited, deriving from it at best what in psychopathology we call "secondary gains" of devious dominance. This fact, however, could be satisfactorily explained only within a new kind of biocultural history which (and this is one of my main points) would first have to overcome the prejudiced opinion that woman must be, or will be, what she is or has been under particular historical conditions.

7.

Am I saying, then, that "anatomy is destiny"? Yes, it is destiny, insofar as it determines not only the range and configuration of physiological functioning and its limitation but also, to an extent, personality configurations. The basic modalities of woman's commitment and involvement naturally also reflect the ground plan of her body. I have in another context identified "inception" as a dominant modality already in the early lives and in the play of children.[4] We may mention in passing woman's capacity on many levels of existence to actively *include*, to accept, "*to have and to hold*"—but also to *hold on*, and *hold in*. She may be protective with high selectivity and overprotective without discrimination. That she must protect means that she must rely on protection—and she may demand overprotection. To be sure, she also has an organ of intrusion, the nipple which nurses, and her wish to succor can, indeed, become intrusive and oppressive. It is, in fact, of such exaggerations and deviations that many men—and also women—think when the unique potentials of womanhood are discussed.

As pointed out, however, it makes little sense to ask whether in any of these respects a woman is "more so" than a man, but how much she varies within womanhood and what she makes of it within the leeway of her stage of life and of her historical and economic opportunities. So far I have only reiterated the physiological rock-bottom which must neither be denied nor given exclusive emphasis. For a human being, in addition to having a body, is *somebody*, which means an indivisible personality and a defined member of a group. In this sense, Napoleon's dictum that history is destiny, which Freud, I believe, meant to counterpoint with his dictum that destiny lies in anatomy (and one often must know what dicta a man tried to counterpoint with *his* most one-sided dicta), is equally valid. In other words: anatomy, history, and personality are our combined destiny.

Men, of course, have shared and taken care of some of the concerns for which women stand: each sex can transcend itself to feel and to represent the concerns of the other. For even as real women harbor a legitimate as well as a compensatory masculinity, so real men can partake of motherliness—if permitted to do so by powerful mores.

In search of an observation which bridges biology and history, an extreme historical example comes to mind in which women elevated their procreative function to a style of life when their men seemed totally defeated.

This story was highlighted for me on two occasions when I participated in conferences in the Caribbean and learned of family patterns prevailing throughout the islands. Churchmen have had reason to deplore, and anthropologists to explore, the pattern of Caribbean family life, alternately interpreted as African or as an outgrowth of the slavery days of plantation America, which extended from the northeast coast of Brazil through the Caribbean half circle into the southeastern part of the present United States. Plantations, of course, were agricultural factories owned and operated by gentlemen whose cultural and economic identity had its roots in a supraregional upper class. They were worked by slaves, that is, by men who, being mere equipment, were put to use when and where necessary and who often had to relinquish all chance of becoming the masters of their families and communities. Thus the women were left with the offspring of a variety of men who could give neither provision nor protection, nor provide any identity except that of a subordinate species. The family system which ensued is described in the literature in terms of circumscriptions: the rendering of "sexual services" between persons who cannot be called anything more definite than "lovers"; "maximum instability" in the sexual lives of young girls, who often "relinquish" the care of their offspring to their mothers; and mothers and grandmothers who determine the "standardized mode of coactivity" which is the minimum requirement for calling a group of individuals a family. These are, then, the "household groups"—single dwellings occupied by people sharing a common food supply and administered "matrifocally"—a word which understates the grandiose role of the all-powerful grandmother-figure, who will encourage her daughters to leave their infants with her, or at any rate to stay with her as long as they continue to bear children. Motherhood thus became community life, and where churchmen could find little or no morality, and casual observers little or no tradition at all, the mothers and grandmothers had to become fathers and grandfathers in the sense that they exerted the only continuous influence resulting in an ever newly improvised set of rules for the economic obligations of the men who had fathered the children. They upheld the rules of incestuous avoidance. Above all, it seems to me, they provided the only superidentity which was left open after the enslavement of the men, namely, that of the worth of a human infant irrespective of his parentage.

It is well known how many little white gentlemen benefited from the extended fervor of the nurturant Negro woman—southern mammies, Creole *das*, or Brazilian *babas*. This phenomenal caring is, of course, being played down by the racists as mere servitude, while it is decried by moralists as African sensualism or idolized as true femininity by white refugees from "continental" womanhood. One may, however, see at the roots of this maternalism a grandiose gesture of human adaptation which has given the area of the Caribbean (now searching for a political and economic pattern to do justice to its cultural unity) both the promise of a positive maternal identity and the threat of a negative male one, for the fact that identity relied on the mere worth of being born has undoubtedly weakened economic aspiration in many men.

That this has been an important historical issue can be seen in the life of Simon Bolivar. This "liberator of South America" was born in the coastal region of Venezuela, which is one anchor point of the great Caribbean half circle. When, in 1827, Bolivar liberated Caracas and entered it in triumph, he recognized the Negro Hipolita, his erstwhile wetnurse, in the crowd. He dismounted and "threw himself in the arms of the Negro woman who wept with joy." Two years earlier, he had written to his sister: "I enclose a letter to my mother Hipolita so that you give her all she wants and deal with her as if she were my mother; her milk fed my life, and I knew no other father than she" (translation not mine). Whatever personal reasons there were for Bolivar's effusiveness toward Hipolita (he had lost his mother when he was nine, etc.), the biographic importance of this item is amply matched by the historical significance of the fact that he could play up this relationship as a propaganda item within that peculiar ideology of race and origin which contributed to his charisma throughout the continent he liberated— from his ancestors.

That continent does not concern us here. But as for the Caribbean area, the matrifocal theme explains much of a certain disbalance between extreme trustfulness and weakness of initiative which could be exploited by native dictators as well as by foreign capital and has now become the concern of the erstwhile colonial masters as well as of the emancipated leaders of various island groups. Knowing this, we should understand that the bearded group of men and boys who have taken over one of the islands represents a deliberately new type of man who insists on proving that the Caribbean male can earn his worth in production as well as in procreation without the imposition of "continental" leadership or ownership.

This transformation of a colorful island area into an inner space structured by woman is an almost clinical example to be applied with caution. And yet it is only one story out of that unofficial history which is as yet to be written for all areas and eras: the history of territories and domains, markets and empires; the history of women's quiet creativity in preserving and restoring what official history had torn apart. Some stirrings in contemporary historiography, such as attempts to describe closely the everyday atmosphere of a given locality in a given historical era, seem to bespeak a growing awareness of a need for, shall we say, an integrated history.

THERE IS a real question then, whether any one field can deliver the data on which to base valid assumptions regarding the differences between the sexes. We speak of anatomical, historical, and psychological facts, and yet it must be clear that facts reliably ascertained by the methods of one of these fields by the same token lose a most vital interconnection. Man is, at one and the same time, part of a somatic order of things as well as of a personal and a social one. To avoid identifying these orders with established fields, let me call them Soma, Psyche, and Polis, for at least they can serve attempts to designate new fields of inquiry such as the psychosomatic field already existing and the psychopolitical one sure to appear. Each order guards a certain intactness and also offers a leeway of optional or at least workable choices, while man lives in all three and must work out their mutual complementation and their "eternal" contradictions.

Soma is the principle of the organism living its life cycle. But the female Soma is not only comprised of what is within a woman's skin and the variety of appearances suggested by modish changes in her clothes; it includes a mediatorship in evolution, genetic as well as sociogenetic, by which she creates in each child the somatic (sensual and sensory) basis for his physical, cultural, and individual identity. This mission, once a child is conceived, must be completed. It is woman's unique job. But no woman lives or needs to live only in this extended somatic sphere. The modern world offers her ever-greater leeway in choosing, planning, or renouncing her somatic tasks more knowingly and responsibly. So she can and must make, or else neglect, decisions as a citizen and worker and, of course, as an individual.

In the sphere of Psyche, we have discussed the organizing principle called ego. It is in the ego that individualized experience has its organizing center, for the ego is the guardian of the indivisibility of the person. Ego organization mediates between somatic and personal experience and political actuality in the widest sense. To do so it uses psychological mechanisms common to both sexes—a fact which makes intelligent communication, mutual understanding, and social organization possible. Militant individualism and equalitarianism have inflated this core of individuality to the point where it seems altogether free of somatic and social differences. But it stands to reason that the active strength of the ego, and especially the identity within the individuality, needs and employs the power of somatic development and of social organization. Here, then, the fact that a woman, whatever else she may also be, never is not-a-woman creates unique relations between her individuality, her somatic existence, and her social potentials and demands that the feminine identity be studied and defined in its own right.

I call the sphere of citizenship Polis because I want to emphasize that it reaches to the borders of what one has recognized as one's "city." Modern communication makes such a communality ever larger—if not global. In this sphere women can be shown to share with men a close sameness of intellectual orientation and capacity for work and leadership. But in this sphere, too, the influence of women will not be fully actualized until it reflects without apology the facts of the "inner space" and the potentialities and needs of the feminine psyche. It is as yet unpredictable what the tasks and roles, opportunities and job specifications will be once women are not merely adapted to male jobs in economics and politics but learn to adapt jobs to themselves. Such a revolutionary reappraisal may even lead to the insight that jobs now called masculine force men, too, into inhuman adjustments.

It should be clear, then, that I am using my definitions concerning the central importance of woman's procreative endowment not in a renewed male attempt to "doom" every woman to perpetual motherhood and to deny her the equivalence of individuality and the equality of citizenship. But since a woman is never not-a-woman, she can see her long-range goals only in those modes of activity which include and integrate her natural dispositions. A truly emancipated woman, I should think, would refuse to accept comparisons with more "active" male proclivities as a measure of her equivalence, even when, or precisely when, it has become quite clear that she can match man's performance and competence in most spheres of achievement. True equality can only mean the right to be uniquely creative.

Most verifiable sex differences (beyond those intrinsic to sexuality and procreation) establish for each sex only a range of attitudes and attributes which to most of its members "come naturally," that is, are predispositions, predilections, and inclinations. Many of these can, of course, be unlearned or relearned with more or less effort and special talent. This is not to be denied; with ever-increasing choices given her by the grace of technology and enlightenment, the question is only how much and which parts of her inborn inclinations the woman of tomorrow will feel it most natural to preserve and to cultivate—"natural" meaning that which can be integrated and made continuous in the three basic aspects mentioned.

As a body, then, woman passes through stages of life that are interlinked with the lives of those whose bodily existence is (increasingly so by her own choice) interdependent with hers. But as a worker, say, in a field structured by mathematical laws, woman is as responsible as any man for criteria of evidence that are intersexual or, better, suprasexual. As an individual person, finally, she utilizes her (biologically given) inclinations and her (technologically and politically given) opportunities to make the decisions that would seem to render her life most continuous and meaningful without failing the tasks of motherhood and citizenship. The question is how these three areas of life reach into each other—certainly never without conflict and tension and yet with some continuity of purpose.

To consider, in conclusion, one of the frontiers of women's work: the nature of engineering and science, for example, is well removed from the workers' sex differences, even as also scientific training is more or less peripheral to the intimate tasks of womanhood and motherhood. I am reasonably sure that computers built by women would not betray a "female logic" (although I do not know how reasonable this reasonableness is, since women did not care to invent them in the first place); the logic of the computers is, for better or for worse, of a suprasexual kind. But what to ask and what not to ask the monsters, and when to trust or not to trust them with vital decisions—there, I would think, well-trained women might well contribute to a new kind of vision in the differential application of scientific thinking to humanitarian tasks.

But I would go further. Do we and can we really know what will happen to science or any other field if and when women are truly represented in it—not by a few glorious exceptions, but in the rank and file of the scientific elite? Is scientific inspiration really so impersonal and methodbound that personality plays no role in scientific creativity? And if we grant that a woman is never not a woman, even if she has become an excellent scientist and co-worker, and especially when she has grown beyond all special apologies or claims, then why deny so strenuously that there may also be areas in science (on the scientific periphery of some tasks, and maybe in the very core of others) where women's vision and creativity may yet lead, not to new laws of verification, but to new areas of inquiry and to new applications? Such a possibility, I suggest, could be affirmed or denied only if and when women are sufficiently represented in the sciences so that they may relax about the task and the role and apply themselves to the unknown.

My main point is that where the confinements are broken, women may yet be expected to cultivate the implications of what is biologically and anatomically given. She may, in new areas of activity, balance man's indiscriminate endeavor to perfect his dominion over the outer spaces of national and technological expansion (at the cost of hazarding the annihilation of the species) with the determination to emphasize such varieties of caring and caretaking as would take responsibility for each individual child born in a planned humanity. There will be many difficulties in a new joint adjustment of the sexes to changing conditions, but they do not justify prejudices which keep half of mankind from participating in planning and decision making, especially at a time when the other half, by its competitive escalation and acceleration of technological progress, has brought us and our children to the gigantic brink on which we live, with all our affluence.

New strength of adaptation always develops in historical eras in which there is a confluence of emancipated individual energy with the potentials of a new technical and social order. New generations gain the full measure of their vitality in the continuity of new freedoms with a developing technology and a historical vision. There, also, personal synthesis is strengthened and with it an increased sense of humanity, which the children will feel, too, even if new adjustments are demanded in the sphere of motherhood. Social inventiveness and new knowledge can help plan necessary adjustments in a society that is sure of its values. But without these values, behavioral science has little to offer.

We may well hope, therefore, that there is something in woman's specific creativity which has waited only for a clarification of her relationship to masculinity (including her own) in order to assume her share of leadership in those fateful human affairs which so far have been left entirely in the hands of gifted and driven men, and often of men whose genius of leadership eventually has yielded to ruthless self-aggrandizement. Mankind now obviously depends on new kinds of social inventions and on institutions which guard and cultivate that which nurses and nourishes, cares and tolerates, includes and preserves.

IN MY last conversation with him, Paul Tillich expressed uneasiness over the clinical preoccupation with an "adaptive ego" which, he felt, might support (these are my words) further attempts at manufacturing a mankind which feels so "adapted" that it would be unable to face "ultimate concerns." I agreed that psychoanalysis was in danger of becoming part of such vain streamlining of existence, but that in its origin and essence it intends to *free* man for "ultimate concerns." For such concerns can begin to be ultimate only in those rare moments and places where neurotic resentments end and where mere readjustment is transcended. I think he agreed. One may add that man's Ulti-

mate has too often been visualized as an infinity which begins
where the male conquest of outer spaces ends, and a domain
where an "even more" omnipotent and omniscient Being must
be submissively acknowledged. The Ultimate, however, may
well be found also to reside in the Immediate, which has so
largely been the domain of woman and of the inward mind.

CHAPTER
VIII

Race and the Wider Identity

1.

THE CONCEPT OR AT LEAST THE TERM IDENTITY seems to pervade much of the literature on the Negro revolution in this country and to have come to represent in other countries as well something in the psychological core of the revolution of the colored races and nations who seek emancipation from the remnants of colonial patterns of thought. Whatever the word suggests, it does seem to speak to the condition of many serious observers at this junction of history. When, for example, Nehru said (as I have been told) that "Gandhi gave India an identity," he obviously put the term into the center of that development of a non-violent technique, both religious and political, by which Gandhi strove to forge a unique unity among Indians while insisting on their complete autonomy within the British Empire. But what did Nehru mean?

Robert Penn Warren, in his *Who Speaks for the Negro?*, reacts to the first mention of the word by one of his informants with the exclamation:

I seize the word *identity*. It is a key word. You hear it over and over again. On this word will focus, around this word will coagulate, a dozen issues, shifting, shading into each other. Alienated from the world to which he is born and from the country of which he is a citizen, yet surrounded by the successful values of that new world, and country, how can the Negro define himself? [1]

It is, of course, impossible to say how often the mere use of the term identity connotes anything resembling the meaning we ascribe to it. Where the term "crisis" appears in conjunction with it, a congruence of meaning is more likely. And, indeed, a national or racial crisis is often implied which forces a people into a kind of *revolution of awareness*. In India, as elsewhere, the context is that of an awakening from what Gandhi has called the "fourfold ruin" wrought by colonization in any form: political and economic, as well as cultural and spiritual ruin.

It would seem justifiable, then, to restate some of the dimensions of the problem of identity and to relate them to this sudden emergence of national awareness of the position of the Negro in the United States.

To begin with biographies, I pointed out at the beginning of this book that positive statements such as William James's exuberant and Sigmund Freud's solemn confession of an inner sense of unity with themselves and some of the world around them could hardly be expected in Negro writers who, to be equally truthful, must with equal fervor attempt to formulate the hateful outcome of that psychosocial process which we call identity. And, indeed, corresponding statements of Negro authors are couched in terms so negative that they at first suggest an absence of identity or, at any rate, the almost total prevalence of *negative* identity elements. There is Du Bois's classical statement on the Negro's inaudibility, and Du Bois, one must remember, lived about as "integrated" and, in fact, favored a life in his Berkshire town as any American Negro child can claim to have had. Yet here is his passage:

It is difficult to let others see the full psychological meaning of caste segregation. It is as though one, looking out from a dark cave in a side of an impending mountain, sees the world passing and speaks to it; speaks courteously and persuasively, showing them how these entombed souls are hindered in their natural movement, expression, and development; and how their loosening from prison would be a matter not simply of courtesy, sympathy, and help to them, but aid to all the world. One talks on evenly and logically in this way but notices that the passing throng does not even turn its head, or if it does, glances curiously and walks on.

It gradually penetrates the minds of the prisoners that the people passing do not hear; that some thick sheet of invisible but horribly tangible plate glass is between them and the world. They get excited; they talk louder; they gesticulate. Some of the passing world stop in curiosity; these gesticulations seem so pointless; they laugh and pass on. They still either do not hear at all, or hear but dimly, and even what they hear, they do not understand. Then the people within may become hysterical. They may scream and hurl themselves against the barriers, hardly realizing in their bewilderment that they are screaming in a vacuum unheard and that their antics may actually seem funny to those outside looking in. They may even, here and there, break through in blood and disfigurement, and find themselves faced by a horrified, implacable, and quite overwhelming mob of people frightened for their very own existence.[2]

From Du Bois's *inaudible* Negro there is only one step to Baldwin's and Ellison's very titles suggesting *invisibility, namelessness, facelessness*. But I would not interpret these themes as a mere plaintive expression of the Negro American's sense of "nobodyness," a social role which, God knows, was his heritage. Rather, I would tend to interpret the desperate yet determined preoccupation with invisibility on the part of these creative men as a supremely active and powerful demand to be heard and seen, recognized and faced as *individuals with a choice* rather than as men marked by what is all too superficially visible, namely, their color. In a haunting way they defend a latently existing but in some ways voiceless identity against the stereotypes which hide it. They are involved in a battle to reconquer for their people, but first of all (as writers must) for themselves, what Vann Woodward calls a "surrendered identity." I like this term because it does not assume total absence, as many contemporary writings do—something to be searched for and found, to be granted or given, to be created or fabricated—but something to be recovered. This must be emphasized because what is latent can become a living actuality, and thus a bridge from past to future.

The widespread preoccupation with identity, therefore, may be seen not only as a symptom of "alienation" but also as a corrective trend in historical evolution. It may be for this reason that revolutionary writers and writers from national and ethnic minority groups (like the Irish expatriates or our Negro and Jewish writers) have become the artistic spokesmen and prophets of identity confusion. Artistic creation goes beyond complaint and exposure, and it includes the moral decision that a certain painful identity-consciousness may have to be tolerated in order to provide the conscience of man with a critique of conditions, with the insight and the conceptions necessary to heal himself of what most deeply divides and threatens him, namely, his division into what we have called *pseudospecies*.

In this new literature, previously not conscious or unverbalized facts are faced and symbolized in a way which often resembles the process of psychoanalysis; but the "case" is transcended by human revolt, the inner realignment by intense contact with historical actuality. And, in the end, are these writers not proclaiming also an essential superiority of identity-in-torment over those identities which feel as safe and remote as a bland suburban home?

What is at stake here is nothing less than the realization of the fact and the obligation of man's specieshood. Great religious leaders have attempted to break through the resistances against this awareness, but their churches have tended to join rather than shun the development which we have in mind here, namely, man's deep-seated conviction that some providence has made his tribe or race or caste, and, yes, even his religion "naturally" superior to others. This, we have pointed out, seems to be part of a psychosocial evolution by which he has developed into *pseudospecies*. This fact is, of course, rooted in tribal life and based on all the evolutionary peculiarities which brought about man. Among these is his prolonged childhood during which the newborn, "naturally" born to be the most "generalist" animal of all and adaptable to widely differing environments, becomes specialized as a member of a human group with its complex interplay of an "inner world" and a social environment. He becomes indoctrinated, then, with the conviction that his "species" alone was planned by an all-wise deity, created in a special cosmic event, and appointed by history to guard the only genuine version of humanity under the leadership of elect elites and leaders. Now, "pseudo" suggests pseudologia, a form of lying with at least transitory conviction; and, indeed, man's very progress has swept him along in a combination of developments in which it seems hard to bring to bear what rationality and humanity he can muster against illusions and prejudices no longer deserving of the name mythology. I mean, of course, that dangerous combinations of technological specialization (including weaponry), moral righteousness, and what we may call the *territoriality of identity*, all of which make *hominem hominis lupum* far exceeding anything typical for wolves among wolves.[3] For man once possessed by this combination of lethal weaponry, moral hypocrisy, and identity panic is not only apt to lose all sense of species, but also to turn on another subgroup with a ferocity generally alien to the "social" animal world. Technological sophistication, in fact, seems to escalate the problem just at the time when (and this would seem to be no coincidence) a more universal, more inclusive human identity seems forcefully suggested by the very need for survival. National-socialist Germany is the most flagrant manifestation of the murderous mass pseudologia which can befall a modern nation.

While we all carry with us trends and tendencies which anchor our identities in some pseudospecies, we also feel in our bones that the Second World War has robbed such self-indulgence of all innocence, and that any threat of a third one would lead man's adaptative genius to its own defeat. But those who see what the "compact majority" continues to deny and dissimulate must also attempt to understand that for man to realize his specieshood and to exchange a wider identity for his pseudospecies, he must not only create a new and shared technological universe, but also outgrow prejudices which have been essential to all (or almost all) identities in the past. For each *positive identity* is also defined by *negative* images, as we have seen, and we must now discuss the unpleasant fact that our God-given identities often live off the degradation of others.

2.

In support of my insistence on the constructive role of the Negro writer's emphasis on the negative and the confused, I almost quoted Ellison as saying that his writing was indeed an attempt to transcend conditions "as the blues transcended the painful conditions with which they deal," but I stopped myself; and now I have quoted him to show up a difficulty attending the aggravated self-consciousness which we have called identity-consciousness. Except for extraordinary moments of lucid conversation, the whole imagery which was once the currency of exchange between the Negro American's world and ours, and especially such seemingly innocent items as the blues, are being devaluated or transvaluated with kaleidoscopic speed before our eyes. The blues may have been at one time an affirmation of a positive identity and a superior uniqueness, even as they "dealt with" feelings of depression and hopelessness. No writer of today can escape using or agreeing to use old images which now have become a sign of discrimination, as if one meant to say that the Negro had better stick to his blues or some other thoughtless accommodation to the postslavery period from which we are all emerging. But what before was a more unconscious mixture of guilt and fear on the white side, and a mixture of hate and fear on the other, is now being replaced by the more conscious and yet not always more practical sentiments of remorse and mistrust. We have, at the moment, no choice but to live with those stereotypes and affects: confrontation will disprove some of them, history dissolve others. In the meantime, it may be helpful to bring some such concept as identity-consciousness to bear on this problem so that the kaleidoscope may reveal patterns as well as bewildering changes.

Identity-consciousness is, of course, overcome only by a sense of identity won in action. Only he who "knows where he is going and who is going with him" demonstrates an unmistakable if not always easily definable unity and radiance of appearance and being. And yet just when a person, to all appearances, seems to "find himself," he can also be said to be "losing himself" in new tasks and affiliations: he transcends identity-consciousness. This is surely so in the early days of any revolution and was so in the case of the young of the Negro revolution who found themselves and, in fact, found their generation in the very decision to lose themselves in the intensity of the struggle. Here identity-consciousness is absorbed in actuality. There are vivid and moving descriptions of this state, none more so than in Howard Zinn's account of the early days of SNCC.[4] Afterward, no doubt, these at first anonymous heroes faced redoubled self-consciousness, a kind of doubletake on the stage of history, and must now sacrifice the innocent unity of living to a revolutionary awareness.

That such "psychologizing" is not always welcome is all too understandable, and the fate of having to cultivate theories while unself-conscious action is called for is not always comfortable. The controversial issue of the "Moynihan Report," a long and at first secret report to President Johnson making him acquainted with the malignant consequences of the absence of the father in so many lower-class Negro homes, brought such resistances to the fore. Whatever the methods employed, Patrick Moynihan's intentions could not be doubted. But at critical times, any explanation pointing to a result of past history as nearly irreversible is perceived as and may, indeed, have the effect of yet another attempt at foreclosing the future fatalistically—as racial prejudice had done.

Nor should it be overlooked that these are only aggravated resistances present in all of us against the sudden awareness of our identity problems in their more unconscious aspects. Even students most eager for enlightenment and most imbued with the ideology of unrestricted inquiry cannot help asking: if unconscious determinants should, indeed, prove operative in our very sense of self and in the very pathos of our values, does this not carry the matter of determination to a point where free will and moral choice would seem to be illusory? Or: if a man's individual identity is said to be linked to communal identities, are

we not faced with another crypto-Marxism which makes man's
very sense of destiny a blind function of the dialectics of history? Or, finally: if such unconscious determinants could, indeed, be demonstrated, is such awareness good for us?

Philosophers no doubt have answers to these questions. But it
must be clear that nobody can escape such scruples, which are
really only part of a wider trend in the scrutiny of human motivation ranging from Darwin's discovery of our evolutionary
animal ancestry and Marx's uncovery of classbound behavior to
Freud's systematic exploration of the unconscious.

3.

In a recent discussion of the Negro family, a highly informed
and influential American Jew blurted out *his* kind of ethnic in-
credulity: "Some instinctive sense tells every Jewish mother that
she must make her child study, that his intelligence is his pass to
the future. Why does a Negro mother not care? Why does she
not have the same instinctive sense?" I suggested that, given
American Negro history, the equivalent "instinctive sense" may
have told the majority of Negro mothers to keep their children,
and especially the gifted and the questioning ones, *away* from
futile and dangerous competition—that is, for survival's sake to
keep them in their place as defined by an indifferent and hateful
"compact majority."

That the man said "mothers" immediately marks one of the
problems we face in approaching Negro identity. The Jewish
mothers he had in mind would expect to be backed up by their
husbands or, in fact, to act in their behalf; many Negro mothers
would not. Negro mothers are apt to cultivate the "surrendered
identity" forced on Negro men for generations. This, so the literature would suggest, has reduced many Negro men to a reflection of the "negative" recognition which surrounds them like an
endless recess of distorting mirrors. How his positive identity has
been systematically undermined—first under the unspeakable
system of slavery in North America and then by the system of
enslavement perpetuated in the rural South and the urban

North—has been extensively, carefully, and devastatingly documented.

Here the concept of a negative identity may help to clarify a number of related complications:

Every person's psychosocial identity, as we have outlined, contains a hierarchy of positive *and* negative elements, the latter resulting from the fact that throughout his childhood the growing human being is presented with evil prototypes as well as with ideal ones. These, we said, are culturally related: in a Jewish background which gives prominence to intellectual achievement, some such negative roles as the *"Schlemihl"* will not be wanting. The human being, in fact, is warned *not* to become what he often had no intention of becoming so that he can learn to anticipate what he must avoid. Thus the positive identity, far from being a static constellation of traits or roles, is always in conflict with that past which is to be lived down and with that potential future which is to be prevented.

The individual belonging to an oppressed and exploited minority, which is aware of the dominant cultural ideals but prevented from emulating them, is apt to fuse the negative images held up to him by the dominant majority with the negative identity cultivated in his own group. Here we may think of the many nuances of the way in which one Negro may address another as "nigger."

The reasons for this exploitability (and temptation to exploit) lie in man's very evolution and development as pseudospecies. There is ample evidence of "inferiority" feelings and of morbid self-hate in all minority groups, and no doubt the righteously and fiendishly efficient way in which the Negro slave in America was forced into and kept in conditions preventing in most the incentive for independent ambition now continues to exert itself as a widespread and deep-seated inhibition against utilizing equality even where it is "granted." Again, the literature abounds in descriptions of how, instead, the Negro found escape into musical or spiritual worlds or expressed his rebellion in compromises of behavior now viewed as mocking caricatures, such as obstinate meekness, exaggerated childlikeness, or superficial submissiveness. And yet is "the Negro" not often all to summarily and all too exclusively discussed in such a way that his negative identity is defined *only* in terms of his defensive adjustments to the dominant white majority? Do we (and can we) know enough about the relationship of positive and negative elements *within* the Negro personality and *within* the Negro community? This alone would reveal how negative is negative and how positive, positive.

But there is the further fact that the oppressor has a vested interest in the negative identity of the oppressed because that negative identity is a projection of his own unconscious negative identity—a projection which, up to a point, makes him feel superior but also, in a brittle way, whole. This discussion of the pseudospecies may have clarified some of this theoretically, but a historical emergence forces immediate application—to oneself.

One comes to wonder, for example, about the ways in which a majority, suddenly aware of a vital split in itself over the fact that it has caused a near-fatal split in a minority, may, in its sudden zeal to regain its moral position and to "face the facts," inadvertently tend to *confirm* the minority's negative image of itself and this in the very act of dwelling exclusively and even self-indulgently upon the majority's sins. A clinician may be forgiven for questioning the restorative value of an excessive dose of moral zeal. The very designation "culturally deprived," for example, would seem somewhat ironic (although one may admire much of the work done under this banner) if one is aware of the fact that the middle-class culture of which the slum children are deprived also deprives some of the white children of experiences which might prevent much neurotic maladjustment. There is, in fact, more than poetic justice in the historical fact that many young white people who feel deeply deprived *because* of their family's "culture" find an identity and a solidarity in living and working with those who are said to be deprived for lack of such culture. Such confrontations (paralleled by experiences in the Peace Corps) are, of course, an important step in any creation of a wider identity, and I have not, in my lifetime, heard anything approaching the immediacy of common human experience revealed in stories from today's South, except perhaps what I have learned in my study of the early Gandhians' discovery of the Indian masses.

4.

Even a remorseful majority, then, must be watchful lest it persist unconsciously in habitual patterns. It seems that hidden prejudice is even to wilt into the very measurements by which the damage done is to be gauged. And diagnosis, it must be remembered, defines the prognosis.

Thomas Pettigrew, in his admirable compilation *A Profile of the Negro American*, employs identity terms only in passing. He offers a wealth of solid and all the more shocking evidence of the disuse of the Negro American's intelligence and of the disorganization of his family life. If I choose from the examples reported by Pettigrew one of the most questionable and even amusing, it is only in order to clarify the relation of single testable *traits* to a people's history.

Pettigrew, following Burton and Whiting, discusses the problem that

[Boys] from fatherless homes must painfully achieve a masculine self-image late in their childhood after having established an original self-image on the basis of the only parental model they have had—their mother. Several studies point to the applicability of this *sex-identity problem* to lower-class Negro males.

He reports that

Two objective test assessments of widely different groups—Alabama jail prisoners and Wisconsin working-class veterans with tuberculosis—found that Negro males scored higher than white males on a *measure of femininity*. . . . This measure is a part of the Minnesota Multiphasic Inventory (MMPI), a well-known psychological instrument that requires the respondent to judge the applicability to himself of over five hundred simple statements. Thus, Negroes in these samples generally agreed more often with such "feminine" choices as "*I would like to be a singer*" and "I think that *I feel more intensely* then most people do." [5]

Pettigrew wisely puts "feminine" in quotation marks. We will assume that the MMPI is, as it claims, an "objective test assessment for widely different groups," including Alabama jail prisoners and patients on a tubercular ward, and that, at any rate, incidental test blemishes in the end all "come out in the wash" of statistics. The over-all conclusions may, indeed, point to significant differences between Negroes and whites and between indices of femininity and of masculinity. That a test, however, singles out as "feminine" the wish to be a singer and feeling "more intensely than most people do" suggests that the choice of test items and the generalizations drawn from them may say at least as much about the test and the testers as about the subjects tested. To "want to be a singer" or "to feel intensely" seems to be something only a man with feminine traits would acknowledge in that majority of respondents on whom the test was first developed and standardized. But why, one wonders, should a lower-class Negro locked up in jail or in a tuberculosis ward not admit to a wish to be a man like Sidney Poitier or Harry Belafonte, and grant that he feels more intensely (if, indeed, he knows what this means) than most people in his present surroundings? To be a singer and to feel intensely may be facets of a masculine ideal gladly admitted if you grew up in a southern Negro community (or, for that matter, in Naples), whereas it would be a blemish in a majority having adjusted to other masculine ideals. In fact, in Harlem and in Naples an emphasis on artistic self-expression and intense feeling—and this is the point to be made—may be close to the core of one's positive identity, so close that the loss or devaluation of such emphasis by way of "integration" may make one a drifter on the murky sea of adjustable "roles." In the case of the compact white majority, the denial of "intense feelings" may, in turn, be part of a negative identity problem which contributes significantly to the prejudiced rejection of the Negro's intensity. Tests harboring similar distinctions may be offering "objective" evidence of racial differences and yet may also be symptomatic of them. If this is totally overlooked, the test will only emphasize, the tester will only report, and the reader of the report (white or Negro) will only perceive the distance between the Negro's "disintegrated" self-imagery and what is assumed to be the white's "integrated" one.

As Pettigrew (in another connection) says starkly, putting himself in the shoes of a Negro child to be tested:

. . . After all, an intelligence test is a middle-class white man's instrument; it is a device whites use to prove their capacities and get ahead in the white world. Achieving a high test score does not have the same meaning for a lower-status Negro child, and it may even carry a definite connotation of personal threat. In this sense, scoring low on intelligence measures may for some talented Negro children be a rational response to perceived danger.[6]

The whole *test event* itself thus underlies a certain historical and social relativity calling for clarification in terms of the actuality of different identity configurations. By the same token, it is by no means certain that a child undergoing such a procedure will be at all the same person when he escapes the predicament of the test procedure and joins, say, his peers on the playground or a street corner. On the other hand, it is all too often taken for granted that the *investigator*, and his identity conflicts, invisibly blends into his method even when he himself belongs to a highly, and maybe defensively, verbal subgroup of whites and is perceived as such (both consciously and "subliminally") by subjects who are near-illiterate or come from an illiterate background.

In this connection, I would like to quote Kenneth Clark's moving characterization of the sexual life of the "marginal young people in the ghetto." As a responsible father-figure, he knows he must not condone what he nevertheless must also defend against deadly stereotypes.

Illegitimacy in the ghetto cannot be understood or dealt with in terms of punitive hostility, as in the suggestion that unwed mothers be denied welfare if illegitimacy is repeated. Such approaches obscure, with empty and at times hypocritical moralizing, the desperate yearning of the young for acceptance and identity, the need to be meaningful to someone else even for a moment without implication of a pledge of undying fealty and foreverness. . . . To expose oneself further to the chances of failure in a sustained and faithful relationship is too large to risk. The *intrinsic value* of the relationship is the only value because there can be no other.[7]

This places a legal or moral item in its "actual" context, a context which always also reveals something about those who would judge and stereotype rather than understand: for is not the *intrinsic value of the relationship* exactly that item (hard to define, hard to test, and legally irrelevant) which may be lost in some more privileged youths who suffer under a bewildering and driving pluralism of values? [8]

5.

To turn now to the new young Negroes: "My God," a Negro woman student exclaimed the other day in a small meeting, "what am I supposed to be integrated *out of?* I laugh like my grandmother—and I would rather die than not laugh like her." There was a silence in which you could hear the stereotypes click, for even laughter has now joined those aspects of Negro culture and Negro personality which have become suspect as the marks of submission and fatalism, delusion and escape. But the young girl did not hastily give in with some such mechanical apology as "by which I do not mean, of course . . ." and the silence was pregnant with that immediacy which characterizes moments when an identity conflict becomes palpable. It was followed by laughter—embarrassed, amused, defiant.

To me, the young woman had expressed one of the anxieties attending a rapid reconstitution of identity elements: "supposed to" reflects a sense of losing the active, the choosing role which is of the essence in a sense of identity as a continuity of the living past and the anticipated future. I have indicated that single items of behavior or imagery can change their quality within new identity configurations, and yet these same indices once represented the only then possible inner integration for which the Negro is now "supposed to" exchange an unsure outer integration. Desegregation, compensation, balance, reconciliation—do they not all sometimes seem to save the Negro at the cost of an absorption which he is not sure will leave much of himself? Thus what Ellison calls the Negro writer's "complicated assertions and denials of identity" have simpler antecedents, no less tragic for their simplicity.

The young woman's outcry reminds us that identity development has its time, or rather two kinds of time: a *developmental stage* in the life of the individual, and a *period* in history. There is, as we have outlined, a complementarity of life history and history. Unless provoked prematurely and disastrously (and the biographies of Negro writers as well as direct observations of Negro children attest to such tragic prematurity) the identity crisis is not feasible before the beginning, even as it is not dispensable after the end of adolescence, when the body, now fully grown, grows together into an individual appearance; when sexuality, matured, seeks partners in sensual play and, sooner or later, in parenthood; when the mind, fully developed, can begin to envisage a career for the individual within a historical perspective—all idiosyncratic developments which are immediately apparent as so many conflicts in the case of a minority-group child.

But the crisis of youth is also the crisis of a generation and of the ideological soundness of its society: there is also a complementarity of identity and ideology. And if we said that the crisis is least marked in that segment of youth which in a given era is able to invest its fidelity in an ideological trend associated with a new technical and economic expansion, such as mercantilism, colonialism, or industrialization, we recognize the catastrophic consequences of any systematic exclusion from such trends. Youth which is eager for, yet unable to find access to, the dominant techniques of society will not only feel estranged from society, but also upset in sexuality, and most of all unable to apply aggression constructively. It may be that today much of Negro youth as well as an artistic-humanistic section of white youth feel disadvantaged and, therefore, come to develop a certain solidarity in regard to "the crisis" or "the revolution": for young people in privileged middle-class homes as well as in underprivileged Negro homes may miss that sameness and continuity throughout development which makes both a grandmother's warmth and a simple technical aspiration part of an identical world. One may go further and say that this whole segment of American youth is attempting to develop its own ideology and its own rites of confirmation by following the official call to the external frontiers of the American way of life (Peace Corps), by going to the internal ones (deep South), or by attempting in colleges (California) to fill an obvious void in their lives. But when will young Americans be able to share the realism, solidarity, and conviction which welds together a functioning radical opposition?

Identity, then, also contains a complementarity of past and future both in the individual and in society: it links the actuality of a living past with that of a promising future. Any romanticizing of the past or any salesmanship in the creation of future "postures" will not fill the bill. It fits this spirit that Pettigrew's "Profile," for example, fails to list such at any rate untestable items as (in alphabetical order) companionability, humor, motherhood, music, sensuality, spirituality, and sports. They all are suspect as traits of an accommodation romanticized by whites. But this makes the presently available "profiles" really the correction of caricatures rather than attempts at even a sketch of a portrait. And, one must ask, can a new or renewed identity emerge from corrected caricatures? One thinks of all those who are unable to derive identity gains from the "acceptance of reality" at its worst (as writers do, and researchers) and to whom a debunking of *all* older configurations *may* add up to a further *confirmation* of worthlessness and helplessness.

It is in this context also that I must question the fact that in many an index the Negro father appears *only* under the heading of "absence." Again, the relationship between family disintegration, father absence, and all kinds of social and psychiatric pathology is overwhelming. "Father absence" does belong in every index and in the agenda of national concern, but as the *only* item related to fatherhood or motherhood does it not do grave injustice to the presence of many, many mothers, and at least of some fathers? Whatever the historical, sociological, or legal interpretation of the Negro mother's (and grandmother's) saving presence in the whole half circle of plantation culture from Venezuela through the Carribbean into our South, is it an item to be omitted from the agenda of the traditional Negro identity? Can Negro culture afford to have the "strong mother" stereotyped as a liability? For a person's, and a people's, identity begins in the rituals of infancy, when mothers make it clear with many preliterate means that to be born is good and that a child (let the bad world call it colored or list it as illegitimate) is deserving of warmth. Even the "invisible man" says:

. . . Other than Mary I had no friends and desired none. Nor did I think of Mary as a "friend"; she was something more—*a force, a stable, familiar force like something out of my past which kept me from whirling off into some unknown which I dared not face.* It was a most painful position, for at the same time, Mary reminded me constantly that something was expected of me, some act of leadership, some newsworthy achievement; and I was torn between resenting her for it and loving her for the nebulous hope she kept alive.[9]

The systematic exploitation of the Negro male as a domestic animal and the denial to him of the status of responsible fatherhood are, on the other hand, two of the most shameful chapters in the history of this Christian nation. For an imbalance of mother-and-father presence is never good, and becomes increasingly bad as the child grows older, for then the trust in the world established in infancy may be all the more disappointed. Under urban and industrial conditions it may, indeed, become the gravest factor in personality disorganization. But, again, the "disorganization" of the Negro family must not be measured solely by its distance from the white or Negro middle-class family with its one-family housing and legal and religious legitimizations. Disintegration must be measured and understood also as a distortion of the *traditional* if often unofficial *Negro family pattern.* The traditional wisdom of the mothers will be needed as will the help of the Negro men who (in spite of such circumstances) actually did become fathers in the full sense.

In the meantime, the problem of the function of both parents, each strong in his or her way and both benignly present in the home when needed most, is a problem facing the family in any industrial society, anywhere. The whole great society must develop ways to provide equality of opportunity in employment and yet also differential ways of permitting mothers and fathers to attend to their duties toward their children. The maternal-paternal dimension may well also serve to clarify the fact that each stage of development needs its own optimum environment, and that to find a balance between maternal and paternal strength means to assign to each a period of dominance in the children's life. The mother's period is the earliest and, therefore, the most basic. As we have seen, there is a deep relation between the first "identity" experienced in the early sensual and sensory exchanges with the mother(s)—the first recognition—and that final integration in adolescence when all earlier identifications are assembled and the young person meets his society and his historical era.

6.

In his book *Who Speaks for the Negro?* Warren records another exclamation by a young woman student:

. . . The auditorium had been packed—mostly Negroes, but with a scattering of white people. A young girl with pale skin, dressed like any coed anywhere, in the clothes for a public occasion, is on the rostrum. She is leaning forward a little on her high heels, speaking with a peculiar vibrance in a strange irregular rhythm, out of some inner excitement, some furious, taut elan, saying: "—and I tell you I have discovered a great truth. I have discovered a great joy. I have discovered that I am black. I am black! You out there—oh, yes, you may have black faces, but your hearts are white, your minds are white, you have been white-washed!"

Warren reports a white woman's reaction to this outburst and surmises that if this woman

at that moment heard any words in her head, they were most likely the echo of the words of Malcolm X: "White devils." And if she saw any face, it must have been the long face of Malcolm X grinning with sardonic certitude.[10]

Although she sees only one of Malcolm X's faces, I think we understand this fear. She has witnessed what we have called a "totalistic" rearrangement of images which is indeed basic to some of the ideological movements of modern history. As totalism we have described an inner regrouping of imagery, almost a *negative conversion*, by which erstwhile negative identity elements become totally dominant, while erstwhile positive elements come to be excluded totally.[11] This, we have said, can happen in a transitory way in many young people of all colors and classes who rebel and join, wander off or isolate themselves; it can subside with the developmental storm or lead to some total commitment. Depending on historical and social conditions, the process has its malignant potentials, as exemplified in "confirmed" pervert-delinquent or bizarre-extremist states of mind and forms of behavior.

The chill which this process can give us in its political implications refers back to our sense of historical shock when post-Versailles German youth, once so sensitive to foreign critique, but then on the rebound from a love of *Kultur* which promised no realistic identity, fell for the Nazi transvaluation of civilized values. The transitory Nazi identity, however, based as it was on a *totalism* marked by the radical *exclusion* of foreignness and especially Jewishness, failed to integrate the rich identity elements of Germanness, reaching instead for a pseudologic perversion of history. Obviously both radical segregationism, with its burning crosses, and Black Muslimism are the counterparts of such a phenomenon in this country. In the person of Malcolm X the *specific rage* which is aroused wherever identity development loses the promise of a traditionally assured wholeness was demonstrated theatrically, although as a person and a leader this fascinating man obviously pointed beyond the movement from which he originated. And yet, the Black Muslims, too, were able to call on some of the best potentials of the individuals who felt "included."

This country as a whole, however, is not hospitable to such totalistic turns, and the inability or, indeed, unwillingness of youth in revolt to come to systematic ideological conclusions is in itself an important historical fact. We as yet lack the ingredients for a significant "loyal opposition" which would combine radicalism with the wish to govern. The temporary degeneration of the Free Speech Movement in California into a revolt of "dirty" words was probably an intrusion of an impotent totalism into a promising radicalism. This reluctance to be regimented in the service of a political ideology, however, can make the latent violence in our disadvantaged youth that much more destructive to personal unity and, sporadically, to "law and order." But note also, that the rate of crime and delinquency in some southern counties was reported to have dropped sharply when the Negro population became involved in social protest. Unfortunately, a violent society takes nonviolence for weakness and enforces violent solutions.

The alternative to an exclusive totalism, we have suggested, is the wholeness of a *more inclusive identity*. What *historical actuality* can the Negro American count on and what wider identity will permit him to be self-certain as a Negro (or a descendant of Negroes) *and* integrated as an American? For we must know that when all the *realities* are classified and investigated, and all the studies assessed, the question remains: what are the *historical actualities* that a developing identity can count on?

In emphasizing once more the complementarity of life history and history, I must register a certain impatience with the faddish equation, never suggested by me, of the term identity with the question "Who am I?" This question nobody would ask himself except in a more or less transient morbid state, in a creative self-confrontation, or in an adolescent state sometimes combining both; wherefore on occasion I find myself asking a student who claims that he is in an "identity crisis" whether he is complaining or boasting. The pertinent question, if it can be put into the first person at all, would be, "What do I want to make of myself, and what do I have to work with?" But such awareness of inner motivations is at best useful in replacing infantile wishes and adolescent fancies with realistic goals. Beyond that, only a restored or better-trained sense of historical actuality can lead to a deployment of those energies which both activate and are activated by potential developments. How potential developments become historical fact is demonstrated by the way in which "culturally deprived" Negro children meet a sudden historical demand with surprising dignity and fortitude. Robert Coles has made significant contributions to this problem by studying the life histories of Negro children "integrated" in the early days. The "data" available, if interpreted according to widespread psychiatric usage, would easily have led any of us to predict, for example, for a lone Negro boy of very pathological background an inevitable and excusable failure in his task of personifying the desegregation of a hostile high school. But Coles describes, having witnessed it as a new kind of "participant observer," how the boy stood up unforgettably and saw it through to graduation.[12]

In many parts of the world the struggle now is for anticipatory and *more inclusive identities:* what has been a driving force in revolutions and reformations, in the founding of churches and in the building of empires, has become a contemporaneous worldwide competition. Revolutionary doctrines promise the new identity of peasant-and-worker to the youth of countries which must overcome their tribal, feudal, or colonial past: new nations attempt to absorb regions; new markets, nations; and world space is extended to include outer space as the proper "environment" for a universal technological identity.

At this point, we are beyond the question (and Gandhi did much to teach this at least to the British) of how a remorseful or scared colonialist may dispense corrective welfare in order to appease the need for a wider identity. The problem is rather how he includes himself in the wider pattern, for a more inclusive identity is a development by which two groups who previously had come to depend on each other's negative identities (by living in a traditional situation of mutual enmity or in a symbiotic accommodation to one-sided exploitation) join their identities in such a way that new potentials are activated in both.

What wider identities, then, are competing for the Negro American's commitment? Some, it seems, are too wide to be "actual," some too narrow. I would characterize as too wide the identity of a "human being" bestowed, according to the strange habit of latter-day humanist narcissism, by humans on humans, patients, women, Negroes, and so on. While this strange phraseology of being "human beings" may at times represent a genuine transcendence of the pseudospecies mentality, it often also implies that the speaker, having undergone some revelatory hardships, is in a position to grant membership in humanity to others. I would not be surprised to find that our Negro colleagues and friends often sense such a residue of intellectual colonialism in the "best" of us. But it tends to take all specificity out of "human" relations. For even within a wider identity man meets man always in categories (be they adult and child, man and woman, employer and employee, leader and follower, majority and minority) and "human" interrelations can truly be only the expression of divided function and the concrete overcoming of the specific ambivalence inherent in them: that is why I came to reformulate the Golden Rule as one that commands us always to act in such a way that the identities of both the actor and the one acted upon are enhanced.

Probably the most inclusive and most absorbing identity potential in the world today is that of *technical skill*. This is, no doubt, what Lenin meant when he advocated that first of all the *mushik* be put on a tractor. True, he meant it as a preparation for the identity of a class-conscious proletarian. But it has come to mean more today, namely, the participation in an area of activity and experience which (for better or for worse, and I think I have touched on both potentials) verifies modern man as a worker and planner. It is one thing to *exclude oneself* from such verification because one has proven oneself gifted in nonmechanical respects and able to draw professionally and esthetically on the traditional verification provided by Humanism or the Enlightenment—at least sufficiently so that alienation from technology adds up to some reasonably comfortable "human identity." It is quite another to *be excluded* from it, for example, by literacy requirements which prevent the proof that one is mechanically gifted or by prejudicial practices of employment which preclude the use of the gift after such proof is given. Israel, a small country with a genius for renewing identities, has shown in the use of its army as an educational institution, under admittedly unique conditions, that illiteracy can be corrected in the process of putting people where they feel they are needed, and that combat morale is none the worse for it.

The *African identity* is a strong contender for the American Negro identity, as Harold Isaacs has shown. It offers a highly actual setting for the solidarity of black skin color, and probably also provides the American Negro with an equivalent of what all other Americans could boast about or, if they chose to, disavow: a homeland, if ever so remote. For the American Negro's mode of separation from Africa even robbed him of the identity element *"immigrant."* There seems to be a question, however, whether to Africans a Negro American is more black or more American, and whether the Negro American, in actual contacts with Africans, wants to be more American or more black. Even the Black Muslims called themselves members of Islam to emphasize the wider mystical unity which all totalism calls for (see the German "Aryans").

The great *middle class* as the provider of an identity of consumers, for whom, indeed, Pettigrew's all-healing prescription of "dollars and dignity" seems to be most fitting, has been discussed in its limitations by many. The middle class, preoccupied as it is with matters of real estate and consumption, of status and posture, will include more and more of the highly gifted and the fortunate, but if it does not yield to the wider identity of the Negro American it obviously creates new barriers between these few and the mass of Negroes, whose distance from white competition is thereby only increased. "Work and dignity" may be a more apt slogan, provided that work dignifies by providing a "living" dollar as well as a challenge to competence, for without both all opportunity is slavery perpetuated.

But here as everywhere the question of the Negro American's

identity imperceptibly shades into the question of what *the* American wants to make of himself in the technology of the future. In this sense, the greatest gain all around may be what the doctors at Howard University have discussed as *prosocial action* on the part of Negroes.[13] I mean the fact that Negro protest, pervaded as far as is justifiable by the nonviolent spirit and yet clearly defying socialized law and custom, has been accepted by much of the nation as American. Executive oratory as well as judiciary and legislative action have attempted to absorb "the revolution" on a grand scale. But absorption can be merely adjustive and, in fact, defensive, or it can be adaptive and creative; this must as yet be seen.

In the meantime, the success of prosocial action should not altogether obscure the significant *antisocial* element which has been so relevantly recounted in the autobiographies of Negro Americans—I mean the tragic sacrifice of youth designated as delinquent and criminal. They, no doubt, often defended whatever identity elements were available to them by revolting in the only way open to them—a way of vicious danger and yet often the only way of tangible self-respect and solidarity. Like the outcast heroes of the American frontier, some antisocial types among the Negroes are not expendable from the history of their people—not yet.

Our genuinely humanist youth, however, will continue to extend a *religious identity element* into race relations, for future over-all issues of identity will include the balance within man of technological strivings and ethical and ultimate concerns. I believe (but you must not tell them for they are suspicious of such words) that the emergence of those youths who stepped from utter anonymity right into our national affairs does contain a new *religious element* embracing nothing less than the promise of a mankind freer of the attitudes of a pseudospecies: that utopia of universality proclaimed as the most worthy goal by all world religions and yet always re-entombed in new empires of dogma which turn into or ally themselves with new pseudospecies. The churches, too, have come to the insight that earthly prejudices—fanatical or hiding in indifference—feed into that deadly combination which now makes man what Loren Eiseley calls "the lethal factor" in the universe. This factor, as we have seen, ties limitless technical ambition (including the supremacy of weapons of annihilation) and the hypocrisy of outworn moralistic dogma to the territoriality of mutually exclusive identities. The counterforce, *nonviolence*, will perhaps be a compelling and creative actuality only at critical moments, and only for "the salt of the earth." But Gandhi took the first steps toward a worldwide application to politics of principles once purely religious.

The worldwide fate of *postcolonial* and *colored identities* is hard to predict in view of the clash of new national interests in Africa and Asia. Here one cannot ignore the possible implications of continued American action in Vietnam for a worldwide identification of colored people with the naked heroism of the Vietcong revolutionaries. The very demand that North Vietnam give in (even if it were nearly on her own terms) to a superorganized assault by a superfluity of lethal weapons may simply be too reminiscent of the function of firepower in colonial expansion in general; of police power in particular; and of a certain (implicitly contemptuous) attitude which assumes that "natives" will give in to pressures to which the master races would consider themselves impervious (*vide* the British in the blitz). It must be obvious that differences of opinion in this country in regard to American military involvement in Asia are not merely a matter of the faulty reading of facts or of lack of moral stamina on one side or the other, but also of a massive identity conflict. Intrinsic to the dominant political-technological nucleus of an American identity is the expectation that such power as can now be unleashed can be used to advantage in limited employment and has built-in safeguards against an unthinkable conflagration. Paradoxically, a significant section of the Negro population registers an identity gain from the fact that so many Negro soldiers prove themselves in battle as well as in technical services where their country denied them nonmilitary opportunities to do so. But there will be urgent voices abroad and sincere protest at home expressing the perplexity of those who perceive only one active moral frontier of equality and peace extending from the center of the daily life of America to the peripheries of its foreign concerns. Here the Negro American shares the fate of a new American dilemma.

AT THE BEGINNING of this book I promised to demonstrate the indispensability of such concepts as "identity" and "identity confusion" in case history, life history, and history. Where I have made my point, I have probably also succeeded in leading the reader into problems so actual that it seems callous to leave them in mid-discussion. And yet most of the uses of the concept suggested here arose from workshoplike symposia in which the psychoanalyst attempted to contribute a dimension, not a conclusion. Such participation is, in itself, a "sign of the times"— but the dimension to be contributed remains the same. Even when turning to issues under concerted discussion, and thus closer to the historical "surface" and to the worker's partisanship, the psychoanalytic viewpoint remains focused on what is most apt to become or remain unconscious at the very time when a new awareness illuminates a previously neglected aspect of human experience. That in this process our very concepts come under the scrutiny of a new historical awareness I have gropingly indicated in the more theoretical passages of this book. But even where it is applied to the assessment of a social problem our approach remains clinical in methodology, that is, it can be used only to focus the thinking of an interdisciplinary team. In the clinic, the assessment of identity problems calls for the "taking of history," the localization and the diagnostic assessment of disintegration, the testing of intact resources, tentative prognosis, and the weighing of possible action—each based on specialties of approach and often of temperament. Social application is not less demanding in calling for an analogous variety of methods. As the clinical and the developmental, the social and the historical endeavor to come closer to each other, some new terms are needed; but a concept is only as good as the preliminary order which it brings into otherwise baffling and seemingly unrelated phenomena—an order, furthermore, which reveals forces of restoration in the anarchy of crisis.

Writings on Which This Book Is Based

CHAPTER I. Transcript of a Workshop on Identity, San Francisco Psychoanalytic Institute (1966). Letter to the Committee on the Year 2000 (1967).

CHAPTER II. Ego Development and Historical Change (1946). On the Sense of Inner Identity (1951). Wholeness and Totality (1954).

CHAPTER III. Growth and Crises of the "Healthy" Personality (1950).

CHAPTER IV. The Problem of Ego Identity (1956). The Dream Specimen of Psychoanalysis (1954). The Syndrome of Identity Confusion (1955). Ego Identity and the Psychosocial Moratorium (1956). Preface to *Emotional Problems of the Student* (1961).

CHAPTER V. The Problem of Ego Identity (1956) and unpublished notes.

CHAPTER VI. Youth: Fidelity and Diversity (1962).

CHAPTER VII. The Inner and the Outer Space: Reflections on Womanhood (1964).

CHAPTER VIII. The Concept of Identity in Race Relations (1966).

Notes

I PROLOGUE

1. Erik H. Erikson, "A Combat Crisis in a Marine," *Childhood and Society*, Second Edition, New York: W. W. Norton, 1963, pp. 38–47.
2. *The Letters of William James*, edited by Henry James (his son), Vol. I, Boston: The Atlantic Monthly Press, 1920, p. 199.
3. Sigmund Freud, "Address to the Society of B'nai B'rith" [1926], *Standard Edition*, 20:273, London: Hogarth Press, 1959.
4. See Chapter VIII.
5. See Chapter IV, section 5.
6. Joan M. Erikson, "Eye to Eye," *The Man Made Object*, Gyorgy Kepes (ed.), New York: Braziller, 1966.
7. See Chapter VIII.
8. Erik H. Erikson, "Psychoanalysis and Ongoing History: Problems of Identity, Hatred and Nonviolence," *The American Journal of Psychiatry*, 122:241–250, 1965.

II FOUNDATIONS IN OBSERVATION

1. See Chapter V.
2. In Fenichel's comprehensive volume, *The Psychoanalytic Theory of Neurosis*, New York: W. W. Norton, 1945, the subject of social prototypes is only introduced toward the end of the chapter on mental development, and then in the form of a negation: "Neither a belief in 'ideal models' nor a certain degree of 'social fear' is necessarily pathological." The problem of the superego's origin in social mores is not discussed until page 463, in the chapter on character disorders.
3. Sigmund Freud, "On Narcissism: An Introduction" [1914], *Standard Edition*, 14:73–102, London: Hogarth Press, 1957.
4. Sigmund Freud, *An Outline of Psychoanalysis* [1938], New York: W. W. Norton, 1949, pp. 122, 123.
5. Erik H. Erikson, "Hunters Across the Prairie," *Childhood and Society*, 2nd ed., New York: W. W. Norton, 1963, pp. 114–165.

6. See "Hunters Across the Prairie"; also, Erik H. Erikson, "Observations on Sioux Education," *Journal of Psychology*, 7:101–156, 1939.

7. Erik H. Erikson, "On Submarine Psychology," written for the Committee on National Morale for the Coordinator of Information, 1940, unpublished.

8. Erik H. Erikson, "Hitler's Imagery and German Youth," *Psychiatry*, 5: 475–493, 1942.

9. Bruno Bettelheim, in "Individual and Mass Behavior in Extreme Situations," *Journal of Abnormal and Social Psychology*, 38:417–452, 1943, has described his experiences in a German concentration camp of the early days. He reports the various steps and external manifestations (such as affectations in posture and dress) by which the inmates abandoned their identity as antifascists in favor of that of their tormentors. He himself preserved his life and sanity by deliberately and persistently clinging to the historical Jewish identity of invincible spiritual and intellectual superiority over a physically superior outer world: he made his tormentors the subject of a silent research project which he safely delivered to the world of free letters.

10. This case history is presented in more detail in *Childhood and Society*, pp. 25–38.

11. " 'Civilized' Sexual Morality and Modern Nervousness" [1908], *Collected Papers*, 2:76–99, London, Hogarth Press, 1948.

12. For a typical case history, see "A Combat Crisis in A Marine," *Childhood and Society*, pp. 38–47.

13. Anna Freud, *The Ego and the Mechanisms of Defence* [1936], New York: International Universities Press, 1946.

14. This basic plan was established in Freud's publication " 'Civilized' Sexual Morality and Modern Nervousness" [1908] and in his habitual references to the cultural and socioeconomic co-ordinates of his own existence whenever he published illustrations from his own life.

15. H. Nunberg, "The Synthetic Function of the Ego" [1931], *Practice and Theory of Psychoanalysis*, New York: International Universities Press, 1955, pp. 120–136.

16. See the papers of H. Hartmann, E. Kris, D. Rapaport, and others in D. Rapaport, *The Organization and Pathology of Thought*, New York: Columbia University Press, 1951.

17. See Erik H. Erikson, *Childhood and Society*, Chapter II (esp. pp. 147ff.) and Chapter IV.

18. Erik H. Erikson, "Ontogeny of Ritualization in Man," *Philosophical Transactions of the Royal Society of London*, Series B, 251:337–349, 1966.

19. See Chapter III.

20. In individuals as well as in groups I prefer to speak of a "sense of identity" rather than "character structure" or "basic character." In nations too, clinical concepts would lead me to concentrate on the conditions, experiences, and behavior patterns which heighten or endanger a national sense of identity, rather than on a static national character.

III THE LIFE CYCLE: EPIGENESIS OF IDENTITY

1. Marie Jahoda, "Toward A Social Psychology of Mental Health," *Symposium on the Healthy Personality*, Supplement II: Problems of Infancy and Childhood, Transactions of Fourth Conference, March, 1950, M. J. E. Benn (ed.), New York: Josiah Macy, Jr. Foundation, 1950.

2. See Erik H. Erikson, *Childhood and Society*, 2nd ed., New York: W. W. Norton, 1963, Part I.

3. My participation in the longitudinal research of the Institute of Child Welfare at the University of California has taught me the greatest respect for the resiliency and resourcefulness of individual children who, with the support of an expansive way of life and of a generous immediate group, learned to compensate for early misfortunes of a kind which in our clinical histories would suffice to explain malfunctioning rather convincingly. The study gave me an opportunity to chart a decade of the life histories of about fifty (healthy) children, and to remain somewhat informed about the future fortunes of some of them. Much of what is recorded here I owe to that study, but only the identity concept helped me to understand the personality development of these children. See J. W. Macfarlane, "Studies in Child Guidance," I, Methodology of Data Collection and Organization, *Society for Research in Child Development Monographs*, Vol. III, No. 6, 1938, pp. 254ff; also, Erik H. Erikson, "Sex Differences in the Play Configurations of Preadolescents," *American Journal of Orthopsychiatry*, 21: 667–692, 1951.

4. R. A. Spitz, "Hospitalism," *The Psychoanalytic Study of the Child*, 1:53–74, New York: International Universities Press, 1945.

5. Benjamin Spock, *The Common Sense Book of Baby and Child Care*, New York: Duell, Sloan & Pearce, 1945.

6. For a systematic exposition see my chapter "The Human Life Cycle" in *The International Encyclopedia of the Social Sciences* (in press).

7. See Erik H. Erikson, "Ontogeny of Ritualization in Man," *Philosophical Transactions of the Royal Society of London*, Series B, 251:337–349, 1966.

8. One of the chief misuses of the schema presented here is a dominant connotation given to the sense of trust, and to all the other "positive" senses to be postulated, as *achievements*, secured once and for all at a given stage. In fact, some writers are so intent on making an achievement scale out of these stages that they blithely omit all the "negative" potentials, basic mistrust, etc., which not only remain the dynamic counterpart of the positive potentials throughout life, but are equally necessary to psychosocial life. A person devoid of the capacity to mistrust would be as unable to live as one without trust.

What the child acquires at a given stage is a certain *ratio* between the positive and the negative which, if the balance is toward the positive, will help him to meet later crises with a predisposition toward the sources of vitality. The idea, however, that at any stage a goodness is achieved which is impervious to all new conflicts within and changes without is a projection on child development of that success-and-possession ideology which so dangerously pervades some of our private and public daydreams.

9. See Erik H. Erikson, *Young Man Luther*, New York: W. W. Norton, 1958, for the echo of both of these convictions in Luther's revelatory experiences.

IV IDENTITY CONFUSION IN LIFE HISTORY AND CASE HISTORY

1. G. B. Shaw, *Selected Prose*, New York: Dodd, Mead, 1952.

2. F. O. Matthiessen, *The James Family*, New York: Alfred A. Knopf, 1948, p. 209.

3. *The Letters of William James*, edited by Henry James, his son, Boston: Atlantic Monthly Press, 1920, p. 145.

4. Matthiessen, p. 161.

5. *Ibid.*, p. 162.

6. *The Letters of William James*, p. 147.

7. *Ibid.*, p. 148. (Italics mine)

8. *Ibid.*, p. 169.

9. Child Guidance Study, Institute of Child Welfare, University of California. See footnote 3, Chapter III.

10. H. Hartmann, *Ego Psychology and the Problem of Adaptation*, New York: International Universities Press, 1958.

11. William James speaks of an abandonment of "the old alternative ego," and even of "the murdered self." See "The Will to Believe," *New World*, V, 1896.

12. For another approach, see Anna Freud's and Sophie Dann's report on concentration camp children, "An Experiment in Group Upbringing," *The Psychoanalytic Study of the Child*, 6:127–168, New York: International Universities Press, 1951.

13. Edward Bibring, "The Mechanism of Depression" in *Affective Disorders*, P. Greenacre (ed.), New York: International Universities Press, 1953, pp. 13–48.

14. I owe my orientation in this field to Robert Knight, "Management and Psychotherapy of the Borderline Schizophrenic Patient" in *Psychoanalytic Psychiatry and Psychology*, Austen Riggs Center, Vol. I, R. P. Knight and C. R. Friedman (eds.), New York: International Universities Press, 1954, pp. 110–122; and Margaret Brenman, "On Teasing and Being Teased: and the Problem of 'Moral Masochism'" also in *Psychoanalytic Psychiatry and Psychology*, pp. 29–51.

15. This example illustrates well the balance which must be found in the interpretation given to such patients between sexual symbolism (here castration) which, if overemphasized by the therapist, can only increase the patient's magic sense of being endangered; and the representation of dangers to the ego (here the danger of having the thread of one's autonomy cut off), the communication of which is, in fact, a condition for the safe discussion of sexual meanings.

16. D. Burlingham, *Twins*, New York: International Universities Press, 1952.

17. Anna Freud, *The Ego and the Mechanisms of Defence*, New York: International Universities Press, 1946.

18. See Kai T. Erikson, "Patient-Role and Social Uncertainty—A Dilemma of the Mentally Ill," *Psychiatry*, 20:263–274, 1957.

19. August Kubizek, *The Young Hitler I Knew*, Boston: Houghton Mifflin Company, 1955.

20. Organized by Professors S. Eisenstadt and C. Frankenstein at the Hebrew University in 1955.

21. We may state tentatively that the elites which emerge from historical change are groups which out of the deepest common identity crisis manage to create a new style of coping with the outstanding danger situations of their society. In doing so, they free the "revolutionary" energies of the underprivileged and dispossessed.

22. I.e., relative communism within the individual community, which, however, in its relation to the national economy, rather represents a capitalist co-operative.

23. See Erik H. Erikson, *Young Man Luther*, New York: W.W. Norton, 1958, for a partial fulfillment of this incautious announcement.

24. A last reference to the chart. The return of confusion in later stages would be "located" in VI.5, VII.5, and VIII.5. In the first of these, identity confusion takes the form of a disturbing carryover of identity problems into relations of intimacy and solidarity as indicated in Chapter III. The other two are illustrated in what follows: in Freud's dream, identity confusion *and* a sense of isolation (VI.5), while in James's dream, the despair of old age is experienced in an acute confusion (VIII.5) overcome only by a reassertion of professional identity, generativity, and integrity.

25. Sigmund Freud, "The Interpretation of Dreams," *The Basic Writings of Sigmund Freud*, A.A. Brill (ed.), New York: Modern Library, 1938, pp. 195–207.

26. Erik H. Erikson, "The Dream Specimen of Psychoanalysis," *Journal of the American Psychoanalytic Association*, 2:5–56, 1954.

27. Sigmund Freud, *Aus den Anfangen der Psychoanalyse*, London: Imago Publishing Co., 1950, p. 344; published in English as *The Origins of Psychoanalysis: Letters to Wilhelm Fliess, Drafts and Notes: 1887–1902*, edited by Marie Bonaparte, Anna Freud, and Ernst Kris, New York: Basic Books, 1954.

28. Sigmund Freud, *The Origins of Psychoanalysis*.

29. William James, "A Suggestion About Mysticism," *Journal of Philosophy, Psychology and Scientific Methods*, 7:85–92, 1910.

30. G.B. Blaine and C.C. McArthur, *Emotional Problems of the Student*, New York: Appleton, 1961, pp. xiii–xxv.

V THEORETICAL INTERLUDE

1. George H. Mead, *Mind, Self and Society*, Chicago: University of Chicago Press, 1934.

2. Harry S. Sullivan, *The Interpersonal Theory of Psychiatry*, New York: W.W. Norton, 1953.

3. P. Schilder, *The Image and Appearance of the Human Body*, New York: International Universities Press, 1951.

4. P. Federn, *Ego Psychology and the Psychoses*, New York: Basic Books, 1952.

5. Heinz Hartmann, "Comments of the Psychoanalytic Theory of the Ego," *The Psychoanalytic Study of the Child*, 5:74–96, New York: International Universities Press, 1950.

6. Sigmund Freud, "On Narcissism: An Introduction" [1914], *Standard Edition*, 14:73–102, London: Hogarth Press, 1957.

7. Sigmund Freud, "The Anatomy of the Mental Personality," Lecture 31 in *New Introductory Lectures on Psychoanalysis*, New York: W.W. Norton, 1933, pp. 95, 96.

8. Sigmund Freud, "On Narcissism," p. 101.

9. Heinz Hartmann, *Ego Psychology and the Problem of Adaptation*, New York: International Universities Press, 1958.

10. H. Hartmann, E. Kris, and R.M. Loewenstein, "Some Psychoanalytic Comments on 'Culture and Personality,'" *Psychoanalysis and Culture*, G.B. Wilbur and W. Muensterberger (eds.), New York: International Universities Press, 1951, pp. 3–31.

11. In *Insight and Responsibility* (New York: W.W. Norton, 1964) I have subsequently called this mutual activation *actuality*, separating this aspect of what, all in all, is *reality* from the mere recognition of the *factual*.

12. Anna Freud, "Indications for Child Analysis," *The Psychoanalytic Study of the Child*, 1:127-149, New York: International Universities Press, 1945.

13. See my forthcoming *Instrument of Peace: Origins of Gandhi's Militant Non-Violence*.

VI TOWARD CONTEMPORARY ISSUES: YOUTH

1. Virtue once connoted "inherent strength" and "active quality." In this sense, I consider the following vital virtues to be anchored in the successive stages of life: Hope, in infancy; Will and Purpose, in the play age; Skill in the school age; Fidelity, in youth; Love, in young adulthood; Care, in adulthood; Wisdom, in old age. For an evolutionary and genetic rationale of this concept of the life cycle, see the writer's "The Roots of Virtue" in *The Humanist Frame*, Sir Julian Huxley (ed.), London: Allen and Unwin, 1961. This appeared in revised form as "Human Strength and the Cycle of Generations" in the writer's *Insight and Responsibility*, New York: W.W. Norton, 1964.

2. Ernest Jones, *Hamlet and Oedipus*, New York: W.W. Norton, 1949.

3. Saxo Grammaticus, *Danish History*, translated by Oliver Elton, 1894. Quoted in Jones, *op. cit.*, pp. 163, 164.

4. The classical psychoanalytic works concerned with psychosexuality and the ego defenses of youth are: Sigmund Freud, "Three Essays on the Theory of Sexuality," *Standard Edition*, 7:130-243, London: Hogarth Press, 1953; and Anna Freud, *The Ego and the Mechanisms of Defense*, New York: International Universities Press, 1946. For a newer work, see Peter Blos, *On Adolescence, A Psychoanalytic Interpretation*, New York: Free Press of Glencoe, 1962.

5. B. Inhelder and J. Piaget, *The Growth of Logical Thinking from Childhood to Adolescence*, New York: Basic Books, 1958.

6. Jerome S. Bruner, *The Process of Education*, Cambridge: Harvard University Press, 1960.

7. Erik H. Erikson, *Young Man Luther*, New York: W.W. Norton, 1958.

8. Sigmund Freud, "Fragment of an Analysis of a Case of Hysteria," *Standard Edition*, 7:7-122, London: Hogarth Press, 1953.

9. *Ibid.*, p. 50.

10. Erik H. Erikson and Kai T. Erikson, "The Confirmation of the Delinquent," *The Chicago Review*, 10:15-23, Winter 1957.

11. January 24, 1967. As I reread this, the *London Times* reports the following self-confirmation of a negative suggestion. A twenty-three-year-old prospective heir to £40,000 is in serious trouble. According to his foster father's will this fortune would be his at the age of forty-eight "provided he is not sentenced meanwhile to imprisonment for a two-year period or more." This condition, the Recorder in charge said, "had an appalling effect and made him utterly useless to himself and society." And indeed, the young man had already worked up fifteen months' imprisonment (for receiving stolen checks) when the Court of Criminal Appeal, apparently noticing some self-defeating impulse in the young man, substituted a three-year probation under the condition that he enter a psychiatric hospital.

But, alas, it took him only two weeks to be expelled by a committee of doctors and patients for distributing drugs on the ward: "A person who does this," was the verdict, "does not want to remain here." Will the young man succeed in outwilling his foster father's will?

VII WOMANHOOD AND THE INNER SPACE

1. Preface, *Youth: Change and Challenge*, Erik H. Erikson (ed.), New York: Basic Books, 1963.
2. For sketches of typical play constructions, see Erik H. Erikson, *Childhood and Society*, 2nd ed., New York: W. W. Norton, 1963, Chapter II.
3. Three films taken in Kenya, 1959: *Baboon Behavior, Baboon Social Organization*, and *Baboon Ecology*.
4. *Childhood and Society*, p. 88.

VIII RACE AND THE WIDER IDENTITY

1. Robert Penn Warren, *Who Speaks for the Negro?*, New York: Random House, 1965, p. 17.
2. W. E. B. Du Bois, *Dusk of Dawn*, New York: Harcourt, Brace & Co., 1940, pp. 130, 131.
3. Erik H. Erikson, "Psychoanalysis and Ongoing History: Problems of Identity, Hatred and Nonviolence," *The American Journal of Psychiatry*, 122:241–250, 1965.
4. Howard Zinn, *SNCC, The New Abolitionists*, Boston: Beacon Press, 1964.
5. Thomas F. Pettigrew, *A Profile of the Negro American*, Princeton: Van Nostrand, 1964, p. 19. (Italics added)
6. *Ibid.*, p. 115.
7. Kenneth B. Clark, *Dark Ghetto*, New York: Harper and Row, 1965, p. 73. (Italics added)
8. New stereotypes are apt to enter the imagery of the most thoughtful. In *Crisis in Black and White* (New York, Random House, 1964), C. E. Silberman discusses S. M. Elkin's basic book *Slavery* and, half quoting and half editorializing, uses the stereotype "childlike" as a common denominator of Negro personality and the transient regressions of inmates in concentration camps. Along with truly *childish* qualities, such as silliness, we find fawning, servile, dishonest, mendacious, egotistic and thievish activities all summed up under "this childlike behavior" (p. 76). Here childlike replaces childish or regressed, as feminine often replaces effeminate, which is both misleading and destructive of the image of the genuine article.
9. Ralph Ellison, *Invisible Man*, New York: Random House, 1947, p. 225.
10. Robert Penn Warren, *Who Speaks For the Negro?*, pp. 20, 21.
11. See Robert J. Lifton, *Thought Reform and the Psychology of Totalism*, New York: W. W. Norton, 1961.
12. Robert Coles, *Children of Crisis: A Study of Courage and Fear*, Boston: Atlantic-Little, Brown, 1967, Part II, Chapter 4.
13. See J. Fishman and F. Solomon, "Youth and Social Action," *Journal of Social Issues*, 20:1–27, October, 1964.

Index